# INVESTING IN JAPAN

### THERE IS NO STOCK MARKET AS UNDERVALUED AND AS MISUNDERSTOOD AS JAPAN

Steven Towns

Copyright © 2012 Steven Towns

All rights reserved.

ISBN: 1475013507
ISBN-13: 978-1475013504

*In memory of all the victims
of the March 11, 2011,
earthquake and tsunami
in Japan*

# CONTENTS

|   | Preface | vii |
|---|---|---|
| 1 | Shrouded in Doubt | 1 |
| 2 | Japan Mutual Funds, ETFs, and ADRs | 26 |
| 3 | Japanese Mutual Funds | 51 |
| 4 | Japanese Stock Market: Nuts and Bolts I | 69 |
| 5 | Japanese Stock Market: Nuts and Bolts II | 91 |
| 6 | Bullish Take on Japan | 124 |
| 7 | There's Always Something to Do | 155 |
| 8 | Corporate Governance in Japan | 177 |
|   | Index | 192 |

What I must do is all that concerns me, not what the people think. This rule, equally arduous in actual and in intellectual life, may serve for the whole distinction between greatness and meanness. It is the harder, because you will always find those who think they know what is your duty better than you know it. It is easy in the world to live after the world's opinion; it is easy in solitude to live after our own; but the great man is he who in the midst of the crowd keeps with perfect sweetness the independence of solitude.
--- Ralph Waldo Emerson, *Self-Reliance*

# PREFACE

I have long wanted to write a book about investing in Japan. I began writing about Japanese stocks in 2005 (just as the Nikkei was beginning to take off with then Prime Minister Koizumi's reform efforts), for a now leading financial news and analysis company, Seeking Alpha. However, interest in Japan faded after that rally lost steam, and it wasn't until the tragic triple-disaster of March 11, 2011, that Japan really reappeared on investors' radars. Unfortunately, the limited news and opinions of the Japanese economy and stock market are often overly negative. This has caused investors to lose interest or become completely disinterested in Japan. To repeat the subtitle of this book: "There is no stock market as undervalued and as misunderstood as Japan."

As a value investor, it is *not* unfortunate that Japan is so misunderstood because it allows one to buy great companies at bargain prices. No, I am not looking for trades to make a quick buck. Rather, I view the valuations available in Japan as offering outstanding potential gains for years to come for the patient, disciplined investor. Value investing is time consuming at the outset (identifying and analyzing companies), but once due diligence is complete there is virtually no need to watch tickers, follow the latest economic data release, or worry about analyst estimates ahead of earnings. There is no need for instant validation, nor does it matter that some other stock is up big on the day. No need to have an opinion on everything going on in the market.

Looking at my life to-date, I have been fortunate with an upbringing during my formative years in an American environment in Japan – fortunate given the opportunity to learn the Japanese language and culture. Further, I learned immensely from my experiences working alongside Japanese diplomats in commercial and economic development. Having lived in Japan more than twelve years and from the many visits I've made from the U.S. in recent years, I feel that I have great appreciation for what works and what doesn't on both sides of the Pacific. As for being a value investor, beyond Benjamin Graham, if I had to name the investors that have been most influential to me I'd have to offer the late Peter Cundill (fearlessness and perseverance), Martin Whitman (unwilling to conform to convention; keen perspective), and Scott Callon (dedication and focus; he is among the very few fund managers that specializes in Japan).

*Investing in Japan* is intended for a broad audience of readers. Although it is written from the bias of a value investor, the contents will surely be of interest to all types of market participants and watchers, services professionals, researchers, and students. There are no comments of substance on specific value investing styles since value investors tend to embrace their own approaches, and since equities are so undervalued that any value style should do well over time.

In the pages that follow, among other things I provide background on value investing (the beauty of value investing is that practitioners never tire of hearing about its merits and newcomers are intrigued by its commonsensical approach) and discuss some of the key criticisms of Japan in Chapter 1; the substantially similar investment style of U.S.-based Japan mutual funds and the universe of New York-listed Japanese companies in Chapter 2; an overview of Japanese mutual funds marketed to Japanese investors in Chapter 3; an in depth look at investing in Japanese stocks in Chapters 4 and 5; key reasons to bullish in Chapter 6; hedge funds' investments in Chapter 7; and proof that Japan's corporate governance is no worse than corporate governance in the U.S. in Chapter 8.

By the end of the book I am certain readers will look at Japan and Japanese stocks in a new way and will have gained a strong working knowledge of the Japanese stock market – which will also be applicable to how one analyzes and considers other stocks and investment funds. Readers will be convinced they cannot afford to not invest in Japan.

STEVEN TOWNS
March 2012

---

To contact the author please visit his website, http://steventowns.com.

*Every effort has been taken to ensure accuracy of information and to provide citations and web links that are active at the time of publishing. This book does not constitute investment advice. Before purchasing or transacting in any securities it is always important to conduct one's own due diligence. Some may wish to consult an investment adviser.*

# CHAPTER 1

# SHROUDED IN DOUBT

"It is extraordinary to me that the idea of buying dollar bills for 40 cents takes immediately with people or it doesn't take at all. It's like an inoculation. [Some people] just don't seem able to grasp the concept, simple as it is."
--- Warren Buffett, "Superinvestors of Graham and Doddsville," 1984.

Imagine if business majors interested in a career in capital markets, specifically in investing, could opt out of certain classes and have better access to others? Forget about all the nonsense of beta in CAPM[1], rational players, and market efficiency, and instead learn more about capital structures, valuation based more on the balance sheet than income statement, and how companies go through a restructuring. Imagine if analyst price targets weren't based on so many assumptions and instead more so on asset values. Well, the good news is that there aren't too many value-focused business (finance) programs or analysts, which means there's naturally less competition. It is also helpful that value investors are also a minority in Japan, even more than they are in the U.S. It is a great time indeed to be a value investor following the

---

[1] CAPM stands for Capital Asset Pricing Model. If CAPM is unfamiliar, know in short that the so-called cost of equity when trying to determine a company's cost of capital (otherwise known as WACC, Weighted Average Cost of Capital), is based on the risk free rate (e.g. 10 year U.S. Treasury), the equity risk premium (usually 5-6%), and the beta (or historical price volatility) of the company's stock. If this sounds confusing, forget everything and keep reading.

2008 financial crisis and ongoing uncertainty across the globe. And despite (or rather thanks to) the uncertainty and bearishness, it may be a once in a lifetime opportunity to be value investing in Japan amid such widespread undervaluation. The entire market trades at a discount to net assets. Cash is plentiful and goodwill is light on many corporate balance sheets.

I had an ah-ha moment several years ago when contemplating the point of CAPM and even discounted cash flow (DCF)[2] analysis when there were so many assumptions to be made. I serendipitously came across a shareholder letter written by the "Oracle of Omaha," Warren Buffett, which included some of his counterintuitive thoughts on the use of beta as an input to calculate the cost of capital. It resonated with me and I'm sure it has with others familiar with his line of thinking. Before I share Buffett's thoughts, know that CAPM and DCF are even more dubious in an environment where interest rates are manipulated with near-term rates close to zero, and long-term rates being so low as to be out of line with reality and history. The prolonged recessionary, deflationary periods in recent Japanese history have featured for many years an official zero interest rate policy (known in short as ZIRP).

Post-2008, a hot question in the U.S. has been whether the country was following Japan's footsteps down the notorious path of zero interest rates, low growth, and ostensibly no hope. The U.S.-Japan comparisons persisted throughout 2011, but it is intriguing to consider the work of Nomura Research Institute's chief economist Richard Koo, who argues Japan and now the U.S. was/is facing a *balance sheet recession* (his work is discussed again later in the book). Lending rates may be next to zero, but there is limited borrowing taking place due to ongoing widespread shoring up of balance sheets, whether by the banks themselves, corporations, individuals, and now even if for show politically at the government level. That is not to say that banks, companies, and people that are creditworthy and desire credit, cannot

---

[2] Discounted Cash Flow is utilized as a means of estimating the value of expected cash flows (e.g. free cash flow) by projecting out the source of income and discounting by a certain rate (10%, for instance). The danger of DCF is twofold, but of the same tributary: estimating the rate of growth of the cash flows for years 1 through X and a terminal value (into perpetuity) and estimating the discount rate.

borrow, though they may face more lender scrutiny. In fact, a time of near-zero short-term rates and historically low long-term rates is precisely the time to contemplate borrowing – just be sure to monitor asset/liability durations. In Japan, we have a situation in which yields on government bonds of durations up to ten years remain below 1%.

Back to financial theory and my aforementioned ah-ha moment, which involves the elusive measure of a stock's beta, or its price volatility as measured against the market's benchmark (the S&P 500 Index). Curiously, the higher the beta, the higher the possible return, but also the higher the risk. Thus, if a stock is falling sharply, say for having missed earnings – even though it was otherwise profitable, had free cash flow generation, paid a dividend, whatever positives there may be – and its beta is spiking, it would be regarded as a very risky investment. While in traders' parlance you certainly don't want to "catch a falling knife," and ideally a value investor's due diligence would afford a proper margin of safety, assuming that there is such a high beta ought to be a buy signal. The relatively higher beta (as a result of the reaction to quarterly earnings) has nothing to do in this case with a higher cost of capital. I can attribute to Warren Buffett a pithy statement enlightening me on this matter and ending my meaningless contemplation of the meaninglessness I perceived of CAPM.

> "[...] under beta-based theory, a stock that has dropped very sharply compared to the market - as had Washington Post when we bought it in 1973 - becomes "riskier" at the lower price than it was at the higher price. Would that description have then made any sense to someone who was offered the entire company at a vastly-reduced price?" (Berkshire Hathaway, "Chairman's Letter to Shareholders," 1993)[3]

A quick review of an all-time Washington Post (WPO) stock chart via Google Finance, which dates back to 1978, shows nearly a 2,200% return through mid-February 2012 (not including dividend returns) and that's despite a depressed stock price in terms of it being less than one-half its all-time high set in 2004 and effectively trading at 1997 price levels. No doubt the return dating back to 1973 is even more significant. With the WACC,

---

[3] See: http://www.berkshirehathaway.com/letters/1993.html.

CAPM, and even DCF guesswork behind beta, I'd like to share an observation in Warren Buffett's 1993 letter to Berkshire Hathaway shareholders within which he said:

> "In their hunger for a single statistic to measure risk, however, they forget a fundamental principle: It is better to be approximately right than precisely wrong."

Later in this chapter I will introduce Warren Buffett's, "Superinvestors of Graham and Doddsville." But with regards to beta one last time, consider the following short passage: "Our Graham & Dodd investors, needless to say, do not discuss beta, the capital asset pricing model or covariance in return among securities. These are not subjects of any interest to them. In fact, most of them would have difficulty defining those terms."

## Mr. Market or a crotchety old uncle

The news, whether in its 24/7 nonstop, or local we have lots of bad news to report, varieties (this of course includes web-based news, sites, social media, and the so-called blogosphere), is something you don't really want to live with, but sometimes can't live without. It is nice after all to know the weather forecast once or twice a week, even if it's wrong. The same with stock prices – it's nice to have quotes when you want them (especially if they're *wrong* and you're able to buy at a discount). Borrowing again from Buffett's 1993 letter to Berkshire Hathaway's shareholders:

> "In fact, the true investor *welcomes* volatility. Ben Graham explained why in Chapter 8 of *The Intelligent Investor*. There he introduced "Mr. Market," an obliging fellow who shows up every day to either buy from you or sell to you, whichever you wish. The more manic-depressive this chap is, the greater the opportunities available to the investor. That's true because a wildly fluctuating market means that irrationally low prices will periodically be attached to solid businesses. It is impossible to see how the availability of such prices can be thought of as increasing the hazards for an investor who is totally free to either ignore the market or exploit its folly."

Jim Rogers, the outspoken commodities guru, formerly of Soros Fund fame, puts it this way:

> "In a way, buying any security on the public market is like having a crotchety old uncle as a partner. When things are tough, all you hear from him is that the two of you should get out of the business; it never was any good; only a fool would have gone into it in the first place. Let things turn around, however; let a few years of profits roll in and his tune changes: This is the greatest business in the world; things will go well forever; let's not give this up. In fact, now that our shares have tripled, let's buy out everybody else."
>
> (As appears in excerpted form in the forward to *Contrarian Investing* (Prentice Hall, 1998), originally published as an article by Jim Rogers).

## March 11, 2011

Following the March 11, 2011, Tohoku (Northeastern Japan) earthquake, tsunami, and nuclear accidents, cheap stocks (and a cheap overall market) got much cheaper, indiscriminately, and irrespective of underlying value and the real economic impact of the disaster – the Tohoku region had most recently accounted for 6.4% of GDP accordingly to media reports. Fast forward to September 2011, amidst an unsurprising continuation of domestic and international political and economic uncertainty, and the benchmark Nikkei 225 was actually trading at March 11 post-earthquake low levels. Sadly, rather than just point this out, a *Wall Street Journal* journalist begins her story (entitled "Japanese Stocks Hit Post-Quake Low") as follows, "So much for those folks thinking they were getting a deal scooping up Japanese stocks during the worst of the post-earthquake sell off."[4] Hyperlinked within the article is a *Barron's* article published a week after the earthquake entitled, "Buy Japanese Stocks," which made a case for stocks citing Japan's resilience and

---

[4] "Japanese Stocks Hit Post Quake Low," WSJ Blogs: Market Beat, Sept. 6, 2011. http://blogs.wsj.com/marketbeat/2011/09/06/japanese-stocks-hit-post-quake-low/

valuations that had fallen to very cheap 2008 crisis levels.[5] Perhaps there was no ill will intended by her statement, but it is odd since she's writing for the WSJ and referencing an article within the Dow Jones family. Nevertheless, unfortunately for value investors, post-March 11 Japanese stocks never fell to anywhere near the low levels of the trough of the 2008 crash.

Readers that followed financial news coverage (TV or online) of the disaster may have felt pressure to sell their stocks, not only the likes of ADRs such as Sony and Toyota, but also "American" stocks and ETFs or mutual funds. Let's review the headlines on the days surrounding the triple-disaster on a leading independent financial news and analysis website, Seeking Alpha (dot-com). Seeking Alpha is a great financial media platform and has some excellent contributors. However, no matter your information source it's important to be able to sift the information. In the month prior to the disaster, a total of fifteen articles were published on Seeking Alpha's Japan country page.[6] There were more articles published on March 14th, twenty-two in total, than in the entire month prior. Even between March 11 and March 13, there were already twelve articles published, so in a four-day period, which includes the weekend (a slow time for re-posting contributors' articles at Seeking Alpha) there was a real flurry of activity – a lot of pundits sure came out from behind paper screen doors.

See the following page for a table of article titles concerning Japan published on Seeking Alpha (dot-com) between March 11 - 14.[7]

---

[5] "Invest in Japan," *Barron's*, Mar. 21, 2011.
http://online.barrons.com/article/SB5000142405297020375760457620452350106900 8.html
[6] At the time of publishing, country-specific pages are no longer available in their former/original layout. Now apparently they are only available based on macro-economic themed articles. See:
http://seekingalpha.com/articles?filters=economy,japan,articles
[7] Some titles edited for formatting purposes.

| March 11 Friday | March 12 Saturday | March 13 Sunday | March 14 Monday | March 14 cont. | March 14 cont. |
|---|---|---|---|---|---|
| Earthquake Sparks Yen Sell-Off | Economic Aftershocks of the Earthquake | Earthquakes as Bullish on Country & Currency | Nikkei Collapses 6% as Aftermath Sets In | 8 Stocks Could Be Rocked by Earthquake | 2nd Biggest One-Day Decline Ever for Japan ETF |
| Insurers Hit Hard, but Yen Rebounds | Manulife Relatively Unscathed, Q2 Impact? | Quake Thru Macro Lens: 3 Recovery Plays | Quake: Boon for Refiners, Bane for Nuc. Stocks | Glbl econ. Implications of Japan's Tragedy | Dumping Japanese Stocks Is Short-Sighted |
| Japan's Stock Mkt Post-Kobe Earthquake in 1995 | Has the Tsunami Destroyed (sic) Japan's Economy? | Japan: Restructuring With ETFs | Earthquake Hits Japan: Why Is the Yen Rallying? | Internet a Comm. Lifeline as Telephone Lines Fail | How Japan's Quake Will Rattle the Global Economy |
| How Will the Market React to the Quake? | Economic Impact of Monster Quake | Mkt & ETF Reactions to Japan's Quake | 6 Market Aftershocks of the Japan Disaster | Nuclear Backlash May Benefit Solar | Retail's Exposure to Japan |
| | | | Investment Implications of a Nuclear Meltdown | Too Early to Assess Effect on Insurers | What Does Quake Mean for Japan's Fiscal Future? |
| | | | The Earthquake & the Broken Window: | Japanese Equities: The Buy of the Decade! | Investing After Disaster Strikes: Eyeing Japan Stocks |
| | | | JP Investmt. During Devastating Times | JP's High Debt Load May Slow Reconstruct. | |
| | | | Becoming Bullish on Japan | Tepco: In Eye of Storm | |

It only gets better with the sixteen articles that appear on the 15th, with my favorites in bold font: Natural Disasters Are Not Black Swans: Japan Will Overcome; Japan Default Risk; Investors Finally Taking Note of Contagion From Japan; Expecting a Pullback on the Nikkei; Buy Japan - But Beware of These 3 Investment Aftershocks; Japan's Cheap Stocks Will Rise Again; **Japan Is a Different Type of Dip**; Research Roundup: Credit Rating Agencies on Japan Earthquake Impact; **14 Reasons Japan's Economic Collapse Has Begun**; Fears About Japan Are Overdone; Why Would Japan Sell Treasuries?; Japan, Inc. on Sale - At Double-Discounts; A Look at the Nikkei's Fall; Now in a Bear Market; **Bank of Japan Continues Printing Money: Bad News**; Fukushima: The Perfect Nuclear Crisis Storm; iShares MSCI Japan ETF (EWJ) Stabilizes.

The first bold-font title includes the following ostensibly expert commentary: "Japan is a buying opportunity IF (and that's a big IF) they can contain the nuclear reactors. Barring that, they may face a huge demographic shift out of nearby cities and in the short term will face a recession or depression that will make their 20 year slow moving recession seem quaint."

The "14 Reasons" piece even comes with a picture of a reactor billowing smoke, and begins, "The economic collapse of Japan has begun." Yes, it really does have 14 reasons. And it includes some classic fear mongering: "Sadly, as the economy of Japan goes down it is going to have a huge affect on the rest of the world as well. For example, Japan is no longer going to be able to buy up huge amounts of U.S. Treasuries. So who is going to pick up the slack? Will our government officials beg China to lend us even more money? Will the Federal Reserve just "buy" even more of our government debt?"

The last one about the BOJ printing money being bad news also has a lot of fear mongering: "One must assume that the Japanese insurers are all insolvent." And, "In the short term, the BOJ is likely to produce a serious contractionary force along with a collapse in government tax funding. The risk is that if you print into that, as the BOJ is doing, the possibility of a severe, sustained and successful speculative financial attack goes up materially. This would then cross-link to the United States, since Japan owns a huge passel of U.S. Treasury bonds."

On the 16th, a Wednesday, I'm a little disappointed that we only have twelve articles. Where have all my pundits gone? We've suffered a 25% day-over-day decline. Titles include: Japan Crisis: The Catalyst for Alternative Energy; The Market and Nuclear Crises; SanDisk, Orbotech and Orckit: The Ties That Bind With Japan; Japan's Struggle to Recover; Japanese Stocks: Cheapest Fundamental Value on Record; Spotlight: Japan ETFs; Bank of Japan Ready to Intervene in Yen Markets; The iShares Japan ETF in Focus; Strong Buying in Japan ETFs Drives Premium to NAV; Japan Stock Market Crash: Keep an Eye on Microchip Companies; How to Play Post-Disaster Currency Moves in Japan; ETFs as a Hedge Against Japanese Volatility; The Great Japanese Unwind and How It Will Play Out Globally.

On the 17th, by which time I was ready to quit this exercise, there are thirteen articles (an uptick, of one), including: "The End of Japan as an Industrial Power?" and "Are We Headed for a Global Meltdown?" Some coverage continues over the weekend and into Monday the 21st (note that it was a three-day weekend in Japan in "celebration" of the vernal equinox) when sixteen articles appeared. Something happened on Tuesday, as only eight articles were published. A time for reflection, perhaps; here are a couple titles: "Japan - And Its Capital Market - Need a Break" and "Death of Japanese Economy: Severely Overhyped." The downtrend continues on Wednesday as only four articles appear. I did finally give up on Friday, when seven articles were published, including: "The Insidious Effects of Japan's Disaster," "What Should the Bank of Japan Do Now?" and "Why 'Buy Japan' Is Now a Joke."

## Graham-and-Doddsville

I largely went off the financial TV news grid a few years ago – I can only imagine what the coverage of the earthquake must have been like; to be fair, I'm still trying to erase from memory the 100-point font headlines during the 2008 financial crisis that were displayed on MarketWatch and other sites' homepages. However, like all investors I must come up with ideas. I take in a lot of information, but it's more reviewing (financials) than reading per se. I find such things as the tone of headlines, biggest advancers/decliners lists, stock screeners, and tweets to be good sources of preliminary information. I rarely use sell-side research, but I do find investor materials published by companies helpful – Japanese investor presentations can be quite detailed, sometimes a little too much so.[8] I must say that I'm most intrigued by the approach of the late Walter Schloss[9] (who enjoyed a highly successful 47-year career as a value practitioner) as Warren Buffett described him in his classic story of the "Superinvestors of Graham-and-Doddsville," which appears as a chapter in the latest edition of *The Intelligent Investor*.

> "He [Schloss] has no connections or access to useful information. Practically no one in Wall Street knows him and he is not fed any ideas. He looks up the numbers in the manuals and sends for the annual reports, and that's about it."[10]

One has to appreciate the inherent humor in a lot of what Buffett has to say. Another passage from "Superinvestors":

> "The common intellectual theme of the investors from Graham-and-Doddsville is this: they search for discrepancies between the *value* of a business and the *price* of small pieces of that business in the market. Essentially, they exploit those discrepancies without the efficient market theorist's concern as to whether the stocks are bought on Monday or Thursday, or whether it is January or July, etc."

---

[8] Visiting companies' Investor Relations websites is a must when investing in Japan since there are limited alternatives to obtaining original information (such as press releases and regulatory filings) in English unless one has a paid subscription with a proprietary vendor. Try a web search consisting of a company's name and "investor relations." As a matter of reference, Sony's IR page is available at: http://www.sony.net/SonyInfo/IR/. There is a wealth of information there, including a spreadsheet with robust financial data from 1960 – 2000 and another for 2001 – 2011. See: http://www.sony.net/SonyInfo/IR/financial/fr/historical.html.
[9] Sadly, just prior to publishing, Walter Schloss passed away on Sunday, February 19, 2012, at the age of 95. See coverage by Bloomberg, http://www.bloomberg.com/news/2012-02-20/walter-schloss-superinvestor-who-earned-buffett-s-praise-dies-at-95.html and a resource page on his career by Value Walk, http://www.valuewalk.com/walter-schloss/.
[10] For those without a handy copy of *The Intelligent Investor*, visit: http://www.grahamanddoddsville.net/ or http://www.valuewalk.com/.

This is an opportune time to mention "margin of safety," a concept value investors should already be very well familiar with, and for any investors that are not, it's a must-grasp and practice or else. Graham & Dodd, the pioneers of value investing (*Security Analysis*, 1st ed. 1934), describe margin of safety as a "basic characteristic of true investment ... its touchstone or distinguishing feature." (pg. 54) As pertains to common stock investing, an analyst is targeting, with conviction, stocks whose worth is more than that is to be paid for them, with reasonable optimism about companies' futures. Such stocks can be bought at times when the overall market is *low*, and also on an individual basis, when a stock is under, or within a conservative value range. (pg. 431) From the latter comes the often heard reference to "intrinsic value" (versus market value, i.e. stock price). And what's important to note is Graham & Dodd's use of ranges, which is duly noted in Wall Street historian Rodney G. Klein's compilation of Graham's earliest writings in, *Benjamin Graham on Investing: Enduring Lessons from the Father of Value Investing* (McGraw-Hill, 2009; pg. 6). It is not uncommon to see even value investors arriving at precise valuations, similar to how sell-side analysts arrive at nice and neat share price targets. Warren Buffett himself (borrowing from the long-deceased but very much of the current times economist, John Maynard Keynes; himself a successful *speculator*, a point unbeknown to most today) has said he'd rather be "approximately right than precisely wrong."

It will not come as a surprise that price targets are used in Japan by the sell-side and their upgrades and downgrades can move stocks. Interestingly, but also somewhat sadly, the business press and magazine publishers in Japan hardly hold back selling publications that make reference to some sort of target and/or intrinsic stock price that is to serve as a point of reference for retail investors. I suspect very few (comparatively less than Western investors) do their homework or due diligence. A visit to any decent-sized bookshop will yield as many as a half-dozen usually monthly magazines on the shelf that concern stocks. This does not include quarterly publications of thick books of all publicly-traded stocks nor the cornucopia of annual publications.[11] The

---

[11] An English version known as the "Japan Company Handbook," is available from leading publisher, Toyo Keizai. It currently retails for ¥9,600 (or $148 when ordered from the U.S.). For ordering details see:
http://www.toyokeizai.net/shop/magazine/jch/ and

quarterly books serve as market bibles for many investors and can be very useful to have a consolidated reference, not to mention the commentary and outlooks by editors. It's quite possible that commentary on a stock popular amongst individual investors could be influenced on the day(s) following publishing. Any non-Japanese investor researching Japanese stocks for the first time or planning to put together a portfolio of Japanese stocks may want to purchase the English-language version. That said, a visit to a Japanese bookstore may make non-Japanese investors jealous and yearn for such variety of information, but the truth is that correspondingly there is far less being published on the web. In addition, online pay walls are pervasive, further limiting information, especially of the timeliest and best of content. The magazines, by the way, are not exactly cheap either, typically costing $7.50 and up.

Keep in mind Walter Schloss, the so-called "superinvestor," who needed none of this mountain of information, let alone such things as channel checks. The late Peter Cundill was another highly successful value investor with minimal needs.

## Nikkei, Japan, not well understood

Perhaps trivial, but suggestive of how little American investors and likely investors elsewhere know about the Japanese stock market and companies is Jim Cramer, the former hedge fund manager turned TV personality of "Mad Money" on CNBC, whom I vividly remember had developed an itch for Japanese stocks. He once talked about the 7 samurai (January 2006), including Matsushita (now Panasonic), Mitsubishi, Kirin, Kubota, Kyocera, Honda, and Toyota, all large/mega-cap stocks and all but one with exchange-listed ADRs at that time.[12] No problem here except these are not dissimilar to the usual

---

http://www.toyokeizai.net/shop/magazine/jch/docs/order/index.html. Purchasing four-quarters worth at the same time costs $528. Note for readers competent in Japanese, the Japanese language version is much cheaper at Y1,850 ($23 at the Feb. 2012 prevailing exchange rate).

[12] ADRs or American Depository Receipts are shares of a company whose main listing (or ordinary shares) is outside the U.S. ADRs can be one of three types with

suspect biggest holdings of the popular Japan ETFs and mutual funds. (See next chapter for an in depth review.) However, he referred to the Japanese benchmark Nikkei 225 as the *Nye kye* (phonetically) instead of what most, especially those with a hedge fund background, should know is pronounced as the *Knee kay*.

Another case, and more disturbing, was in July 2006, when *BusinessWeek* published an article entitled, "The Toyota Enigma," which mentioned that few American fund managers knew that Toyota shares were accessible on the New York Stock Exchange as an ADR (American Depository Receipt) trading under ticker TM. One value shop executive commented, "We were stunned when Toyota came up [in our screen]. We thought it was a typo." It was a fortuitous buy for said fund, which reportedly started buying at $74 and just over a year later Toyota was around $100. Then with a market capitalization well in excess of $100 billion, its sustained success in the U.S., and its rapid ascent to becoming the world's then largest auto manufacturer, one would presume that fiduciaries would know that Toyota was available to clients as easily as were shares of GM or Ford or any other publicly-traded company in the U.S.[13]

While in this mindset, I may as well share one more piece of disturbing information. Hark back to the 2005 – 2007 period when there was no shortage of reports of the U.S. Big 3 Auto decrying Japan Auto's unfair advantage from its weak yen. At that time, the yen was trading around Y120/US$1, weak, indeed, compared to current levels (February 2012) in the high Y70s. Repeating some of its tactics from yesteryear the Big 3 worked Congress, worked the press, and essentially used the same smoke and mirrors to blame the Japanese while avoiding putting any blame on failed internal strategy. Now, fast forward a few years to the present, a situation in which the yen is at an all-time high. The aforementioned Y120 level was a far cry from

---

the most visible ones tending to be listed on either the New York Stock Exchange or Nasdaq. See next chapter for a detailed look at ADRs.

[13] "The Toyota Enigma: With its cars so popular, why are investors neglecting the stock?" *BusinessWeek*, Jul. 10, 2006.
http://www.businessweek.com/magazine/content/06_28/b3992057.htm

the fixed rate of Y360 post-WWII that did not become free floating until the 1980s, during which time the rate mostly stayed above Y200.

Maybe justifiably, the time to complain was in the 1980s, when it became apparent the Japanese were really starting to eat the Big 3's lunch. At the same time, as Japan's GDP and wealth per capita were experiencing gangbusters growth, many foreign companies and investors felt they were shunned from tapping such growth, wealth, and the opportunities behind an economy that tolerated, in fact, thrived, on cartels. However, by the 2000s, it seems distasteful to blame the Japanese, when there was also a big push by South Korean manufacturers, sustained investment by European manufacturers, and even whispers audible from China about wanting to eventually become a player in the U.S. auto market. Furthermore, Japan had already experienced a so-called "lost decade" (and a half) and was hardly the aggressive force it was until the late 1980s.

Consider how some American manufacturers did not hesitate or refrain from publicly blaming the Japanese (today the Chinese have effectively supplanted them) for their companies' woes (and in the case of politicians, the country's woes). I am not exactly aware of a case when the Japanese have as vociferously publicly decried U.S. behavior that was perceived or actually was harmful to Japanese interests. The sustained war mongering of the U.S., the demise of the U.S. dollar, in which the Japanese hold significant reserves, and the hyper boom-bust of American capital, are all major causes of concern both for the Japanese and the rest of the world. But when is the last time a Japanese company publicly voiced dissatisfaction? How about the auto bailouts of 2008? How about the claims (proven falsified) of malfunctioning brake systems in Toyota autos? How about the fact that no Japanese institutional or alternative investor tries to take board seats or effect change in governance, operations, or use of capital, in U.S. companies. Yet, some American (and other Western) investment companies feel they can complain and act however suits them best. Finally despite all the China bashing in the U.S. Congress, I'm not aware of the same in Japan of the currency management regime in China, even though it seemingly favors the Chinese over the Japanese just as much as it disadvantages the U.S.

Finally, while on the touchy topic of national currencies and sovereign debt, I would like to share the work of investment economist Enzio von Pfeil, author of *Trade Myths: Globalization has left trade balances behind* (2009). Within said book, Enzio argues that international trade accounting is based on an antiquated 16th century framework. Trade deficits are misleading because they do not take into consideration the overseas activities of domestic companies. For example, regarding the highly controversial trade imbalance between China (surplus) and the U.S. (deficit), Enzio argues in fact the imbalance is inversed in an even more exacerbated way because of the presence in China of highly successful U.S. multinational corporations. I reviewed *Trade Myths* in spring 2010 and interviewed Enzio afterward (Enzio and I have been in contact for the past several years given our shared interest in investments and Asia).[14] Putting friendship aside, I can honestly say that his 100-page effort to dispel five common trade myths is an eye-opening read. And his research on the matter extends back more than 25 years. On the topic of currency driving trade and the argument that a strong currency is a disadvantage, Enzio had the following comment:

> "Were exchange rates really as important as some politicians claim, then why do Germany, Japan and Switzerland—whose currencies have appreciated fourfold against the dollar since 1970/71—all have trade surpluses?"

## No interest in Japanese stocks

Japan bears on financial websites are far more common than not when it comes to any Japan coverage. So while there's certainly not a lot of attention being paid to Japan, when there is, there's enough anti-Japan investment sentiment on the web and amongst institutional investors to presumably scare off would-be buyers of quality, low-price (great value) stocks. That said, it is also important to be wary of anyone making grand calls to buy Japan, usually with the suggestion of going long the iShares MSCI Japan Index ETF, EWJ.

---

[14] Review of *Trade Myths* and Q&A with author, Mar. 17, 2010. http://steventowns.proxyexchange.org/2010/03/book-review-trade-myths/

Ironically (as documented above), after the March 11, 2011, earthquake (tsunami and ensuing nuclear reaction meltdown scare), it seemed like there were more market participants on the bandwagon of Japan being cheap and thus it being a buy amidst the heavy selling. I'm sure many of the same individuals were not in the long-Japan camp in recent years prior to 3-11 despite similar or lower valuations. Now in terms of genuine bears, first and foremost, in the blogosphere there's asset manager "Random Roger" (Roger Nusbaum) of the eponymous blog, who as far back as I can remember has unmistakably disliked Japan. Take his June 2007 post on the importance of international investing in which he says:

> "I don't allocate anything to Japan, haven't in the time I've been managing money and have no plans to either. The reason I don't like Japan is pretty simple; years and years of wildly stimulative policy have not wildly stimulated the economy. Something ain't right so I leave it alone."[15]

Fair enough, for macro-minded investing, which is his game, Roger is right since buying Japan, say via the actively traded iShares Japan (EWJ), and holding, would not have worked out very well at all. But buying a basket of stocks is typically not what value investors do; certainly not a basket with upwards of 300 (or more) components. This would be the U.S. equivalent of buying the S&P 500 Index, SPY. Anyway, true to his game, in a March 2011 (post-earthquake) interview with Seeking Alpha (dot-com), he responds to the interviewer's question as follows:[16]

> **SA:** In the wake of the triple disaster there, are Japanese equities undervalued right now?
>
> **RN:** We want no part of Japan, period. I've never owned Japan for clients and have no plans to. I don't believe they can right their ship

---

[15] "Not Just Europe," Jun. 4, 2007. http://randomroger.blogspot.com/2007/06/not-just-europe.html

[16] "Nusbaum Positions for Q2: Bullish on Energy Producers, Avoiding Japan, EU, Munis," Seeking Alpha (dot-com), Mar. 31, 2011. http://seekingalpha.com/article/260913-nusbaum-positions-for-q2-bullish-on-energy-producers-avoiding-japan-eu-munis

and they have a serious demographic problem. Whatever snapback there might be, I am quite certain we can get the same big move up from another part of the market where the fundamentals are far more favorable. I don't want to put client money into something where I think the fundies stink.

Japan's so-called "demographic disaster" is among the top reasons given for why investors' capital should not flow into Japan. Another has to deal with its lethargic economy – there's actually a *positive* demographic tie-in. And a third involves companies' low returns on capital, especially equity as far as investors are concerned. Let's tackle the demographic and GDP issues first and visit the matter of ROE later in the book.

## So-called demographic disaster

The oft-cited demographic disaster has become a chief concern for non-Japanese largely as a result of semi-sensational reporting (sometimes by the government itself perhaps to compel action) and self-reinforcement from overuse. Japan's situation of a graying society with fewer and fewer children is not exactly unique, rather it is Japan that's having to deal with such problems first. Not far behind are some of the member states of the European Union, with China reportedly on course to face similar issues stemming from its longtime one-child policy. (See data table below.) One possible bright spot for Japan is the relative good health of elderly Japanese, which means they will not be as big a financial burden on society as may be the case elsewhere where demographics are thought to be a lesser concern. The government is also providing free or reduced price services such as fitness and cultural activities to keep senior citizens active and hopefully healthier than they would be otherwise. Healthcare spending in Japan as a percent of GDP was 8.1% in 2006 and increased slightly to 8.3% in 2009. In the U.S., it was 14.8% and 16.2%, respectively. Most EU members were in the 11% - 12% range, with Italy and Spain at 9.5% and 9.7%, respectively, in 2009.[17]

---

[17] "Health expenditure, % of GDP," The World Bank. http://data.worldbank.org/topic/health

See the following table for: 2010 – 2015 UN Population Division estimate of births per 1,000 persons (bottom-10)[18], 2011 *CIA World Factbook* population growth rate (%)[19], and 2007 – 2011 World Bank Dependency Ratio (people age 0-15 and 64+ vs. working-age)[20]

| Country | Birth rate | Growth rate | Dependency |
| --- | --- | --- | --- |
| Bosnia and Herzegovina | 8.2 | 0.01% | 41% |
| Japan | 8.5 | (0.28%) | 56% |
| Austria | 8.6 | 0.03% | 48% |
| Germany | 8.7 | (0.21%) | 51% |
| Portugal | 8.8 | 0.21% | 49% |
| Hong Kong | 8.8 | 0.45% | 32% |
| Italy | 9.1 | 0.42% | 52% |
| Malta | 9.1 | 0.38% | 41% |
| Channel Islands | 9.3 | n/a | n/a |
| Singapore | 9.5 | 0.82% | 36% |

The estimated world average birthrate per 1,000 persons is 19.2. The U.S. is estimated at 13.7 (ranked number 136 of 196). And China is estimated at 11.9 (ranked number 152). In terms of population growth, the 2011 *CIA World Factbook* listed 30 some countries that experienced a decline. The U.S. is estimated at 0.96% growth and China at 0.49%. As for the dependency ratio, the U.S. came in at 50% and China at 38%.

---

[18] "List of sovereign states and dependent territories by birth rate."
http://en.wikipedia.org/wiki/List_of_sovereign_states_and_dependent_territories_by_birth_rate.
[19] "List of countries by population growth rate."
http://en.wikipedia.org/wiki/List_of_countries_by_population_growth_rate
[20] "Age dependency ratio (% of working-age population)."
http://data.worldbank.org/indicator/SP.POP.DPND

While there is no question Japan faces challenges encouraging families to have more children, it seems somewhat alarmist to call the situation dire or a disaster. Japanese are keenly aware of their graying and reversed-pyramid (shaped in terms of the proportion of elderly vs. youth) society. After two decades of low economic growth, which followed three decades of very robust growth, the negativity surrounding economic headlines may itself have become self-reinforcing to some extent – and naturally impacted individuals' decisions on marriage and having children. Part of the matter in some instances may involve antiquated beliefs and behaviors between husband and spouse; similarly, old-fashioned thinking of putting company before family can also be partially blamed. It's also ridiculous to assert that a place as sexually open as Japan will see a majority of its young couples favor abstinence or childless marriages.

At the same time however, companies must increase compensation to younger professionals in order to help facilitate more marriages and childbirths. Interestingly, as more senior employees retire or accept voluntary retirement, companies will realize increasingly more savings by virtue of not having to pay such high salaries to them. These savings really need to be redirected to younger employees, especially with the abundance of net-cash corporate balance sheets. With the government already offering child subsidies and corporate executives well aware of the need for domestic consumers, it should, hopefully, be a matter of time before attitudes towards work-life balance begin to change meaningfully. Furthermore, I would argue that Japan is poised for better economic times as its proximity to China and the rest of Asia with the region's favorable growth prospects afford it ample opportunity to maintain exports, while domestically, substantial capital in companies' coffers and savers' various deposit accounts could be much better utilized. Thus, I believe it is more likely a normalization of family creation is on the horizon than there is a possibility of Japan's population halving. A longwinded debate on demographics is beyond the scope of this book; therefore beyond also mentioning that a more open immigration policy (as complex and controversial a topic it is) could be at least a partial solution for Japan, I will say no more.

# A closer look at GDP

As much as Japan's low-growth pales in comparison to the highflying BRIC economies (Brazil, Russia, India, and China), it turns out that Japan is doing fairly well despite all of its problems. A growth comparison to BRIC economies is very much apples-to-oranges, there's just no way that productivity growth combined with economic growth in an advanced economy can outpace robust commodity and capital investment-driven growth in economies with much lower bases. Therefore, let's see how Japan compares to a similarly advanced economy like the U.S.

Following the 2008 Great Financial Crisis and the sharp decline in the S&P 500 benchmark the past decade came to be regarded as a "lost" one in the U.S. Japan meantime, based on its benchmark Nikkei 225 Stock Average, has entered its third lost decade. Somewhat ironically, it was real estate that did in the U.S. in 2008, similar to Japan in 1990 – and it could be what does in China next if bears' assessments are proven correct. The pre-crash global boom in construction and consumption helped Japan enjoy its longest post-war stretch of economic growth of 69-consecutive months from early 2002 until October of 2007 – exceeding previous records of 50-plus months set in the mid/late 1980s bubble and the tremendous growth achieved in the decade through the late 1960s.

In recent years, very quietly economic analyses have been published showing in fact, Japan's GDP growth has approached or even exceeded America's. Most recently, on November 14, 2011, *The Economist*, in its "Free Exchange" blog noted between 1984 and 2008, GDP growth in Japan was 1.2% versus 3.0% in the U.S. However, when taking into account a declining work force of 0.4% per annum since the mid-'90s while America's was growing by 1.2%, the GDP gap is narrowed to a difference of only 0.4%, which *The Economist* says is due to Japan's overregulated and inefficient service sector. Annual increases in productivity were the same, 2.1%.[21]

---

[21] "Two things to remember about Japan," *The Economist*, Nov. 14, 2011. http://www.economist.com/blogs/freeexchange/2011/11/america-following-japan

*****

A pet peeve of mine is the blanket statements one hears now and then that Japan's service sector productivity is low or is detracting from growth. I think this is partially misleading, as it portrays a look more at efficiency than effectiveness. It reminds me of attempts at measuring GNH, or gross national happiness, instead of GNP or GDP, which I think could prove enlightening. For Japan, anyone that has spent even a short time there will likely readily agree that Japan's quality of services rendered is top-notch. It is debatable whether there needs to be such politeness, wrapping of goods purchased, and deliberateness. But I don't think that many will claim that such service is not preferable to say, indifference on the part of workers, or worse, such as the exact opposite of Japan in terms of the unpredictable and sometimes downright horrible service found in the U.S.

Yes, it can be argued that Japan has an easier job of providing standardized high-quality services, since it is much smaller, and has a lower population, than the U.S., in addition to having a history of explicitly and implicitly valuing social harmony. However, we're not talking the impossible when it comes to seeing more smiles, a greeting here and there, and more courteous handling and bagging of merchandise. So while productivity may be reported to be higher in the U.S., I believe the numbers miss important points such as customer satisfaction, errors, and future problems such as product returns. Customers are typically highly satisfied in Japan, errors in my experience are quite few, and ditto for returns. One longstanding complaint heard amongst foreigners in Japan is about the availability of ATMs. The situation has improved greatly in recent years and even so, ATM fees of more than around a $1 are rare while $3 charges are fairly common in the U.S. Need I comment on the quality of ATMs, services available at ATMs, and personal (as well as identity) safety in the U.S.

*****

*The Economist's* next print edition, November 19, 2011, featured an article entitled, "Japan's economy works better than pessimists think – at least for the elderly." It begins as follows:

"The Japanese say they suffer from an economic disease called "structural pessimism". Overseas too, there is a tendency to see Japan as a harbinger of all that is doomed in the economies of the euro zone and America ...."

How true; but how sad! Nevertheless, the article mentions Japan's Q3-2011 GDP has snapped back to a very respectable annualized 6%, ahead of other advanced economies and a positive development post-March 11. Most importantly, the article shows that contrary to popular belief, Japan's GDP has exceeded America's and the EU's based on GDP per capita over the past decade. With similar levels of productivity growth as mentioned above, combined with lower levels of unemployment, Japan appears to be doing *better* than its Western counterparts.

*The Economist* has really done its homework with this story as it goes on to provide value investors with invaluable information to weigh against all the doom and gloom headlines and data.[22] While this sort of information is after all of secondary importance to fundamental analysis, the extra knowledge doesn't hurt. Other key points from the article include:

- Japan is the world's largest creditor nation, with Y253 trillion ($3.3 trillion) in net foreign assets (NB: No, it's not enough to erase its national debt and in practice could not be used to do so anyway, but this data point is often lost in the Japan-is-doomed talk. At least these days more investors understand that unlike the U.S., Japan's government borrowing is nearly completely domestically funded.)

- Japan need only fix its taxation system, and the hurdle is no higher than implementing a high-tax European nation's rates, and it could immediately erase its fiscal deficit. Japan has the lowest tax take of any OECD country: 17% of GDP.

- Admittedly, implementing reforms and tax hikes is far easier said than done (especially facing powerful lobbies and interest groups),

---

[22] "Japan's economy works better than pessimists think -- at least for the elderly." *The Economist*, Nov. 19, 2011. http://www.economist.com/node/21538745/

but the self-acknowledged overly pessimistic Japanese need to be sold in a different way. In short, it's a matter of framing: don't tell the people they're mired in stagnation, but instead explain the realities of an aging society, and don't compare oneself to more rapidly growing China (different stage of growth), but more appropriately to the U.S. and EU.

## Japan: "A bug searching for a windshield." Really?

Juxtapose the above with the following comments from a July 2010 presentation by John Mauldin, editor of the finance and economics newsletter, *Thoughts From the Frontline*, which he says his publisher says has over 1.5 million subscribers. The instance below is not the only one in which Mauldin makes a similarly diagnosed fatal call on Japan. Though to be fair, a description of his 2011 book, *End Game: The End of the Debt Supercycle and How it Changes Everything*, indicates that he's essentially saying the outlook for the global economy is not good, and there are no good choices of escaping this downturn for the developed economies – though his book will provide a framework to help countries make difficult choices.

> "Maybe we'll do it like Japan? Japan is a disease. They're like a bug searching for a windshield. It's a dying country. Nominal GDP is where it was 17 years ago. Plus, the population is very old. When they stop funding their own debt [as a result of retirees ceasing to save], it's going to get ugly. You're going to see the yen valued against the dollar go to 100, and then 120, and then 250, 300. They won't care how low it goes. They can sell more Hondas and Toyotas to us. They're just going to print money. 40% of their budget right now is borrowed. Think about that. They're in deep dire trouble with a government that has no clue. I think Japan will implode within the next two to three years. It will not be good for the world."[23]

---

[23] John Mauldin, presentation at the Agora Financial Investment Symposium, Vancouver, British Columbia, Jul. 22, 2010. See coverage by way of the Motley Fool, which published an article of his speech (Mauldin's speech was entitled "The End Game of the Debt Super Cycle"), which the Motley Fool author entitled, "John

That Japan will implode by 2012 – 2013 is a rather bold prediction. It seems that the typical market naysayer is macro-minded, often effectively a self-proclaimed pundit that feels compelled to share his or her expert knowledge of not only Japan (and its dire demographics, deflation, poor governance, or whatever else happens to be a negative story in the news) but practically anything related to markets and economies.

Given all the conflicting viewpoints on Japan, I highly encourage those who have not been to Japan before to visit and experience it for themselves. Japan is sometimes compared to California in approximate size and shape, but Japan has a population of over three times (3.4x to be more exact) California's. (California: total area of 424,000 km$^2$ compared to Japan: 378,000 km$^2$, while California's population was 37.25 million per the 2010 census, versus Japan's 127 million per the 2011 *CIA Factbook*). Japan is a graying nation, more akin to Florida than California, but despite all its headline and real problems, consider that unemployment of 4.6% compares favorably to the 8.6% rate in the U.S. (February 2012). It's not my intent to argue about specific figures when many are simply imprecise to begin with. My point is for readers not to be misled to believe that Japan is so gray as to be on its last breath and in such dire straits that masses of unemployed youths pass time by occupying ubiquitous internet cafes.

Hopefully from prior or future travel to Japan, as well as from internet browsing, readers will recognize that Japan is quite an amazing place. For all its presumed problems, you can enjoy safe travels throughout the country, anytime day or night, and you will come across the most modern of technology and not far away could be several hundreds of years of preserved history. There are enough English signs, especially in the cities, that getting around is manageable despite the confusion of Japanese-language signs and waves of people coming and going. Similarly, investors will find companies' English-language Investor Relations web pages to be rather good, especially amongst larger companies. That said, the less English-language information a company has available could be a blessing for value investors. Going off the

---

Mauldin: Japan Is a Bug Searching for a Windshield."
http://www.fool.com/investing/international/2010/07/22/john-mauldin-japan-is-a-bug-searching-for-a-windsh.aspx

beaten path or against conventional wisdom is not so foreign to value investors.

One final note here about market participants and watchers who have disparaging comments about Japan. What has happened is that very few among all those in the investment management business are willing to publicly call Japan an attractive investment market. Instead, in fear of leaving the safety of the crowd, and not wanting to be doubted or laughed at by colleagues or clients, few are willing to see or acknowledge the attractiveness of Japan. Without belaboring the point that bad is often good for value investors, such sentiments as these afford value investors more time to study and accumulate stock. And of course, as has happened at irregular frequencies in Japan, enough foreign investors will eventually jump on the buy-Japan bandwagon and ride the momentum of a big rally. The challenge for value investors is how much of a correction there will be post-monster rally; how cyclical the money flows and economic growth appear; how much capital is being returned to shareholders and how those rates compare elsewhere; and of course whether there are more attractive opportunities in other securities. The good news is that some Japanese stocks are so deeply undervalued that there will be much upside despite a future correction, and great opportunities meanwhile to earn dividend income.

# CHAPTER 2

# JAPAN MUTUAL FUNDS, ETFs, AND ADRs

I must disclose upfront that I am not a big fan of mutual funds, not even index funds so much; though there are some respected value fund houses that are worthy of consideration for investors' capital should an investor not have the time or enough capital to manage their own investments, such as Brandes, First Eagle, Third Avenue, and Tweedy Browne, among a select few others. The issue for investors really wanting to dig into the abundance of fertile value in Japan is that while those four shops do invest in Japan, they don't offer a fund that does so exclusively. And amongst the asset management companies that do have funds focused on Japan, the investment style and results are disappointing.

Know that my general dislike of mutual funds in particular includes reasons such as bloat (regarding the number of portfolio holdings), conventions such as typically only paying dividends annually, possibly being subjected to capital gains taxes even if you haven't sold any stock, also possibly being subjected to a dubious practice like "window dressing" (the Japanese refer to month and quarter-end opportunistic buying of winning stocks as "cosmetic buying") and forced selling on the part of the portfolio manager if investors wish to liquidate, and the widespread lack of attention managers pay to proxy voting and governance matters. Index funds of course may be bloated by default. A specific problem with indexes or ETFs that are based on capitalization weighting is that the buying and selling practices go against the credo of the value style.

At its core, investing is not rocket science by any means, in the sense of buying low and selling high or buying high and selling higher, as long as one sells at a higher price than one paid. But that better describes trading than investing. Sometimes I feel the stock market certainly has a Ponzi scheme element to it for those buying on tips, analyst upgrades, or whatever may be sending a stock higher. Naturally, as far as value investors are concerned, it's best to buy as low as possible, not just for the prospect of greater gains, but also (equally as important) to reduce the downside impact of whatever risk (i.e. visible or invisible; known or unknown) a company may be exposed. Determining "low" in light of opportunity and risk, hence working with a margin of safety, is the essence of value investing. Furthermore, investing suggests that holding periods will be longer, allowing for accumulation of dividend income and the possibility of other "resource conversion" activities (I will discuss Martin Whitman's "resource conversion" philosophy later in the book.)

In the preceding chapter, I mentioned margin of safety and other things near and dear to value investors. In the remainder of this chapter I will hopefully convince readers that they probably stand a better chance of success on their own investing in Japan than they would otherwise with Japan-focused mutual or exchange traded funds. We will learn about, and become more familiar with, the workings of the Japanese market and traditional approaches of U.S.-based investors in Japan.

## The Japanese stock market

Before we begin looking at Japan-focused mutual funds in the U.S. and then mutual funds marketed to Japanese investors, let's go over the basic structure of the Japanese stock market.

The Nikkei 225 Stock Average (N225 for short), which is not an exchange or market, but an index rather, is Japan's best-known benchmark irrespective of its shortcomings. Launched in 1950, the N225's familiarity is similar to the Dow Jones Industrial Average or S&P 500 in the United States. Despite said familiarity and how often it's referenced, even in this book, it is quite an imperfect reference. Reason being is that similar to the Dow, the N225 is price-weighted meaning the higher a company's stock price, the greater weight it has on overall value. Market capitalization-weighted indexes, which have their own shortcomings, are discussed later in this chapter. Also similar to the Dow, the N225 maintains a divisor to account for continuity and changes to capital of constituents. All constituents have come from the TOPIX 1st Section and have typically been among the more actively traded issues in Japan.[24] The history of the N225 dates back to 1950.[25]

Regarding price-weighted indexes, a November 2011 article on Bloomberg (dot-com) by stock market historian John Steele Gordon, makes the point that had IBM been left in the Dow in 1939 instead of being replaced by AT&T, the Dow would have reached/exceed it pre-Depression high-water mark years earlier (versus the 25 it actually took) and other milestones (e.g. reaching 1,000) would have happened sooner, too. Between 1939 and 1979, AT&T's share price rose threefold, while IBM's expanded by a whopping 22,000%, says Gordon.[26] More recently, if one were to have equal-weighted the S&P 500 index between March 24, 2000 and December 2, 2010, it would have returned 66% instead of -19% in its original capitalization-weighted form.[27]

The Tokyo Stock Exchange (TSE) is the sponsor of two benchmark indices, the TOPIX 1st Section and TOPIX 2nd Section; both are free-float, market capitalization-weighted indices with base values of 100 as of January

---

[24] See explanation of the Nikkei 225 at http://e.nikkei.com/e/fr/info/nifaq/225.aspx. See constituent list for N225 at http://e.nikkei.com/e/app/fr/market/constituents.aspx.
[25] For a more detailed history, see the Nikkei's website http://e.nikkei.com/e/fr/info/nifaq/history.aspx.
[26] "How the Dow Distorts the History of Wall Street," Bloomberg, Nov. 23, 2011. http://www.bloomberg.com/news/2011-11-23/how-the-dow-distorts-the-history-of-wall-street-echoes.html
[27] "No Lost Decade for S&P 500 as Market Value Bias Masks Rally," Bloomberg, Dec. 5, 2011. http://www.bloomberg.com/news/2011-12-05/no-lost-decade-for-s-p-500-as-market-value-bias-masks-66-rally-since-2000.html

1968. TOPIX stands for Tokyo Stock Price Index. The 1st Section is comprised of larger-capitalization stocks, and is by far the bigger of the two in terms of number of listings and total capitalization. (See figures below.) TOPIX 1 and 2 combined are similar to the New York Stock Exchange's Composite Index, although securing a listing on the respected 1st Section is the equivalent of being listed on the "Big Board," while the more obscure listings of the 2nd Section are the equivalent perhaps to an Amex (American Stock Exchange) listing.

The 2nd Section features primarily smaller-capitalization listings; it has less than one-forth the number of listings and nearly 1/80th the capitalization of the 1st Section (as of November 2011). Note that the TSE also sponsors the Mothers Index (Mothers stands for "Market of the high-growth and emerging stocks), which is calculated in the same manner as the TOPIX indices; it began at a value of 1,000 in 2003, although the actual market for listings was launched in 1999. What's missing is the JASDAQ, owned by the Osaka Securities Exchange (OSE) and the OSE itself, which also has two "sections." Nintendo (7974) is a noteworthy Osaka-listing. JASDAQ is Japan's answer to the Nasdaq in the U.S. (Nasdaq actually launched service in Japan in 2000 but made a quick exit in 2002, which coincided with a very difficult period for tech-related stocks). Note the TSE and OSE are poised to merge in 2012 after years of expectation of firstly that the TSE would itself become a publicly-traded company and secondly that the TSE and OSE would have reached agreement earlier considering the brisk inbound and outbound exchange tie-ups around the world. It remains to be seen whether the TSE's listing and the TSE-OSE merger will happen.

**Stock market listings and market capitalization:**[28]

---

[28] TSE listing and capitalization data:
http://www.tse.or.jp/english/listing/breakdown/index_e.html also available via Morningstar Japan,
http://www.morningstar.co.jp/RankingWeb/IndicesTable.do?market=1. The TSE website contains a large amount of data in both English and Japanese. For English see: http://www.tse.or.jp/english/. The OSE-JASDAQ website also has a variety of

- TOPIX 1 had 1,675 listings as of November 18, 2011, and had an aggregate market capitalization of Y246.3 trillion, $3.15 trillion as of November 28, 2011.

- TOPIX 2 had 431 listings, and had an aggregate market capitalization of Y3.13 trillion, $40 billion as of November 28, 2011.

- Mothers had 178 listings and had an aggregate market capitalization of Y1.624 trillion, $16.2 billion, as of October 31, 2011.

- JASDAQ + OSE 1st and 2nd Sections, had 915 listings and had an aggregate market capitalization of Y78.4 trillion, $1 trillion, as of November 28, 2011.

The JASDAQ in its current form includes the merger of two other, smaller, markets (HERCULES and NEO, similar conceptually to the TSE's Mothers) in October 2010. While the combined OSE-JASDAQ's listings have a total capitalization of $1 trillion, both the OSE and JASDAQ are perceived as inferior to TOPIX 1 in the minds of investors. This may change however, and effectively become a moot point, with the TSE-OSE planned merger. While a third the size (based on market capitalization) of the TSE's TOPIX 1st section, the OSE-JASDAQ is 25-times larger than the TOPIX 2 and dwarfs Mothers. The largest JASDAQ-listed company, Rakuten (4755), which had a market capitalization of Y1.105 trillion ($14 billion) as of intraday November 30, 2011, ranked 42nd largest in all of Japan; Jupiter Telecom (4817) at Y525B ($6.7B) is 2nd largest on JASDAQ and 110th largest in Japan. (See next chapter for a list of the largest companies in Japan.) Note also that the OSE itself leads Japan in futures trading.

---

English information and data, see: http://www.ose.or.jp/e/jasdaq/ and http://www.ose.or.jp/e/market/5067. For daily and historical (up to five years) charts of the TOPIX 1 and 2, Mothers, and JASDAQ, search Bloomberg.com for the following tickers: TPX: IND, TSE2:IND, TSEMOTHR:IND, and JSDA:IND.

Using the TOPIX (composite) as a benchmark does not have much practical use for value investors due to its breadth of constituents (around 1,700) and since it's market-weighted certain sectors and industries (such as bank and non-bank finance) can be weighted quite heavily. What may be of more, albeit still limited, use is firstly to know the Tokyo Stock Exchange's other TOPIX indexes, which are listed below (notably missing are TSE-sponsored sector indexes), and to recognize in the very least there will be index-buying demand for component stocks.[29] Most interesting to value investors (to get away from the usual suspects in autos, banking, and consumer electronics) may be the components of the Dividend and "Active in Asia" indexes – two key areas for Japan and investors in Japanese equities, i.e. yield and growth opportunities. I review the Dividend index in Chapter 5 and the Asia index in Chapter 6.

- Core 30 – The 30 most liquid and highly market capitalized stocks

- Large 70 – After the Core 30, the 70 most liquid and highly market capitalized stocks

- 100 – Component stocks in the TOPIX Core 30 and the TOPIX Large 70

- Mid400 – Excluding TOPIX 100 stocks, inc. the remaining stocks in the TOPIX 500

- 500 – Component stocks in the TOPIX Core 30, the TOPIX Large 70 and the TOPIX Mid 400; growth and value styles of 500 are available

- 1000 – Components of TOPIX 500 and highly market capitalized stocks of TOPIX small

---

[29] See TSE "Indices," http://www.tse.or.jp/english/market/topix/index.html and TSE "Component stocks of TOPIX new index series," http://www.tse.or.jp/english/market/topix/data/component.html.

- Small – Outside the component stocks in the TOPIX 500

- Dividend Focus 100 – The top 100 issues (90 stocks, 10 REITs) which have large market capitalization and high estimated dividend yield, out of constituent issues of the TOPIX 1000 and Tokyo Stock Exchange REIT Index.

- Active in Asia – 25 issues from the TOPIX 500 universe based on criteria such as market value and sales in the Asia/Oceania region

- S&P/TOPIX 150 – A market capitalization weighted index, includes 150 highly liquid securities selected from each major sector of the Tokyo market, and represents approximately 70% of the market value of the Japanese equity market. (There is also a Shariah-compliant 150 Index and a Carbon Efficient 150 Index).

For readers interested in the history of the Tokyo Stock Exchange I recommend taking a look at the Exchange's website.[30] Note the "human" trading floor closed in 1999, and since then trading has been electronic at a redesigned facility called Arrows; "arrowhead," its next-generation trading system, was launched in 2010.[31]

## 33 industry groups of Tokyo Stock Exchange

Japan officially has 33 industry sectors that traditionally have been closely watched and tracked. For instance, the JASDAQ says on its website it has representational listings in 29 of 33 sectors. In recent years, however, perhaps as a way to be less confusing and to offer more liquid exchange-traded products, the TSE has consolidated the 33 sectors into 17.

---

[30] "History of TOPIX," TSE website.
http://www.tse.or.jp/english/market/topix/history/index.html
[31] For particular details of arrowhead, see the TSE's website:
http://www.tse.or.jp/english/rules/equities/arrowhead/info.html

Following is a list of the traditional 33 sectors with the consolidated (17) sectors in brackets.

| | |
|---|---|
| Fishery, Agriculture, & Forestry | [FOODS] |
| Food, Beverage | [FOODS] |
| Mining | [ENERGY RESOURCES] |
| Oil and Coal | [ENERGY RESOURCES] |
| Construction | [CONSTRUCTION & MATERIALS] |
| Glass and Ceramic Products | [CONSTRUCTION & MATERIALS] |
| Metal Products | [CONSTRUCTION & MATERIALS] |
| Textiles, Apparels | [RAW MATERIALS & CHEMICALS] |
| Pulp, Paper | [RAW MATERIALS & CHEMICALS] |
| Chemicals | [RAW MATERIALS & CHEMICALS] |
| Pharmaceutical | [PHARMACEUTICAL] |
| Rubber Products | [AUTOMOBILES & TRANSP. EQUIP.] |
| Transportation Equipment | [AUTOMOBILES & TRANSP. EQUIP.] |
| Iron and Steel | [STEEL & NONFERROUS METALS] |
| Nonferrous Metals | [STEEL & NONFERROUS METALS] |
| Machinery | [MACHINERY] |
| Electric Appliances | [ELECTRIC APPL. & PRECIS. INSTR.] |
| Precision Instruments | [ELECTRIC APPL. & PRECIS. INSTR.] |
| Other Products | [IT & SERVICES, OTHERS] |
| Information & Communication | [IT & SERVICES, OTHERS] |
| Services | [IT & SERVICES, OTHERS] |
| Electric Power and Gas | [ELECTRIC POWER & GAS] |

| | |
|---|---|
| Land Transportation | [TRANSPORTATION & LOGISTICS] |
| Marine Transportation | [TRANSPORTATION & LOGISTICS] |
| Air Transportation | [TRANSPORTATION & LOGISTICS] |
| Warehousing & Harbor Trans. | [TRANSP. & LOGISTICS] |
| Wholesale Trade | [COMM. & WHOLESALE TRADE] |
| Retail Trade | [RETAIL TRADE] |
| Banks | [BANKS] |
| Securities & Commodities Futures | [FINANCIALS (EX BANKS)] |
| Insurance | [FINANCIALS (EX BANKS)] |
| Other Financing Business | [FINANCIALS (EX BANKS)] |
| Real Estate | [REAL ESTATE] |

This is a great point to introduce Japan's ticker system, which consists of strictly of four-digit codes (similar to other Asian exchanges, but differing from the one to four letter tickers investors are familiar with in the U.S.). In the following example, note the similarity of tickers amongst auto stocks; it's often the case that companies of the same sector are grouped.[32]

- Nissan         7201
- Isuzu Motors   7202
- Toyota         7203
- Hino Motors    7205
- Mitsubishi Motors   7211

---

[32] Google Finance and MarketWatch (.com) are two English-language web sites that can be searched using the 4-digit codes.

- Mazda                7261
- Daihatsu Motor       7262
- Honda                7267
- Suzuki Motor         7269

## Japan-focused mutual funds

With the excessive attention on Japan's exports and commonly associated household names (Sony and Toyota, to name two), versus a misperceived uninteresting domestic-demand economy (common reasons provided include poor demographics as discussed above, as well as inefficient distribution networks, and reluctant spending by consumers in the face of deflation), there is a blatant tendency for most U.S. mutual funds focused on Japan to resemble one another closely in composition and performance. I have spent only a little time over the years looking at overseas (ex-U.S.) fund managers focused on Japan, primarily those in the UK, and can say that ostensibly there is less group-think there, perhaps owning to a longer history of such funds and tenure of their managers. The bottom-line is that there is no safety in numbers outside of a bull market. The last thing an investor wants to do is pay unnecessarily high fees for performance that may not be much better than an index fund. Shrewd value investors instead will be poised for outsized rewards by understanding Japan's market dynamics and taking advantage of opportunities missed or unactioned by others.

Some readers might remember the near-euphoric second-half of 2005 in Japan. Following the then post-bubble ultimate trough in 2003 when the benchmark Nikkei 225 breached the 8,000 level (a new low was set in early 2009 when the N225 fell into the 7,000s) there had already been a sharp rally of over 50% as popular Prime Minister Junichiro Koizumi vowed to end the banking system's non-performing loan problem (a massive consolidation had already begun, leading to the creation of so-called "mega banks") and achieved victory to privatize the nation's monolithic postal system. The peoples' belief in Koizumi (very rare indeed for a Japanese prime minister to have had such widespread admiration and support) and the Japan Post privatization win catapulted Japanese stocks up another 50% or so, once again in a very short time frame – in just over 3 years from its 2003 low, the Nikkei 225 had more than doubled to 17,000-plus. For reference, the Nikkei peaked at just below 40,000 at year-end 1989.

It turns out the Nikkei 225 never advanced much further than reaching the 18,000-level a couple of times before correcting, and eventually imploding in late-2008 to 2009. Two key happenings in 2006 put a damper on stocks, especially small-caps: the Livedoor scandal and activist investor Yoshiaki Murakami's insider trading charges.[33] Equally important from the above recapitulation is that many a Japan investor (particularly those using mutual and index funds) was burned, and especially those that put money in after the 2005 rally. The underlying problem with Japan-focused mutual funds then and still now is the crowded, often cyclical, and largely unoriginal investments predominantly consisting of exporters (the automakers and consumer electronics companies being the most common) and banks.

The peril of the hot stock should be well known to value investors. The trouble with chasing hot stocks in Japan is that with the post-bubble Nikkei 225 hammered down to such nominally low levels, it appears there's still much upside ceteris paribus, which is a tenuous argument given the exorbitant unfounded rise in stock prices in Japan into the end of the 1980s. In addition, while hot stocks may look pricey on a trailing earnings basis, their future growth prospects may look promising enough to deserve higher multiples, not to mention that book values may appear relatively attractive, too. So, generally speaking, the easy move for Japan fund managers is to stick with the biggest names, the ones often also with the biggest gains of late, and publicize their performance, hoping it will continue until it doesn't, and then claim that stocks valuations still look good and cling to them for a rebound that may not happen anytime soon. Excluding select strong broad market rallies (e.g. 2003, 2005, and 2009) Japan-focused mutual fund and index performance leaves a lot to be desired.

---

[33] Livedoor was a popular albeit controversial internet company headed by a so-called maverick, Takafumi Horie, a.k.a. "Horiemon." Murakami was also regarded as a maverick. For more on Livedoor, see: http://en.wikipedia.org/wiki/Livedoor.

# Substantially similar

In October 2007 I undertook a study of U.S.-marketed Japan-focused mutual fund holdings. I identified over forty such funds; total assets under management tapered quickly outside of the top-5 or so funds (AUM as of August 31, 2007). For reference, the Fidelity Japan fund (ticker FJPNX) was the largest at $1.72 billion, followed by Fidelity's Japan Smaller Companies fund (ticker FJSCX) at $807 million. T. Rowe Price Japan (ticker PRJPX) at $446 million, Scudder/Nomura Japan fund (ticker: SJPNX) at $364 million, and Matthews Japan fund (ticker MJFOX) at $235 million rounded out the top-5. The next largest fund had assets of $85 million; only three others had assets of more than $50 million. It goes without saying that interest in Japan, at least by way of mutual funds, was somewhat limited, and very concentrated in select funds. The iShares MSCI Japan Index fund (ticker EWJ), an exchange traded fund, has for many years had assets in the many billions of dollars -- $12 billion in October 2007; it is a favorite of both fund managers and individual investors who want exposure to Japan with liquid trading and at a much cheaper expense rate. By comparison, the iShares S&P/TOPIX 150 ETF (ticker ITF), not differing very meaningfully component-wise with EWJ, had assets of just over $300 million.

Toyota (ticker TM; Tokyo: 7203) was the top holding of four of the eight-largest funds and was also held in two other funds. Nintendo (ticker NTDOY.PK; Osaka: 7974) was the second-largest holding in three funds. Mizuho Financial Group (ticker MFG; Tokyo: 8411) was the third-largest holding in three funds and was also held in another fund. Sumitomo Mitsui Financial Group (ticker SMFG; Tokyo: 8316) was the second-largest holding of two funds and was held in three other funds. Mitsubishi UFJ Financial Group (ticker MTU; Tokyo: 8306) and Sony (ticker SNE; Tokyo: 6758) were each the largest holding of one fund and held in another. Canon (ticker CAJ; Tokyo: 7751) was held in three funds. Nomura Holdings (ticker NMR; Tokyo: 8604) and Komatsu (ticker KMTUY.PK; Tokyo: 6301) were held in two funds. Finally, Sumitomo Metal Industries (ticker SMMLY.PK; Tokyo: 5405) was held in four funds.

Fast forward nearly four years and the Fidelity Japan fund, which has a 0.93% expense fee, has assets of $560 million, down by two-thirds, with its top holdings consisting of (in order of size allocation) Toyota, Mitsubishi UFJ, Honda, Sumitomo Mitsui Trust, and Sumitomo Mitsui Financial Group, all very familiar names; for reference note its $11.3 billion average component market capitalization. The iShares Japan Index ETF EWJ's assets are down 40% to $7.2 billion. Its top holdings are Toyota, Honda, Mitsubishi UFJ, Canon, and Sumitomo Mitsui Financial Group, eerily similar to Fidelity Japan's; the market cap of the average component was $16.6 billion. If one is going to buy a basket of Japanese stocks, might as well buy EWJ and save 40% or more on expense fees (EWJ charges 0.54%). If interested, using Google or Yahoo! Finance, readers can compare performance of various durations side-by-side. It's not pretty; I'll save the ink.

Assets of the Fidelity Japan Smaller Companies fund are also down around 40% to $350 million; it charges a 1.09% expense fee and has a high portfolio turnover of 133%. This fund will provide investors with exposure to "smaller" companies (though components still have an average market capitalization around $2 billion) and is one of the few not dominated by the names mentioned above, but for some reason, the $10 billion-plus (market cap) Nintendo appears as its fifth-largest component and none other than Toyota (approximate $120 billion market cap) is its tenth-largest.

T. Rowe Price's Japan fund, which has a 1.13% expense fee – assets down 48% to $214 million – features Toyota, NTT, Mitsubishi UFJ, Honda, and Mitsui & Co. among its top-5 holdings; $11 billion average component market cap. The Scudder/Nomura Japan fund charges a 1.68% expense, three-times that of EWJ; its assets are down 29% to $258 million. Among its top-5 holdings are Sony, Honda, Mitsui & Co., Mitsubishi Electric, and Toyota; its average component market cap of $9.5 billion is lower than the other funds, but its holdings clearly mirror the others. The Matthews Japan fund's assets are down 30% to $165 million; it charges a 1.3% expense fee. While its top-5 holdings, excluding Honda at number four, bear no resemblance at the present to the funds above (Itochu, ORIX, Nissan, Honda, and GMO Payment Gateway), its average component market cap is $4.3 billion (similar to the Fidelity Smaller fund, this is still a fund that favors larger companies over smaller ones).

The ETF iShares S&P/TOPIX 150 charges a 0.5% expense fee, and its assets have since fallen by two-thirds to $101 million. Its top-5 holdings are Toyota, Mitsubishi UFJ, Canon, Honda, and Sumitomo Mitsui Financial Group, identical (name-wise) to EWJ, and its average component market cap is $22.6 billion, the largest of any of the above funds. With all the overlapping holdings, I became curious what exactly PIMCO (the trillion dollar asset management company) was buying after the March 11, 2011, triple-disaster in Japan, when *Barron's* published its bullish take on Japan and Japanese stocks following the disaster and mentioned: "Another buyer was Pimco, which snapped up Japanese ETFs for its Pimco Global Multi-Asset Fund (PGMAX)."[34] Interestingly, the most recently available data (as of June 30, 2011) of fund holdings does not list anything related to Japan. Holdings as of the end of March 2011, were not readily accessible on the web; but Morningstar's Sept. 19, 2011, print version of its *Fund Highlights* shows that no portfolio information was available for the quarter-ended March 31st, while it does indicate that the $4.86B fund had 7% portfolio exposure to Japan. Notice that *Barron's* said it was snapping up ETFs; EWJ is a certainty, but with PIMCO's large asset base, and the low asset levels (and comparatively thin trading) of other Japan ETFs, it's hard to imagine what exactly ended up in PGMAX.

Interestingly enough, rather than look to Japan-focused mutual funds for exposure and ideas, it appears much more efficacious to review the holdings of value-oriented mutual funds.[35] Among funds that have been longer-term investors in Japan include Brandes, Dodge & Cox, First Eagle, Longleaf, Oakmark, and Third Avenue. Brandes in recent years has invested as much as twenty percent of its tens of billions of dollars in assets in Japan – somewhat ironically, Brandes at any time could have more invested in Japan than the

---

[34] "Invest in Japan," *Barron's*, Mar. 21, 2011.
http://online.barrons.com/article/SB50001424052970203757604576204523501069008.html

[35] Visit a fund's website for its latest and archived copies of shareholder letters and portfolio holdings. A site also worth visiting is ValueWalk (dot-com), which among its services offers a page entitled, "Timeless Reading," which contains an amazing collection of value investing-related information. See:
http://www.valuewalk.com/timeless-reading/.

assets in leading Japan ETF, EWJ, and quite possibly of all Japan-focused funds in the U.S.! However, note that many of its Japan holdings (as of year-end 2011) are staple names found atop Japan ETFs and funds, such as NTT (9432), Toyota (7203), Honda (7267), Canon (7751), and Fujifilm (4901). To be fair, NTT is a longstanding compelling value story and the other four companies have traded at cyclically low levels; notice Brandes doesn't report any stakes, at least not big ones, in banks. Leading retailer Seven & I (3382), which most notably owns 7-Eleven and supermarket chain Itoyokado, is a more interesting holding. Otherwise, Brandes also holds a number of Japanese pharmaceutical companies.

Dodge & Cox, a fund manager with over $100 billion under management, often has several Japanese companies in its International Stock fund (DODFX), with most investments being larger than $100 million. As of year-end 2011, DODFX's largest Japanese holdings include: Mitsubishi Electric (6503), Fujitsu (6702), Kyocera (6971), Nintendo (7974), and Fujifilm (4901), all positions in excess of $400 million each. Smaller investments that are less "household" (to non-Japanese) include Aderans (8170; a leading wigmaker that has received a large amount of attention in recent years following activist measures taken by investment firm Steel Partners), NGK Spark Plug (5334), the world's leading manufacturer of spark plugs, and Bank of Yokohama (8332). Regarding activism, Brandes has taken action in Japan, with one area of particular concern being low yielding excess capital.

Longleaf Partners International Fund (LLINX) is another billion-dollar fund, but a more modest one, with assets approaching $1.6 billion at year-end 2011. Similar to Brandes, at times it can have fairly large exposure to Japan. Sadly for Longleaf, however, it found itself among Olympus' (7733) largest shareholders when ousted president Michael Woodford went to the press with his findings of massive financial fraud, which sent Olympus' share price crashing from the Y2,500-level in October 2011, to the Y500-level early the next month. Olympus did rebound to Y1,000-plus, but still faces possible de-listing as of early January 2012. In Longleaf International's Q3 (ended September 30, 2011) commentary, it had almost 18% of its assets in Japan; at year-end 2011, exposure had fallen to just over 7%. Despite the negative impact of Olympus, Longleaf had two positions disclosed earlier in 2011 that are worth reviewing.

Firstly, Nitori Holdings (9843), Japan's leading home furnishing retailer (the "Japanese IKEA," though it competes with IKEA in Japan), has fairly modest debt levels (it could be debt-free in just over a year), years of double-digit top- and bottom-line growth, and an ROE in recent years between the high-teens and low-twenties. As of February 24, 2012, Nitori trades at a not-so-cheap 2.5-times book, however, it trades at under 13-times trailing earnings and is slightly cheaper on a forward basis; and its dividend has been on the rise, too. After a 2002 IPO of around Y2,000 (split-adjusted), Nitori doubled by 2005, tripled by 2006, and has flirted with the Y8,000-level in recent years (see all-time chart below). Nitori has a market cap of Y403 billion or $5 billion. Not deep value, and not a hidden gem, but a fine example nonetheless of an excellent Japanese company. Not priced unreasonably high despite its successes, its stock price growth matches more its growth in revenues since IPO as opposed to its near 10-fold increase in earnings.[36] Longleaf established a position in Nitori after the March 11th disaster.

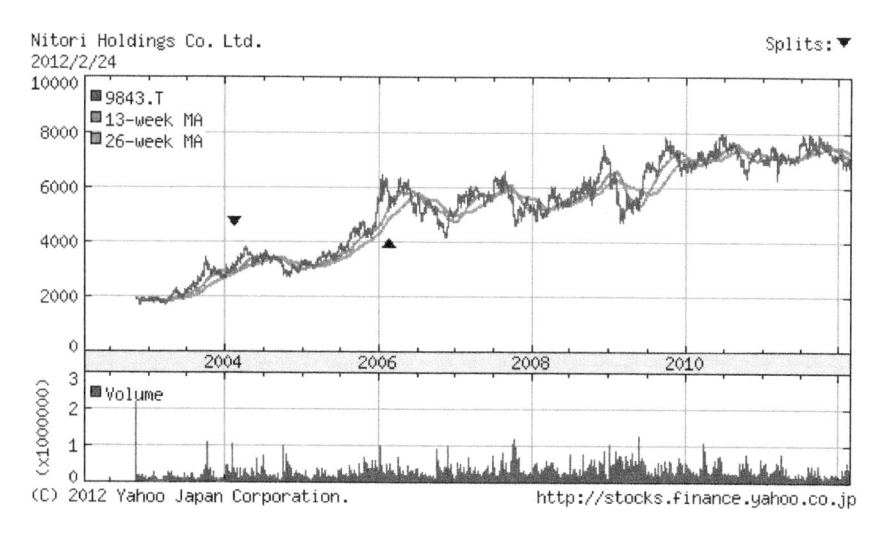

---

[36] Beside visiting a company's Investor Relations website, a reliable English source of Japanese company financial data is MSN Money, which is better than many other free sites since it not only publishes financials, but a whole five years worth and it has ten-year summaries. At http://money.msn.com/stocks/ enter a ticker such as 9843; on the next page choose "Japan" for country, remove the ticker and enter a company name (e.g. Nitori). On the next page financial and fundamental research options appear in the left-margin.

Secondly, Hirose Electric (6806) is a leading manufacturer of electronic connectors for some of the world's top electronics companies. It has not had the impressive growth of the likes of Nitori, but it does have the better valuation in terms of traditional metrics – as of February 24, 2012, it trades at 1.2-times book, and although it's trading at just under 25-times earnings, nearly half of its market value consists of net cash. Also, its forward P/E indicates that at current prices it is trading at closer to 20-times earnings. Hirose's ROE has been around 5% - 6% in recent years. Note, however, that it is debt-free, and it has a dividend yield of over 2.2%, in addition to having bought back around 10% of its shares outstanding over the past five years to March 2011. In spite of all the above, Hirose is trading near ten-year low levels. (See chart below). Hirose also happens to be a holding of Oakmark's International Small Cap fund (OAKEX) and First Eagle Investment Management, another value-oriented shop that has put money to work in Japan.

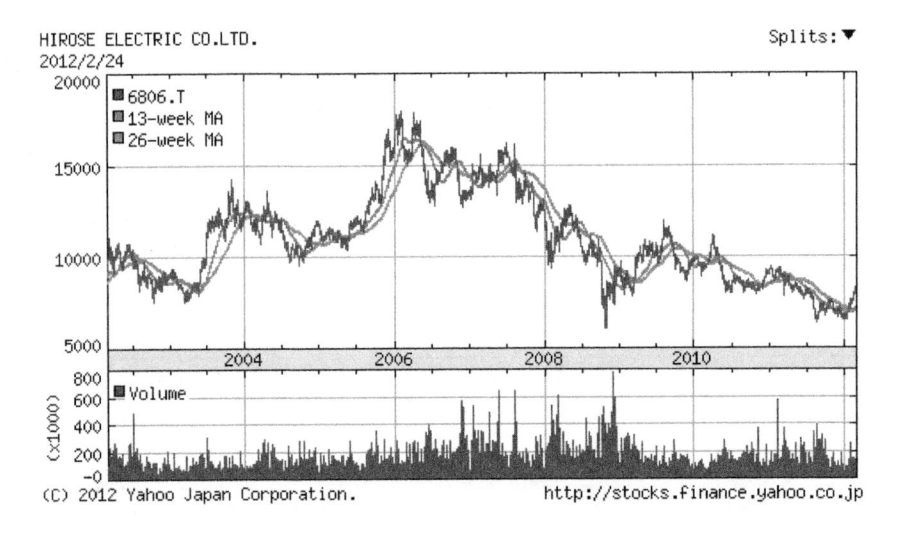

Prior to wrapping up this cursory review of select value funds' investments in Japan, let's take a quick look at some of Oakmark and First Eagle's holdings. Oakmark was another shareholder of Olympus at the time its fraud was revealed by former president Michael Woodford. Oakmark's International Fund (OAKIX) had almost $7.2 billion in assets as of year-end 2011. Just under 24% of assets were invested in Japan, with its largest holdings including large-caps: Toyota (7203), Daiwa Securities (8601), Canon

(7751), and Rohm (6963). Having more interesting holdings than the usual suspects is Oakmark's International Small Cap Fund (OAKEX), which had over $1.3 billion in assets of which 28.5% were in Japan. Its largest Japanese holdings that comprise the fund's top-10 holdings include Hirose Electric (reviewed above), videogame maker Square Enix (9684), and drug store operator Sugi Holdings (7649). Toyota Industries (6201), an affiliate of Toyota, is also a portfolio company – some may recognize this name as one of Third Eagle's longtime favorites, though it has been reducing its stake (more on this in Chapter 5). Very few of Oakmark's remaining Japanese holdings are likely to be familiar to most investors, which is obviously a great thing considering the ubiquity of some names and bias toward large capitalizations in most funds.[37]

## iShares MSCI Japan Index ETF (EWJ)

Let's take a close look at EWJ for reference and clarity since beside the actual Nikkei 225 benchmark itself (and Nikkei futures), EWJ serves as the main proxy for investing and trading Japan. EWJ has been around a lot longer, since 1996, than rival Japan ETFs. EWJ's massive average daily trading volume of some 30 million shares provides high liquidity and narrow bid/ask spreads, much more so than other Japan ETFs, which have a fraction of the volume of EWJ. However, it is important to recognize that the robust trading in combination with the very cyclical trading behavior of leading Japanese stocks also means that EWJ may be among the favorite holdings of institutional investors to sell when the broader market turns negative. Its liquidity and quality assets make selling it easy to raise cash levels.

Fundamentally, know that EWJ does not track the Nikkei 225 (the MAXIS Nikkei 225 Index Fund, ticker: NKY, does; it was launched in summer 2011 and as of February 2012, it had assets of around $175 million and a competitive expense ratio of 0.50%, although weekly volume that has yet to reach one million shares, at a recent $14.25/share, may preclude traders and larger investors). That EWJ tracks the N225 is a basic misconception

---

[37] Visit Oakmark.com for current and past holdings.

shared amongst many retail investors/traders and surely even amongst some professionals. EWJ is based on MSCI's (Morgan Stanley Capital International) own index – EWJ typically has over 300 holdings (310 as of July 31, 2011 or a third more than the N225). While the Tokyo Stock Exchange has long since closed by the time New York opens, MSCI publishes live quotes of its indices, including MSCI Japan, for paying customers via subscription and Bloomberg.

If you are a trader, using leverage, and/or concerned about the minutest of price movements, you're probably disadvantaged by not having such quotes from MSCI or via a Bloomberg terminal. As a value investor, however, just be aware that EWJ does not equal one-for-one the N225. It goes without saying that a strong yen is a positive for the quoted price per share of EWJ itself, but in fact, a strong yen will most often be a negative for the companies that comprise EWJ since amongst those that have overseas sales, the stronger the yen the less those sales and/or repatriated funds are worth denominated in yen. In short, it is possible a rising yen could help the price of EWJ by magnifying any gains or mitigating losses. And a weaker yen, while typically a positive for constituent companies, can limit EWJ's upside and magnify its downside. Know that EWJ is optionable but volume is, or typically may be, light. Also, EWJ can be sold short, but it may not be easy to locate shares at any given time.

Earlier in this chapter I mentioned a key shortcoming of price-weighted indexes. Let's now look at the downside to market value-weighted index funds. *The Economist's* Buttonwood succinctly noted June 2011: "Traditional indices are weighted by market value. As a result, investors will end up having their biggest exposure to a company when its value has reached its peak. They will buy up-and-coming companies when they join the index and sell them again when they drop out; it is a formula for buying high and selling low."[38] The popular EWJ discussed above is market-weighted. An exception among Japan funds is WisdomTree, which sponsors funds based on fundamental factors; it is unique in its dividend-based methodology.[39] My only issue with

---

[38] "On the wrong track: Is there a better way to mimic the stockmarket," *Economist* (Buttonwood), Jun. 4, 2011. http://www.economist.com/node/18774910
[39] See http://wisdomtree.com.

WisdomTree's Japan ETFs is that they have hundreds of holdings, which while offering diversification, dilute performance of real winners, the kind that value investors spend time to identify and analyze. WisdomTree's Japan SmallCap Dividend fund (DFJ) most recently (January 2012) had over 500 holdings, with its largest, Park24 Co (4666) having a portfolio weighting of 0.79% Another matter is that it is a so-called dividend fund, but its trailing 12-month yield of 2.1% comes in lower than TSE 2nd section and JASDAQ trailing yields of more than 2.4%. WisdomTree's Japan Hedged Equity fund (DXJ) meanwhile, which most recently had 629 holdings, is a close replica of most Japan funds and large indexes featuring Japan's mega caps, having portfolio weightings of 0.74% to 4.34% among its top-25 holdings, while a large number of holdings have negligible weightings.

For value investors, the review of Japan-focused funds should inspire confidence in the value approach to investing. The cyclical nature of the economy and funds themselves should serve as a reminder to pay as little as possible for growth. Although disclosure of fund holdings is delayed, a review of top holdings and changes to them, in addition to portfolio manager commentary, can be helpful.[40] Remember that fund managers and analysts often use the same or similar information and resources. Sometimes coattails investing works out well; sometimes it's wise to question the wisdom of consensus, keeping in mind opportunity cost and possible diminishing returns from over-researching. I tend to be skeptical of both mainstream business press reporting and statements from corporate executives. While not as extreme as Walter Schloss in approach (i.e. only relying on the company's

---

[40] Morningstar.com is the source of a majority of the fund data referred to in this chapter. There is usually a lag of one month (up to three months) for component holdings due to the typical quarterly disclosure of mutual fund holdings. As a rule, the best source of fund info is a fund company's website. As an alternative, especially for uniform presentation of information to compare fund options across different fund families, Morningstar.com (subscription-free; paid subscription includes access to in-house analyst fund analysis) has been the most reliable, robust, and timely in my experience. Morningstar lists each fund's top-25 holdings and denotes increases, decreases, and new additions to the top-25. Be sure to look for disclaimers containing dates for select information such as portfolio holdings.

reported financials), I agree with Martin Whitman, who has long said that he essentially trusts the numbers (that companies report) and works with them. Fortunately, the amount of financial disclosure is quite good in Japan, as it is in the U.S.

## Japanese ADRs

The number of Japanese American Depository Receipts (ADRs) has been on the decline for several years; as recently as 2006 there were 30 listed on the New York Stock Exchange and the Nasdaq. As of mid-year 2011 there were 21. Investors have access to Japan's three mega-banks, Mitsubishi UFJ (MTU), Mizuho (MFG), and Sumitomo Mitsui (SMFG), leading investment bank, Nomura (NMR), two of the Big-3 automakers, Toyota (TM) and Honda (HMC), and some of the leading consumer electronics manufacturers, Sony (SNE), Canon (CAJ), and Panasonic (PC).

**Listed ADRs, in alphabetical order, followed by ADR and ordinary tickers, and ordinary-to-ADR listing ratios:**

| | | | |
|---|---|---|---|
| Advantest | (ATE) | (6857) | 1:1 |
| Canon | (CAJ) | (7751) | 1:1 |
| Hitachi | (HIT) | (6501) | 1:10 |
| Honda | (HMC) | (7267) | 1:1 |
| Internet Initiative Japan | (IIJI) | (3774) | 400:1 |
| ORIX | (IX) | (8591) | 2:1 |
| Konami | (KNM) | (9766) | 1:1 |
| Kubota | (KUB) | (6326) | 1:5 |
| Kyocera | (KYO) | (6971) | 1:1 |
| Makita | (MKTAY) | (6586) | 1:1 |

| | | | |
|---|---|---|---|
| Mitsubishi UFJ | (MTU) | (8306) | 1:1 |
| Mizuho | (MFG) | (8411) | 1:2 |
| Nidec | (NJ) | (6594) | 4:1 |
| Nippon Telegraph & Tel. | (NTT) | (9432) | 2:1 |
| Nomura | (NMR) | (8604) | 1:1 |
| NTT DoCoMo | (DCM) | (9437) | 100:1 |
| Panasonic | (PC) | (6752) | 1:1 |
| Sony | (SNE) | (6758) | 1:1 |
| Sumitomo Mitsui | (SMFG) | (8316) | 5:1 |
| Toyota | (TM) | (7203) | 1:2 |
| Wacoal | (WACLY) | (3591) | 1:5 |

Regarding the ordinary-to-ADR ratios, 1:1 means that the Japanese share price is equivalent to the ADR price, but investors must then factor in the prevailing exchange rate. For a simple example, if the yen and dollar were at parity, and Nomura closed at Y400, its ADRs should trade at/around $4.00. There may be arbitrage opportunities on occasion, but in general the opportunities will be hardly worth actively looking for and will likely be hard to capitalize on with a meaningful number of shares. Large ratios are indicative of high ordinary share prices, such as Internet Initiative Japan's Y239,100 close on January 20, 2012, followed by a $7.71 close on the Nasdaq. At an approximate exchange rate of Y77/$1, and adjusting for the 400:1 ratio, IIJ's ordinary share equivalent is $7.76. In years past there were far more diverging ordinary-to-ADR ratios than not. Thankfully, there are increasingly more one-for-one ratios as Japanese companies have undertaken share splits to make it easier for individual investors to buy their shares.

Beyond the aforementioned exchange-listed ADRs, there is a much broader universe of Pink Sheet-traded ADRs. While chances are readers of this book know that quality companies trade on the same Pink Sheets that feature penny stock scams, recently delisted companies, near-bankrupt companies, and companies too small to, or unwilling to, list on the American Stock Exchange, it's still worth a brief overview. In short, there are three levels of ADRs, with the 3rd being the highest and most similar to a domestic listing in terms of being able to raise capital. Ticker symbols of level III ADRs are no different than domestic issues, such as TM for Toyota, HMC for Honda, and SNE for Sony. Similarly, there's GM for General Motors, F for Ford, and AAPL for Apple. Level II ADRs are traded on the Nasdaq or NYSE but companies are not able to raise capital and have fewer disclosure obligations than level III listings. Finally, level I ADRs are traded over the counter often as "Pink Sheets" quotations with .PK suffixes.

One of the most well known Pink Sheets among Japanese ADRs is Nintendo (NTDOY.PK), whose 3-month average trading volume (as of Feb. 2012) is around 190,000 shares (per day). Nissan (NSANY.PK), was previously exchange-listed; its 3-month average daily volume is 92,000-plus shares. Note that both Nintendo and Nissan's tickers end in a 'Y' before the .PK suffix. This indicates they are sponsored ADRs. This is important to know because any foreign companies that have five-letter tickers ending in an 'F' are technically ordinary shares or (ORDs; traded over-the-counter), not ADRs, and are not only usually much less liquid than ADRs, but may also incur hefty trade settlement commissions.

It goes without saying that any orders placed for these ADRs (including ORDs) absolutely must be done by limit order. If you are trying to trade smaller than the minimum required all-or-nothing limit order don't do it; just as you don't want to use a market order. There is no telling whether, how much, or at what price(s) your order will be filled. When possible either transact in exchange-listed shares or ordinary shares traded in Japan. Shares ending in a "Y" are preferable to those ending in an "F." Finally, before you ever transact in any ADR or ORD, if you are referencing the share price of the ordinary listing in Japan, and you should be, you must be aware of the price ratio since it may not be 1:1 (see above section). As of February 2012, there were a total of 258 Japanese ADRs (exchange listed and those with "Y"-

ending symbols) per JPMorgan's ADR.com.[41] A spot check suggests as many as 10% of the ADRs may not be active, some due to mergers.

**Pink Sheets ADRs with decent daily volume as of February 2012:**

- Dai Nippon Printing (DNPLY.PK) 207,000
- Daiwa Securities (DSEEY.PK) 150,000
- Komatsu (KMTUY.PK) 145,000
- Tokio Marine (TKOMY.PK) 127,000
- Takeda Pharma (TKPYY.PK) 111,000
- Sega Sammy (SGAMY.PK) 103,000
- Fanuc (FANUY.PK) 93,000
- Kao (KCRPY.PK) 93,000
- Sekisui House (SKHSY.PK) 91,000
- FujiFilm (FUJIY.PK) 83,000
- KDDI (KDDIY.PK) 51,000
- Shiseido (SSDOY.PK) 39,000
- Daiichi Sankyo (DSNKY) 37,000
- Astellas Pharma (ALPMY.PK) 30,000

---

[41] ADR search by country via JPMorgan's ADR.com website: https://www.adr.com/DRSearch/CustomDRSearch

For reference, following is a list of Japan-related ETFs and closed-end funds (denoted by *) with assets of at least around $100 million as of February 2012. I used a $100 million or thereabouts threshold since it is said that such an amount is a typical breakeven point for fund sponsors. It doesn't make sense to unnecessarily subject oneself to wide bid/ask spreads. I will not review the two close-end funds because I don't believe readers need to spend time on them outside of instances in which they trade at multi-month double-digit discounts and readers intend to watch fund prices and NAVs closely. JEQ's top-holdings are very similar to the usual suspects found in index and Japan-focused mutual funds. JOF offers some unique names, but I would rather use them for idea generation than be in the backseat; annual turnover of portfolio holdings is 57% per Morningstar.com.

- CurrencyShares Japanese Yen Trust (FXY)
- iShares MSCI Japan Index (EWJ)
- iShares S&P/TOPIX 150 (ITF)
- *Japan Equity Fund (JEQ)
- *Japan Smaller Cap Fund (JOF)
- MAXXIS Nikkei 225 Index (NKY)
- SPDR Russell/Nomura SmallCap Japan (JSC)
- Vanguard Pacific Stock (VPL)
- WisdomTree JP SmallCap Dividend (DFJ)
- WisdomTree JP Hedged Equity (DXJ)

# CHAPTER 3

# JAPANESE MUTUAL FUNDS

The Japanese universe of mutual funds (known as trust funds, domestically) is an odd one. Rather than serving as a key component to the domestic equities market as mutual funds do in the U.S., they are not widely embraced by domestic investors. "Individual investors shun investment trusts," an article which appeared in the July 18, 2011, edition of *The Nikkei Weekly*, contains as much overview as one needs. I will summarize briefly and emphasize a couple of my personal observations.

Though mutual funds are by no means new in Japan – they have been around for over 60 years – they only comprise 4% of individuals' assets (Y65 trillion or about $850 billion) and only 8% of the public invests in them. In fact, in the early 1980's the participation rate was in the teens, similar to the U.S. Today, the U.S. mutual fund market is reported to be fifteen-times larger (based on assets) than Japan's, which ranks only eighth in the world. Among the explanations for the comparatively small size include poor fund performance, broad reluctance by the public to invest, lack of a robust 401(k) system like the U.S., over-emphasis on marketing overseas-themed investments, and high fees. Interestingly, it's not for a lack of innovation, such as offering funds that pay dividends on a monthly basis, though some innovation may pose risks via derivative transactions that could prove expensive. That said, there are also unnecessary obstacles preventing more inflows such as minimum trading units, with some ETFs having 1,000-lot minimums that can require investment capital of around $10,000. Over the longer term, fund sponsors may not be able to get away with high fees and minimums as competition increases. There are already ETFs being launched with only 10-lot minimums and fees under 0.10%.

On the matter of performance, it is no secret that Japanese equities as a whole have done very poorly over the past two decades. There have been monster rallies (referred to as "false starts" after the fact), as I referred to earlier, and discuss again later, but the fact is that broad market performance has been unsatisfactory. Take for instance the decade of 2000 - 2010, during which the broad TOPIX benchmark lost thirty percent of its value. And bubble-peak to 2011, the Nikkei 225 benchmark is still down approximately 78%. Nevertheless, *The Nikkei Weekly* article expressly notes that despite the most recent lost decade (i.e. the 30% decline in the TOPIX), 48% of stocks have actually risen in price. While more data would be great, albeit perhaps superfluous, there is clearly merit in fundamental stock analysis.

Which leads me to the point of fund marketing. It has always been puzzling (*disturbing* may be a better way of putting it) to see such a strong desire amongst the investing Japanese public for overseas stocks (not as surprising in the case of bonds and currencies thanks to anemic domestic yields), in light of the great value opportunities at home. A chief complaint in the *Nikkei Weekly* article is the marketing department is calling the shots, creating the funds they want, not necessarily what investors want. This is apparently an ongoing issue, as I have heard anecdotally that in the past (hopefully not true today) it was marketing that also "researched" equities and called the shots for portfolio management. The desire for non-Japanese investments amongst the Japanese is a multi-faceted matter involving somewhat simplistically, a self-reinforcing, at times defeatist mindset as pertains the domestic economy (it doesn't help that bad or negative news and stories seem to sell better than good or upbeat ones). Likewise, it's an attempt to compensate for what Japan does not have, hence an attraction to resource-rich, higher-growth, and higher-yielding (currencies, bonds, and other securities/assets) countries.

As for yield hunger, interest rates in Japan have been at or near zero since 1998, for most of that time under a policy officially called ZIRP or Zero

Interest Rate Policy. The ZIRP was essentially resurrected in 2008/2009 amidst the Great Financial Crisis, a mere two years after the Bank of Japan had raised interest rates for the first time post-ZIRP. In 2006, Japan's economy was riding the global boom of "record" everything such as corporate profits, consumption, debt issuance, M&A, securitization, and trade, all in which the BOJ's ZIRP and near-ZIRP played at least a minor supporting role. The BOJ was the official sponsor of the yen carry trade (for foreigners: borrowing in yen to invest in higher-yielding assets; for Japanese: converting yen into higher-yielding foreign currencies and foreign currency-denominated securities or assets), which was a popular undertaking amongst hedge funds and Japanese housewives (so-called "Mrs. Watanabe" in the collective and an apparent favorite reference of the *Financial Times*), alike; but that does not mean *every* hedge fund and house wife were "punting."

So, amidst the global boom, the yen remained relatively weak against the dollar, around the 120-level (certainly no threat then of reaching parity), compared to current levels (February 2012) in the high-70s to flirting with 80. However, all good things come to an end and the yen carry trade certainly ended badly for those involved, in the mad scramble in late-2008 to liquidate positions for whatever the reason carry traders might have had; the yen has since continued to strengthen to record levels, and subsequently intervention after intervention by the Finance Ministry has not worked to reverse the strength (likely to the dismay of any brave soul willing to short Japanese government bonds) – but it has certainly prevented a catastrophic surge, such as to the 50-level. What is interesting at present, in terms of yield and speaking specifically about equities' dividend yields, is the depressed Japanese stock market now has dividend yields that easily exceed its nation's own benchmark 10-year government bond, and rather than being the runt of the developed world, yields in Japan are very competitive.

Before I share some information on what the Japanese are investing in by way of mutual funds, for a sampling of headlines let's take a look at the home page of Morningstar Japan on a visit made in October 2011, which by and large is no different than one made earlier or more recently. Readers may wish to visit, http://www.morningstar.co.jp/, to see how much noise a Japanese investor has to contend with – reflective also of other internet and magazine content. Below I list some of the articles, advertisements and links on the home page. I suppose the abundance of overseas information is the U.S. equivalent of pumping out (and marketing) ETF after ETF.

> 1. Article: President Obama's 2 major concerns, an unexpected ambush in the coming presidential election
>
> 2. Article: ("Emerging Markets Eye") Russia's Putin announces plan to establish Eurasia bloc
>
> 3. Article: (Re. Mutual funds) The differing actions of Japanese and American investors amidst fluctuating markets
>
> 4. Article: (Chinese stock column) Coming improvements, and dangers, of improving supply and demand of coal
>
> 5. Article: (Fund analysis report) Goldman Sachs' emerging countries' bond funds
>
> 6. Ad block: "Autumn asset management special"; (1) ANZ Bank for asset diversification, into the Australian dollar; (2) Half-off load charge campaign for emerging market stock funds; (3) Accepting reservations for a November, Osaka mutual fund investing event with 4 online brokerages.
>
> 7. Ad block: Morningstar Japan's "Emerging Market Eye"
>
> 8. Ad block: Free invite for 500 people to Fidelity's investor seminar about investing in U.S. REITs
>
> 9. Video reports: (1) Deutsche AM on the return of aggression in markets; (2) Mizuho Trust on the attractiveness of investing in Australian dollar-denominated bonds; (3) The practicality and efficacy of investing, now, in managed futures.
>
> 10. Ad: Half-price campaign for Stock Market newspaper on iPad
>
> 11. Ad: DIAM Asset Management emerging market (sovereign) currency investing

**12. Content: Mutual funds of interest amongst readers:** (1) Emerging market stock funds: China, India, Brazil, Russia, other emerging markets, Vietnam, Indonesia, Southeast Asia, Middle East and Africa; (2) High-yield funds: Brazil real bonds, High-income (yield) bonds, Global REITs, Australian Dollar bonds, Global bonds, **J-REITs**, European bonds, Investment-grade high-yield currency bonds; **(3) Domestic and style stock funds:** Environmental, Natural resources, long-term domestic, SMEs, Bullish/bearish, advanced economies, domestic indices; (4) Index and other funds: Overseas bond indices, Overseas stock indices, Gold and Oil, Currencies, SRI (socially responsible), Emerging country balanced, and convertible bonds.

Outside of the third article, there is no real mention of anything related to Japan until the latter portion of "funds of interest" block!

# Largest Mutual Funds in Japan

Now let's take a look at the top-20 mutual funds in Japan (ranked by assets). We'll then take a look under the hood of two funds for a sampling of individual Japanese stocks.

**Mutual fund ranking by assets (trillions JPY) as of November 16, 2011 (via Morningstar Japan)**

1. Global Sovereign Open (end; monthly yield) –Kokusai; Y1.988T, $25.5B

2. Short-term A$ Debt Open (end; monthly yield) –Daiwa; Y1.134T, $14.5B

3. High-grade Oceania Bond (monthly yield) –Daiwa; Y906.738B, $11.5B

4. Global High-yield Bond (Resource country) –Nomura; Y878.596B, $11.0B

5. Shinko U.S. REIT Open – Shinko; Y676.808 billion, $8.5B

6. Lasalle Global REIT Open (monthly yield) – Nikko; Y667.579B, $8.5B

7. Nikkei 225 Index Fund – Nomura; Y658.194 billion, $8.5B

8. Pictet Global Income Equities – Pictet; Y651.497 billion, $8.5B

9. TOPIX Index Fund – Nomura; Y647.690 billion, $8.5B

10. Brazil Bond Open (monthly yield) – Daiwa; Y646.424 billion, $8.5B

...

20. Daiwa U.S. REIT Fund (monthly yield) – Daiwa: Y363.851 billion, $4.5B

*Values rounded in US$ to nearest $500 million.*

Numbers 11 – 19 are comprised of international (including emerging market) and global (which by definition includes Japan even if a only a very small allocation) bond and REIT funds. Daiwa has six of the top twenty funds ranked by asset size; Nomura has four, Fidelity, two, Kokusai, two, and Nikko, two. There is not a single fund, beside the Nikkei 225 and TOPIX Index funds, that focus on a domestic equity strategy. Another (obvious) observation is the comparatively small assets the top funds manage compared to U.S. counterparts. Recall my earlier mention of comparisons of investor participation. Japan's current largest fund, Global Sovereign, had peak assets approaching Y6 trillion (or $60 billion at Y/$ parity for a simple comparison) at fiscal year-end March 2008. Even that asset level pales in comparison to the assets under management of funds sponsored for example by Pimco, Vanguard, American, and Fidelity, some of which exceed $100 billion.

A December 2011, presentation to Japan's Financial Services Agency by Morningstar Japan's COO, Tomoya Asakura, makes the point that despite amassing such a large asset base (Global Sovereign's assets surged around six-fold between 2002 and 2008), Global Sovereign's sponsor, Kokusai, never lowered fund management fees, which have stayed fixed at 1.31%. This particular management fee is below average in Japan where the average has actually been on the rise; up from a decade low of 1.36% in 2003 nearly unabated (with annual increases) to 1.48% in 2011. Adding insult to injury, the sales (loads) fees charged to investors have been rising in tandem from a decade low of 2.22% in 2002 and 2003 to 2.69% in 2011.[42] Thus, combined, investors must hurdle more than 4% on average! No wonder an unrelated article by leading Japanese magazine publisher Diamond reported of a study that found approximately 60% of Japanese 401(k) accounts were worth less than their principal (invested) value.[43]

One more takeaway from the Morningstar COO's presentation is his lamenting how strong performance fails to attract investor interest, as evidenced by Japan's largest domestic-focused equity fund (non-index), Fidelity Japan Growth Fund, which has lost over 13% year-to-date November 30, 2011, is flat over the past three years, down over 12% in the past five years, and down just under 2% over the past ten years. By comparison, JP Morgan's JF The Japan fund (a growth-oriented fund) is up 9.4% year-to-date (making for a 20%-plus absolute return versus Fidelity), up more than 16% over three years, 1% in the past five years, and nearly 12% in the past ten years. JP Morgan's fund outperformed Fidelity's by more than 10% in each period. Now get ready for this, Fidelity's fund's assets under management as of November 30, 2011: Y224 billion ($2.9 billion) vs. JP Morgan's fund: Y12.6 billion ($164 million). Nearly an 18-fold difference! Fidelity charges a 3.15% load and 1.71% management fee. Interestingly, Morningstar Japan rates the Fidelity fund 4-stars. JP Morgan's fund also charges a 3.15% load and a slightly higher management fee of 1.81%. It is rated 5-stars.

**Top holdings of JP Morgan's JF The Japan fund as of November 30, 2011, valuations based on December 30, 2011 market close.**

- Anritsu (T1: 6754)        2.57x book, 35.2x ttm P/E
- KLab (Mothers: 3656)      17.1x book, 40.7x ttm P/E
- UBIC (Mothers: 2158)      n/a

---

[42] "投資信託に関する現状の課題と対応," Dec. 16, 2011.
http://www.fsa.go.jp/singi/singi_kinyu/w_group/siryou/20111216/01.pdf
[43] "401ｋの運用成績ガタ落ち元本割れ6割の深刻," Dec. 28, 2011.
http://zasshi.news.yahoo.co.jp/article?a=20111228-00015498-diamond-bus_all

- Sanrio (T1: 8136)                  11.3x book, 37.8x ttm P/E

- LeoPalace21 (T1: 8848)          0.82x book, ( - )   ttm P/E

- Gree (T1: 3632)                     16.3x book, 33.2x ttm P/E

- Skymark Airlines (Mothers: 9204)    2.35x book, 11.3x ttm P/E

- Net One Systems (T1: 7518)       1.60x book, 32.6x ttm P/E

- *Shin-Kobe Elec. Machinery (T1: 6934)    3.22x book, 19.2x ttm P/E

- Takuma (T1: 6013)                 1.20x book, 14.3x ttm P/E

*Has received takeover offer from Hitachi Chemical expiring Jan. 19, 2012.

Anritsu comprised 7.1% of the portfolio; Takuma 3.2%; top-10 holdings represent 42.7% of portfolio.

Morningstar Japan provides a ranking of the biggest inflows to funds over the past month. As of October 31, 2011, the top-25 funds ranked by inflows were close to a carbon copy of the above ranking based on assets. Overall, and again, beside the Nikkei 225 and TOPIX Index funds (and one global balanced fund), Japanese individuals are allocating a not insignificant amount of their money earmarked for mutual funds into international bond and REIT funds.

Turning next to fund performance, we start to have a different story. First, based on our value focus, know that the only value-oriented fund among the top-20 performing Japanese mutual funds for the one-year period ended October 31, 2011, is Daiwa SBI's Small Cap Equity (Value) Fund, which returned 27% (5th highest among all mutual funds). Perhaps we should not be surprised that it only had assets of Y3.883 billion (~US$50M) at the end of October. In fact, all but a few of the top-20 funds had assets under US$100 million; none were above $200 million. Before we take a look at the

Daiwa SBI Small Cap value fund, note the top-5 performing funds were the Japan Gold Fund 2x leverage, +43.5%, an Australian-dollar denominated gold futures fund, +36.7%, a Japan-focused emerging (i.e. growth) market fund, +28.7%, a growth-oriented small & mid cap fund, +27.6%. Eleven of the top-20 performing funds were labeled as having domestic growth-oriented strategies. Four commodities funds and a couple balanced domestic securities funds round out the remainder of the top-20.

## Review of Daiwa SBI's Small Cap value fund

Daiwa SBI's Small Cap Equity Value Fund reported its top-10 portfolio holdings last on June 10, 2011. Said holdings each accounted for 2.6% to 5.5% of the overall portfolio, with half the stocks being constituents of the JASDAQ, three from the TOPIX 2nd Section, and two from the 1st Section. There were three retailers, a wholesaler, four broadly-defined services companies, and two real estate-related companies. Overall, services and retailers comprised nearly 45% of the fund's portfolio. Other top sector holdings (above 5%) were IT, real estate, metals, and wholesale – a combined approximate 25%. Specific top-10 holdings as of June 2011 are as follows:

| Company | Code | PPS | MC | B/V | P/E | 52 wk rg |
|---|---|---|---|---|---|---|
| Seria | JQ 2782 | 370,500 | Y28.99B | 1.89 | 12.12 | 140 - 492 |
| Genky | T1 2772 | 1,494 | Y5.129B | 0.76 | 5.67 | 995 - 2755 |
| TOKAI | T1 9729 | 1,659 | Y29.90B | 0.88 | 7.43 | 1125 - 1870 |
| Prestige | JQ 4290 | 620 | Y9.306B | n/a | n/a | 427 - 812 |
| Tsukui | T2 2398 | 880 | Y13.30B | 1.84 | 9.65 | 505 - 1183 |
| Relo | T1 8876 | 1,825 | Y27.67B | 1.46 | 9.48 | 1150 - 1825 |
| Watts | JQ 2735 | 745 | Y52.00B | 0.98 | 4.55 | 436 - 870 |

| | | | | | | | |
|---|---|---|---|---|---|---|---|
| Step | T2 9795 | 461 | Y7.063B | 0.65 | 7.01 | 460 - 504 |
| Senshu Electric | T2 9824 | 906 | Y9.785B | 0.33 | 10.49 | 737 - 1240 |
| Star Mica | JQ 3230 | 71,200 | Y7.049B | 0.69 | 9.05 | 52.5 - 130.0 |

*As of November 17, 2011 market close. Per Yahoo! Finance Japan. PPS = price per share; MC = market capitalization in billions of yen; B/V = price to book value; ttm P/E = trailing twelve-month price-to-earnings; 52 wk rg = 52-week range of stock price.

| Company | Code | S/E Ratio | ROE | ROA | Div |
|---|---|---|---|---|---|
| Seria | JQ 2782 | 35.8% | 19.4% | 6.8% | 0.67% |
| Genky | T1 2772 | 31.0% | 14.1% | 4.4% | 3.01% |
| TOKAI | T1 9729 | 57.9% | 12.8% | 7.1% | 1.81% |
| Prestige | JQ 4290 | 62.5% | 15.6% | 9.7% | n/a |
| Tsukui | T2 2398 | 18.5% | 27.3% | 4.6% | 1.14% |
| Relo | T1 8876 | 42.4% | 17.3% | 6.7% | 3.29% |
| Watts | JQ 2735 | 35.5% | 23.4% | 8.0% | 3.36% |
| Step | T2 9795 | 72.3% | 9.4% | 6.8% | 4.12% |
| Senshu Electric | T2 9824 | 60.8% | 3.3% | 2.0% | 2.21% |
| Star Mica | JQ 3230 | 30.5% | 7.8% | 2.4% | 1.54% |

*As of November 17, 2011 market close. S/E Ration = shareholders' equity ratio; ROE = return on equity; ROA = return on assets; Div = dividend yield.

**Seria** (2782) Japan's second-largest "dollar store" (i.e. Y100 store). Year-to-date November 17, 2011 stock chart:

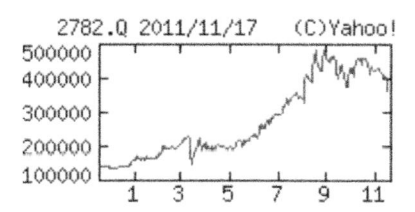

**Genky** (2772) operates regional, suburban drug stores. Food sales are said to be a strength; it is also trying to grow cosmetics sales.

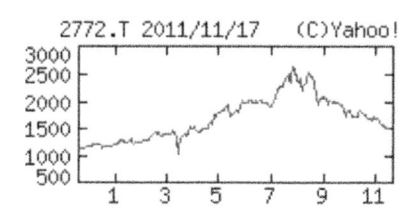

**Tokai** (9729) is a regional (western and central Japan) operator of pharmacies. It is expanding into clinics and nursing homes.

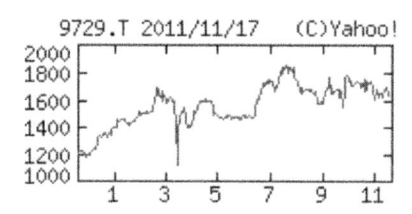

**Prestige International** (4290) is a call center/BPO operator focused on vehicle roadside assistance services and insurance; it also has a real estate arm.

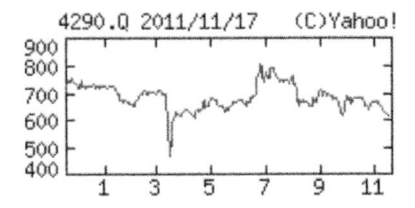

**Tsukui** (2398) based in Yokohama, operates nursing care homes and provides in-home care nationally. Also has staffing arm. March 2011 IPO.

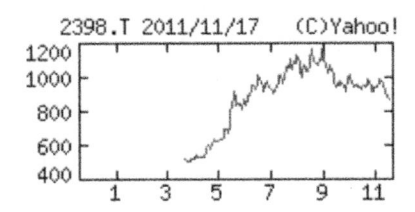

**Relo Holdings** (8876) is a corporate benefits outsourcer and also manages properties. It is expanding to the U.S.

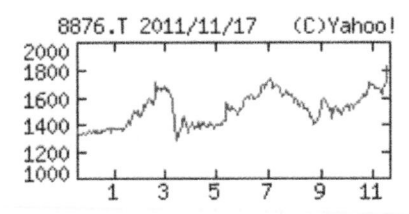

**Watts** (2735) is an operator of "dollar stores" (Y100 shops), of which it reported having 100 of as of August 2010.

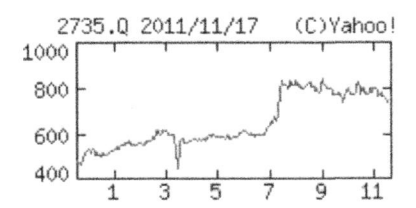

**Step** (9795) is a cram-school operator in Kanagawa prefecture. Last reported September 2010 to have 84 schools for elementary and middle school grades and 16 for high school. September 2011 IPO.

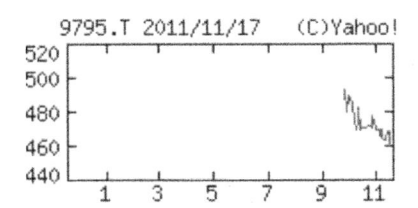

**Senshu Electric** (9824) is a specialized wire/cable trading company.

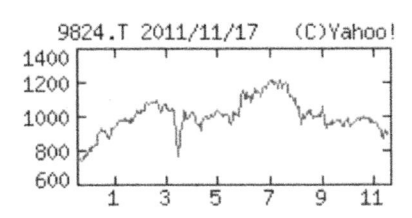

**Star Mica** (3230), apartment refurbishment, management, and sales. Its focus is on older buildings, in which it invests for either lease or sale.

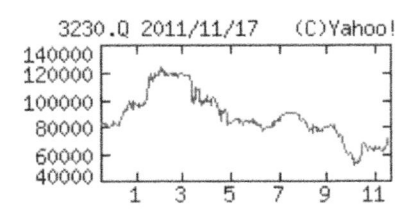

# Hood check of Nomura's "Undervalued Japan" Fund

Nomura Asset Management's Undervalued Japan Stocks fund launched successfully in January 2011, attracting strong investor interest, which pushed its assets under management to over $1 billion (very respectable for a domestic equity-focused fund) at its peak before the March 11th disaster – assets as of October 31, 2011 were Y47.5 billion ($610 million). The name of this fund is very intriguing since it's managed by a leading Japanese asset manager. However, as is always the case with any investment fund, one must not rely upon the name of the fund alone. A deeper look at exactly what the fund invests in is worthwhile.

A closer look shows disappointingly that it is practically a bank-focused fund, with 7 of its top-10 holdings (17%) being banks; overall 30.9% of fund assets were banks as of October 31, 2011. More than 10.5% of the fund is Mitsubishi UFJ Financial Group (Tokyo: 8306) (ADR: MTU) and Mizuho Financial Group (Tokyo: 8411) (ADR: MFG). These two are without doubt sporting cheap valuations, price-to-book ratios of around 0.5 and single-digit P/Es, however, there are better bets in Japan, outside of the banking sector. Beyond banks, another problem is that this fund invests only in TOPIX 1st Section companies, meaning it skips some of the best value of the smaller caps in TOPIX 2 and it ignores the JASDAQ. In fact, the fund's buying is based on a confusing program (which I translate here from Japanese) consisting of eliminating 20% of the TOPIX 1 companies with the lowest trading liquidity, and buying amongst the 50% of the lowest-priced remaining stocks (I believe this to mean the lowest price per share, believe it or not) trading at the highest forward P/Es and current price-to-book ratios (as I believe it says it limits the universe to the "top" 40%).

I find this program a bit unorthodox, although it may encompass some value and contrarian elements. I also think the concentration in banks is unhealthy. Note that while there is some concentration among the fund's top-10 holdings, there is a sizable total of 279 holdings, which means essentially unless there's a strong bank or broad market rally, this fund will not stand out on the merit of its supposed value-bias. The fund's October 2011 monthly report indicates that its portfolio has an average forward P/E of 8.4 and trades a current price-to-book value of 0.6. The market has since faced downward pressure and as of late-November, the Nikkei is trading at over a 2 ½ year low. The TOPIX 1st Section was trading at 14-times forward earnings and 0.88x book value as of November 25th. The banks are undoubtedly what give the fund its comparatively lower valuation. Performance from inception of the fund, January 27, 2011, through October 31, 2011, has been -13.9%.

*****

## Japanese Banks

It is very difficult for banks to earn attractive margins with interest rates having been so low, for so long; companies reluctant to borrow, and many having already shored up their balance sheets; saturation in all segments of banking, suggesting that more consolidation is needed; also in the face of a slowdown in domestic IPOs and inbound M&A.

Readers unfamiliar with recent banking history in Japan should know that the current big-3, otherwise known as the "mega banks," are Mitsubishi UFJ, Mizuho, and Sumitomo Mitsui. Each with trillion dollar-plus asset bases, they are among the largest banks in the world based on assets: Mitsubishi UFJ is top-10 and the other two are top-20. However, their market capitalizations, while in the tens of billions of dollars, fall short of the post-2008/2009 crash $100 billion club (HSBC $128B and JPMorgan $108B, as of the November 23, 2011, market close), which used to be the *$200 billion club* featuring HSBC, Bank of America, and Citigroup, but not JPMorgan (I have omitted solely Hong Kong and Shanghai-listed banks). The mega banks are full-service operations and face fierce competition in each segment.

- Mitsubishi UFJ has a market capitalization of just over Y4.5 trillion ($58B) as of November 25, 2011. Mitsubishi Tokyo Financial Group merged with UFJ Holdings in 2005; UFJ was formed by way of a merger of other once prominent banks in 2001.

- Mizuho has a market capitalization of just under Y2.4 trillion ($31B) as of November 25, 2011. It was formed in 2000, by way of a merger of former banking giants Dai-ichi Kangyo, Fuji, and the Industrial Bank of Japan.

- Sumitomo Mitsui has a market capitalization of nearly Y2.9 trillion ($37.5B) also as of November 25, 2011. It was effectively formed in 2001, when Sumitomo Bank merged with Sanwa Bank.

*****

# 20-Largest Japanese stocks (by market capitalization)

As of December 2, 2011

| Rank | Company | Code | Industry | Market Cap JPY (T) | MC ($B) |
|---|---|---|---|---|---|
| 1. | Toyota | 7203 | Automobiles | 8.944 | 115 |
| 2. | NTT DoCoMo | 9437 | Mobile tele. | 6.063 | 78 |
| 3. | NTT | 9432 | Telecom | 5.094 | 65 |
| 4. | Mitsubishi UFJ | 8306 | Banking | 4.784 | 61 |
| 5. | Canon | 7751 | Electronics | 4.581 | 59 |
| 6. | Honda | 7267 | Automobiles | 4.490 | 57.5 |
| 7. | Japan Tobacco | 2914 | Tobacco/food | 3.515 | 45 |
| 8. | Nissan | 7201 | Automobiles | 3.205 | 41 |
| 9. | Fanuc | 6954 | Machine tools | 3.151 | 40 |
| 10. | SMFG | 8316 | Banking | 3.060 | 39 |
| 11. | Mitsubishi | 8058 | Trading | 2.701 | 34.5 |
| 12. | Softbank | 9984 | IT, web | 2.664 | 34 |
| 13. | Mizuho FG | 8411 | Banking | 2.449 | 31 |
| 14. | Takeda Pharma | 4502 | Pharma. | 2.448 | 31 |
| 15. | KDDI | 9433 | Telecom | 2.287 | 29 |
| 16. | Mitsui & Co. | 8031 | Trading | 2.255 | 29 |

| 17. | Komatsu | 6301 | Constrct. Mchry. | 2.043 | 26 |
| 18. | Hitachi | 6501 | Electronics | 1.971 | 25 |
| 19. | Denso | 6902 | Auto parts | 1.943 | 25 |
| 20. | East JP Railway | 9020 | Railroad | 1.900 | 24 |

## Japan's 20-largest "shareholders"[44]

| Rank | Investment Co. | Assets JPY (T) | Assets ($B) | No. Co's Stock | Top Holding |
|---|---|---|---|---|---|
| 1. | Japan Trustee Svcs | 21.0 | 273 | 1,810 | Toyota |
| 2. | Master Trust Bank JP | 14.7 | 192 | 1,375 | Toyota |
| 3. | Nippon Life | 5.3 | 69 | 711 | Toyota |
| 4. | NTT | 5.0 | 65 | 4 | DoCoMo |
| 5. | State Street | 4.9 | 64 | 249 | Toyota |
| 6. | Ministry of Finance | 3.9 | 51 | 8 | NTT |
| 7. | Toyota | 2.9 | 38 | 66 | Denso |
| 8. | Mitsubishi UFJ FG | 2.2 | 29 | 826 | Honda |
| 9. | Meiji Yasuda Life | 2.1 | 27 | 331 | Honda |

---

[44] See: http://www.ullet.com/stock/search.html#toppage.

| 10. | Dai-ichi Life | 1.7 | 22 | 338 | Canon |
| 11. | SMFG | 1.6 | 21 | 535 | Toyota |
| 12. | Renault | 1.6 | 21 | 1 | Nissan |
| 13. | JPMorgan | 1.5 | 19.5 | 67 | Honda |
| 14. | Tokio Marine | 1.5 | 19.5 | 287 | Toyota |
| 15. | Mizuho | 1.4 | 18 | 316 | Canon |
| 16. | SSTOD05 Omnibus | 1.4 | 18 | 57 | MUFG |
| 17. | Hitachi | 1.2 | 15.5 | 24 | Hit. Chem. |
| 18. | Toyota Industries | 1.2 | 15.5 | 14 | Toyota |
| 19. | Moxley & Co. | 1.0 | 13 | 11 | Sony |
| 20. | SSTOD05 Omnibus | 1.0 | 13 | 45 | SMFG |

Notes: #6 holdings consist primarily of NTT and Japan Tobacco (2914), the latter made the news in autumn 2011 after speculation the government might sell its stake to raise much needed funds. However, as can be imagined, any sale will probably be easier said than done given competing political and commercial interests. NTT's equity holdings, by the way, consist of over 63% of NTT DoCoMo (9437), Japan's largest wireless carrier, 54%-plus of NTT Data (9613), 67%-plus of NTT Urban Development (8933), and more than 24% of Internet Initiative Japan (3774). #16 and #20 appear to be the same, however, research suggests that they are two different China state funds. #19 is affiliated with JPMorgan for ADRs. US$ conversion as of prevailing rate, Jan. 19, 2011; values rounded.

# CHAPTER 4

# THE JAPANESE STOCK MARKET: NUTS AND BOLTS PART I

*There are certain events and developments bound to move the market in Japan that investors should at least be aware of; no need to try and "trade" around them, but it may be helpful at times to understand why the market or a stock may be moving.*

## *Tankan*

A key market focus, fairly synonymous with the ISM Index[45] in the U.S., is the Bank of Japan's *tankan* (formally the *tanki keizai kansoku chousa*, or the Short-term Economic Survey of Enterprises in Japan); both are advanced or leading indicators. For the ISM, a reading of 50 or higher indicates economic expansion, while less than 50, signals a contraction. Published quarterly (pre-market open at the beginning of April, July, and October, and in the middle of December), the *tankan* is very, very closely watched – it uses diffusion indices (DI for short), where the more positive the results, the better. The BOJ has a detailed explanation and other information on its website.[46] I tend not to rely upon the *tankan* for making investment decisions, but it is

---

[45] The Institute of Supply Management's Manufacturing Index is based on a survey of 300-plus manufacturers, re. inventories, deliveries, employment, and new orders.
[46] See: http://www.BOJ.or.jp/en/statistics/outline/exp/tk/faqtk02.htm/.

nevertheless helpful as a barometer, and most importantly in my opinion for companies' outlook for the yen.

The *tankan* survey includes some 11,500 enterprises, which are categorized as manufacturing or non-manufacturing. Within "manufacturing" there are 17 sub-classifications and within "non-manufacturing" there are 14 sub-classifications. All enterprises are further divided by their size of capital: large, Y1 billion (approx. $13 million as of October 2011); medium Y100 million to Y1 billion ($1.3 million to $13 million); and small Y20 million to Y100 million ($260 thousand to $1.3 million). Clearly, most foreign investors and market watchers are primarily concerned with the large enterprise readings. However, post-March 11, 2011, smaller-sized enterprises have been gaining far more attention as the Bank of Japan and Cabinet Office have actively tried to extend credit and ensure businesses do not go under for a lack of available financing.

At the time of writing this section the latest *tankan* was issued the morning of Monday, October 3, 2011.[47] The headlines in the business press initially took advantage of the positive reading, noting it was the first positive reading amongst large enterprises in two quarters. The diffusion index (DI) was +2, up 11 points from June. This positive reading and reversal suggest that the economy has moved from a post-earthquake bottom – despite the ongoing global uncertainty and volatility in markets. News reports duly noted, however, that the fiscal 2011 (ending in March 2012) foreign exchange expectations amongst large manufacturing enterprises of Y81.15/$1, is the highest (referring to yen strength) on record. As the trading day progressed on October 3, the headlines changed to ones reflecting uncertainty amidst such a strong yen forecast as the Nikkei and many other markets were selling off, extending recent weakness, and following a selloff in the U.S. the prior Friday. It is worth mentioning that the foreign exchange forecast could be useful when comparing it to the forecasts that individual companies provide in their quarterly financial reporting. Over the past couple years it is clear that the yen's persistent strength has both surprised and negatively impacted a not insignificant number of Japanese companies.

---

[47] For *tankan* releases see: Bank of Japan, *tankan* website in English, http://www.BOJ.or.jp/en/statistics/tk/index.htm/.

The Japanese market can be influenced by such items as the ISM Index; of course the *tankan* can be market moving depending on the results versus pre-release expectations. It may sometimes be the case that key data out of the U.S. sparks more of a reaction in Japan than does Japanese domestic economic data. This happens because of the impact, whether perceived or real, on exports. Ostensibly U.S. markets react much more directly to data releases, perhaps due to the insanely high amount of trading that takes place in the U.S. So, if you're an investor (or trader) that follows the markets daily and checks prices frequently, be warned that economic data from the U.S. can move the market in Japan. This can be enigmatic for those attracted to, but unfamiliar with, Japan. I once corresponded with a young professional who had spent a summer in Japan as a student and was looking to learn more about the Japanese stock market. This individual, having read my daily market summaries after a few days expressed his surprise that U.S. news impacted Japanese markets so much.

## Market Psychology and Technical Analysis

Similar to the U.S. in some respects, though more extreme overall, key stock market benchmark levels are closely followed and widely reported. References to the Dow Jones (Industrial Average), say at 10,XXX, with 11,000 being a "psychologically important" level, are common, but are not reported anywhere near the frequency of market recaps in Japan in which virtually any whole number in thousand point increments (i.e. 10,000; 11,000; 12,000) is deemed "psychologically important."

One explanation is the prevalence (among market participants) of traders and a trading mindset in Japan where market recaps and individual stock coverage often reference technical trading developments and candlestick chart patterns. I am somewhat sympathetic to the technical analysis crowd given the irrational behavior of the market, which is a reflection of irrational behavior of many a market participant. Thus, I admit to thinking there is some merit to understanding basic technical trading data such as the market and a stock's moving averages. Candlestick charts can be fun to look at, but I would not put much faith into trying to discern an entry/accumulate/exit price when one's investing time horizon is likely measured in years instead of mere days. I have no intention of going into any depth about behavioral economics or finance, but clearly, Mr. Market and his manic depressive behavior exist not just in the U.S., but in Japan, and anywhere securities are traded.

*****

A widely used technical indicator is the 25-day advance-decline ratio, where a reading of 70% or less indicates a situation where stocks are oversold, and a reading of 120% or more suggests stocks are overbought. This is similar to the RSI, formally known as the Relative Strength Index, which also helps traders and investors to discern whether a stock or index is overbought or oversold, based on the *magnitude* of gains and losses over a certain number of trading days (often 14). A reading of 30 or less suggests oversold conditions; 70 or greater indicates likely overbought conditions. Japanese market participants/watchers also like to reference the 50 and 200-day moving averages of prices. Technical analysts consider convergences and divergences of the two as being key indicators of a stock or index's price trend. The MACD, or Moving Average Convergence Divergence, measures moving averages, and is used to discern momentum. The best practice for using technical analysis is said to be to use more than one indicator for confirmation, and the more indicators confirming a trend, the better the likelihood. It sounds self-fulfilling, but obviously at one extreme or the other it will eventually attract or repel traders taking contrarian stances. This is not intended by any means to be a definitive or exhaustive review of technical analysis, which is beyond the scope of this book.

*****

**Nikkei 225 1-year candlestick chart (Nov. 25, 2011 close) with 13 and 26-week moving averages**

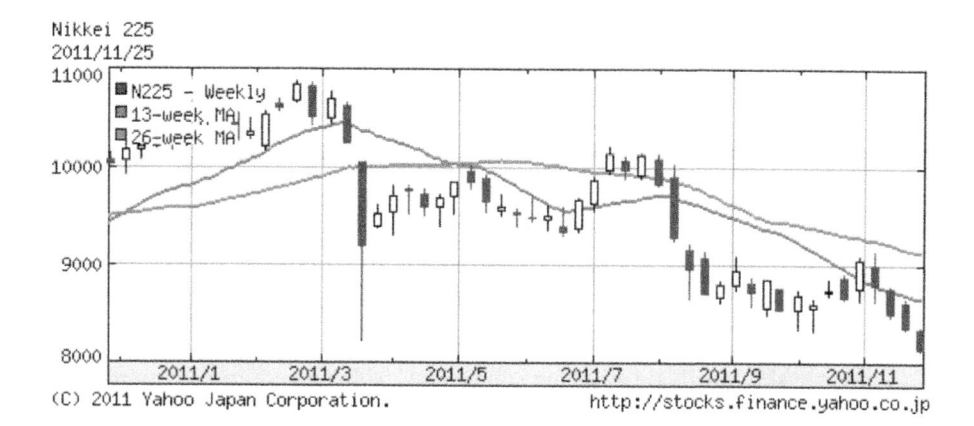

Same chart duration and moving averages but with lines instead of candlesticks:

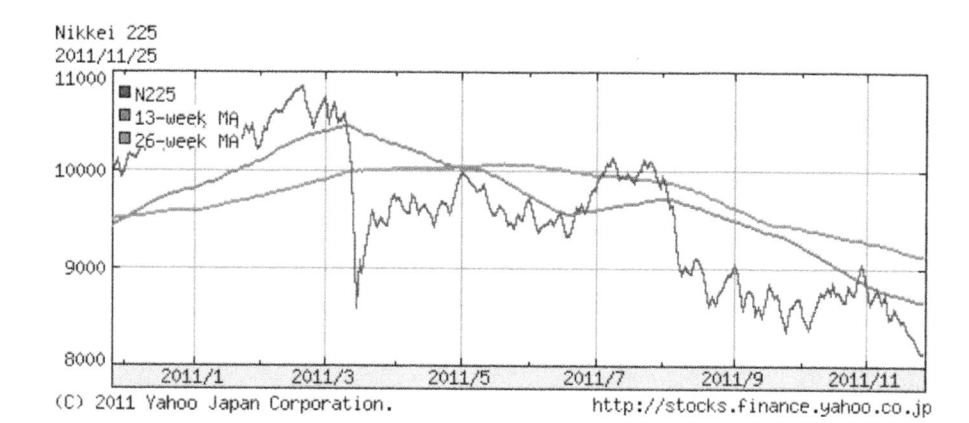

Morningstar Japan maintains daily RSIs for the past month for the TOPIX 1st Section and Nikkei 225.[48] As of November 25, 2011, the N225's RSI was 20.3, suggesting oversold conditions, unsurprising since the Nikkei has been under selling pressure as it recently reached two-year eight-month low levels, falling below the March 11th disaster-induced lows. Its 25-day advance/decline ratio was 76.92.

A second explanation for the Japanese infatuation with so-called "psychologically important" benchmark or index price levels is because of the deleterious decline in such levels since 1989, and the "false starts" in the economy since then that have generated substantial market advances (though well short of the 1989 peak) and sharp subsequent declines. The chart of the Nikkei 225 below, from November 1984 to March 2012, shows: the 400% rise to 1990, the initial collapse from 40,000 to 30,000, a recovery of sorts only to witness a sharper decline to 20,000, a very quick retracement of 5,000 points, which was ultimately lost as the next bottom was under 15,000, followed by two failed attempts to hold the 20,000-level in the 1990s. Following the IT-bust (c. 2000) came the grinding decline to what many would have thought would be the post-bubble trough in 2003, from which point the benchmark would more than double to over 18,000 during the next four years, to only fall all the way through its 2003 low. As of November 2011, the 8,000-level was in jeopardy; let alone trying to attain the 10,000-level. It shouldn't be difficult to imagine how each 1,000-point increment, and especially the levels, of 10, 15, and 20-thousand become closely watched. Adding more suspense, if you will, is the often-accompanying references to key technical support and resistance levels.

---

[48] See the following Morningstar page for N225 RSI readings: http://www.morningstar.co.jp/RankingWeb/IndicesPart.do?indcCode=24. See this Morningstar page for a look at a variety of market data for the five most-recent sessions: http://www.morningstar.co.jp/RankingWeb/IndicesTable.do?market=1.

## Nikkei 225 Stock Average chart c. 1984 – March 2012

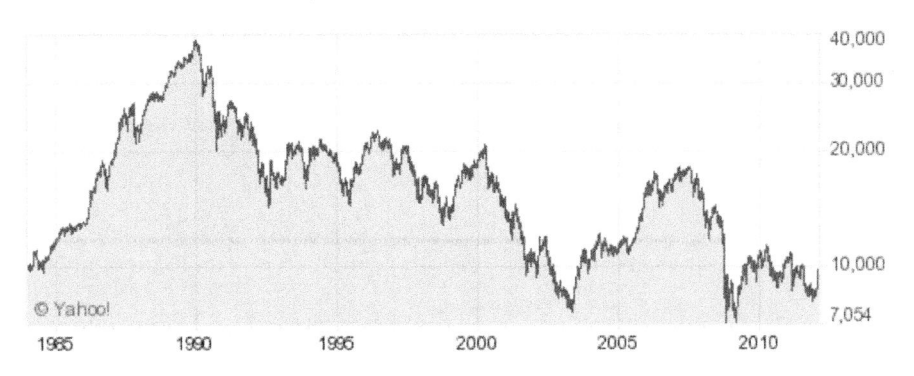

**Sampling of press references to "psychologically" important levels:**

- Sept. 5, 2011: Japan's *Nikkei* 225 index added 1 percent to 9965.09, having breached the *psychologically important* 10000 mark earlier in the day for the first time since ...

- Sept. 1, 2011: A man walks past a stock quotation board displaying the *Nikkei* share average ... as the benchmark approaches the *psychologically important* 10000 level. ...

- Aug. 9, 2011: The benchmark index closed below the *psychologically important* 9000 line for the ... the *Nikkei* average briefly dropped 440 points to 8656 in the morning. ...

- Aug. 1, 2011: ... with the *Nikkei* Stock Average climbing 180.87 points, or 1.84%, ... The benchmark index topped the *psychologically important* line of 10000 during ...

- Jun. 8, 2011: The fact that the *Nikkei* managed to stay above the *psychologically important* 9400 level and key technical support of 9317 -- a March 29 intraday low ...

- Jun. 2, 2009: Japan's *Nikkei* stock average is likely to move ... to push it through resistance to the *psychologically important* 10000 mark. ...

- May 11, 2009: The *Nikkei* 225 Stock Average hovered near the *psychologically important* mark of 9500 points.

- May 8, 2009: Market players say the next targets for the *Nikkei* will be 10500, which is *psychologically important* and also a target level for futures and options, ...

- Apr. 11, 2009: The *Nikkei* briefly topped the *psychologically-important* 9000-point level early in the session for the first time in three months but many investors opted to ...

- Mar. 1, 2000: On the stock market, the *Nikkei* finished above the *psychologically important 20000* level for the first time since Feb. 9. ...

- Mar. 20, 1992: The US stock market was lower earlier in the week after Tokyo's *Nikkei* stock average fell below the *psychologically important 20000* level. ...

- Mar. 21, 1990: The *Nikkei* index came within range of the *psychologically important 30000*-point level and ended the day down 456.05 points at 30807.19, its lowest close ...

# Central Bank Watching

Another closely watched matter, not dissimilar to the situation in the U.S., is the Bank of Japan's interest rate policy meetings, decisions, and meeting notes. The good news is twofold. If you are a central bank watcher you'll be pleased to know that the BOJ has a rather robust website of English language information and publications. That said, the policy meeting notes tend to be quite brief and predictable due to recycling of language and since the bank is essentially handcuffed in terms of its rate setting abilities when rates have been at or near zero for years on end. Thus, if one is truly looking at stocks bottom-up and takes a position that low interest rates are likely here to stay for a period measured in years rather than months or quarters (barring an extreme event such as outright hyperinflation in the U.S. or EU), one can largely ignore the coverage of monetary policy. Hence the good news in this case of being able to save time. About the only time one needs to pay attention is when there is a dissenter, or more than one dissenter, and if one is following U.S. market news with any frequency there is bound to be coverage of this on any of the major financial news websites or TV programs.

Again, while there's no real need to be a central bank or rate watcher, it's worth knowing that there is much apprehension about higher interest rates in Japan. There have only been two rate hikes over the past ten years (zero -> 0.25% in 2006, then prematurely dubbed the end of ZIRP or zero interest rate policy, and 0.25% -> 0.50% in 2007), a deflationary period in which wages have stagnated, government debt has mushroomed, and inflation cannot be bought since even in times of high commodity prices, like those of recent years, the yen has exhibited strength. In short, with regards to interest rates, it is highly unlikely that any future rate increase (barring, again, a hyperinflationary situation for instance) would be more than 25 basis points or 0.25%. Such an increase is not significant for individuals or corporations, meaning it will not sink those who carry debt, or are contemplating debt financing. However, due to the vast Japanese government debt, there's a natural aversion to higher interest rates, and in this case, even a 0.25 point increase could be meaningful absolutely and literally in terms of paying the debt and financing current expenditures.

*****

Richard Koo, chief economist of the Nomura Research Institute, is the author of *The Holy Grail of Macroeconomics - Lessons from Japan's Great Recession* (John Wiley & Sons, 2008) in which he argues that Japan's prolonged economic slump is the result of a "balance sheet recession." He describes the approximate period of 1986 to 1990 as being a debt-financed bubble, and the following sixteen-year period to circa 2006 as one of balance sheet recession. The 1996 - 2006 period was a decade of near-zero interest rates and deleveraging. Borrowing from financial institutions and securities markets by non-financial companies was mostly negative during said period. Koo's key features of balance sheet recessions include:[49]

- Post-debt financed asset bubble leaves private sector with more liabilities than assets

- Necessitating balance sheet repair

- Which changes MO from profit maximization to debt minimization

- Thus even with low or zero interest rates, no borrowers of newly generated savings and debt repayments

- Lack of borrowers means commensurate amount of demand is lost

- Self-sustaining economic growth not possible until private balance sheets repaired

- Fiscal consolidation must wait until certainty that funds NOT borrowed by govt. will be borrowed and spent by private sector

*****

---

[49] "The Age of Balance Sheet Recessions: What Post-2008 U.S, Europe, and China can learn from Japan 1990 - 2005." April 2010. Presentation by Richard Koo. http://www.businessinsider.com/richard-koo-recession-2010-4#-1.

The Bank of Japan has taken its share of blame and then some for hiking rates too aggressively into the Nikkei's crash in 1989 and keeping rates unnecessarily high thereafter. There's also the matter of an ill-timed and counter-effective consumption tax hike in 1997 (see below). Thus, in the past five to ten years of persistent deflation, the Bank of Japan has been very reluctant to move rates much beyond zero. Beside the two rate hikes mentioned above, in 2006 and 2007, the *only* one prior to that after the BOJ's aggressive late-80's hiking, was a very short-lived one of similar magnitude, 0.25%, in 2000. Despite already having suffered a lost decade, 1990 - 2000, Japan was not immune to more suffering emanating from the IT boom turned bust in the U.S. Then there was 9-11 and only in 2003 did the Nikkei hit its then post-bubble trough. In the interim of all this was a record-high yen in the mid-1990s, the Asian financial crisis, the Russian financial crisis, and the failure of Long Term Capital Management, just to name the most publicized developments.

In 1997, the Japanese government succeeded for the first time in raising the nation's consumption tax, to 5%, from 3% previously (the rate at which it was introduced in 1989). The *Wall Street Journal Japan's* "Japan Real Time" blog has written about the fatal end to prime ministers who have pushed for the introduction of a consumption tax to begin with, and hikes, later – whether they were successful in their endeavor or not.[50] The introduction of a consumption tax finally happened 1989, at 3%. Ill-timed, coinciding with the peak of the Nikkei 225 Stock Average and land values, but certainly not *the* reason for the bursting of the "bubble."

The 1997 hike also came at a bad time, ahead of the Asian financial crisis and a series of bank and investment-bank failures domestically. In fact, the timing was so bad that in retrospect, there is now recognition by the BIS (Bureau for International Settlements) that while still erroneous fiscal policy, it was more so a matter of bad luck in terms of the timing. Retrospective, perhaps even revisionist, thinking about the Japanese economy appears to be

---

[50] "Consumption Tax Hikes: A Short, Unhappy History," Jun.2010. http://blogs.wsj.com/japanrealtime/2010/06/17/consumption-tax-hikes-a-short-unhappy-history/

gaining some traction. Remember earlier in the book I discussed the easily missed point of Japan's comparatively strong GDP.[51]

Undoubtedly the day will come for Japan when respectable economic growth returns for more than a few quarters and talk of a rate hike resurfaces. As of February 2012, it seems like a hike is not in the cards even if there were sustained growth since the yen is already at record high levels. Frankly, I am of the opinion that value investors not invest much time on rate-related news and forecasting unless one is involved in financial stocks or a leveraged company. Again it's highly likely that when there is a hike, it will be of the 0.25-point variety, which will be more symbolic and a harbinger of more potential hikes, but not very impactful on debtors or savers. Note in fact, higher interest rates are in Japanese citizens' best interest since they have trillions upon trillions of dollars of savings and they are also buyers of Japanese government bonds whether they like it not – via their Japan Post and other deposit accounts, as well as via their insurance policies. (See Chapter 6 for discussion about assets.) A normalized interest rate environment should, but might not, be welcomed due to fear of government debt repayment. The secret that appears to be slowly getting out of the bag is that Japanese are buyers and will remain buyers of JGBs by way of the 'savings' system in place, and since Japan has the benefit of issuing its own sovereign currency. This means there is ample domestic demand, and the government can easily print money and rollover its government debt. What I've just described actually has been what keeps interest rates low.

Domestic institutional investors learned how damaging foreign currency losses from their overseas debt securities holdings can be following significant yen strength after the Plaza Accord agreement in 1985 (a five-country foreign currency intervention designed to weaken the dollar against the yen and Deutsche mark) and again in 1995 following a devastating earthquake in Kobe, Japan. Fear of forex-induced losses was and remains motivation enough for holding JGBs, despite higher-yielding U.S. Treasuries, for

---

[51] Regarding both Japan's consumption tax hikes and GDP per capita, see the *The Economist's* "Free Exchange" blog of Nov. 14, 2011, "Two things to remember about Japan." http://www.economist.com/blogs/freeexchange/2011/11/america-following-japan.

example, though Japan is among the world's largest holders of Treasuries (since such purchases from the Japanese government's standpoint help to ease yen strength). Finally, consider that in recent years, JGBs have been reinvested at lower rates, which means that even with future inflation, JGB payments will be manageable presuming higher tax receipts; and given notoriously low collection rates, JGB repayment could be far more manageable than currently thought.

## TSE holidays and BOJ policy meetings

For calendar year 2012; holidays and monetary policy meeting (MPM) dates are similar each year and can be reviewed at the TSE and BOJ's websites.

Jan. 1 – New Year's （元日）

Jan. 2 & 3 – TSE holiday

Jan. 9 – Coming of Age Day （成人の日）

Jan. 23 & 24 – BoJ MPM (minutes pub. 2/17)

Feb. 11 – National Foundation Day （建国記念の日）

Feb. 13 & 14 – BoJ MPM (minutes pub. 3/16)

Mar. 12 & 13 – BoJ MPM (minutes pub. 4/13)

Mar. 20 – Vernal Equinox （春分の日、振替休日）

Apr. 9 & 10 – BoJ MPM (minutes pub. 5/7)

Apr. 27 – BoJ MPM (minutes pub. 5/28) and pub. of "The Bank's View"

Apr. 29 – Showa Day （昭和の日）

Apr. 30 – Exchange holiday

May 3 -> 5 – Constitution Memorial Day, Greenery Day, Children's Day（憲法記念日、みどりの日、こどもの日）

May 22 & 23 – BoJ MPM (minutes pub. 6/20)

Jun. 14 & 15 – BoJ MPM (minutes pub. 7/18)

Jul. 11 & 12 – BoJ MPM (minutes pub. 8/14)

Jul. 16 – Marine Day（海の日）

Aug. 8 & 9 – BoJ MPM (minutes pub. 9/24)

Sept. 17 – Respect for the Aged Day（敬老の日）

Sept. 18 & 19 – BoJ MPM (minutes pub. 10/11)

Sept. 22 – Autumnal Equinox（秋分の日）

Oct. 4 & 5 – BoJ MPM (minutes pub. 11/2)

Oct. 8 – Health and Sports Day（体育の日）

Oct. 30 – BoJ MPM (minutes pub. 11/26) and pub. of "The Bank's View"

Nov. 3 – Culture Day（文化の日）

Nov. 19 & 20 – BoJ MPM (minutes pub. 12/26)

Nov. 23 – Labor Thanksgiving Day（勤労感謝の日）

Dec. 19 & 20 – BoJ MPM (minutes pub. TBA)

Dec. 23 – Emperor's Birthday（天皇誕生日）

Dec. 24 – Exchange holiday

Dec. 31 – Exchange holiday: New Year's Eve（大晦日）

## Trading on margin

Another "indicator" closely watched by Japanese investors and the financial press is the long margin balance and to a lesser extent the short balance of companies' shares. Anecdotal evidence suggests that shorting stock in Japan is difficult for larger investors, especially the smaller the short target's capitalization. Further, shorting stock is somewhat anathema to Japanese individual investors, so it is uncommon to see articles touting highly shorted stocks or ones touting stocks that should be sold short. Therefore, the main focus is on margin buying, the level of such buying, and weekly increases or decreases. Psychologically, one wants to see increases in buying as evidence of investor interest and in hopes of more such buying. The key word is "hope." A June 2011 *Nikkei Weekly* article about margin buying of bank stocks mentions margin buying begetting more margin buying, until a stock eventually peaks and the long margin holders begin to sell in order to unwind their positions.[52]

According to Kenichi Hirano of Tachibana Securities (quoted in the *Nikkei Weekly* article), "Stocks don't rise when everyone is buying on margin on expectations of an upswing. In my experience, there is movement only after some investors give up [i.e. shorts] and the long margin balance shrinks." Mr. Hirano's experience is inline with the value investing creed of being contrarian. Sell into strength; buy into weakness. Of course, the financial press and average investor's interest will be in stocks with the largest and/or fastest growing long margin interest. This information could be useful for finding potential short sale candidates, although, again, selling short can be tricky in Japan as some stocks may not be shortable and if they are, they may only be for a six-month duration. It goes without saying that it can be difficult to short stocks with small floats. For larger investors, a short position of 0.25% or more of a company's shares outstanding requires public disclosure via the listing stock exchange.

## Stock price limits

The terms limit-up and limit-down may be foreign to many readers with some exceptions for those who have of course invested in Japan previously,

---

[52] "Does margin buying of bank stocks portend rebound?" *The Nikkei Weekly*. Jun. 27, 2011.

commodities traders, and anybody who remembers the New York Stock Exchange circuit breakers during/after the Great Financial Crisis in 2008/2009. In short, limit-up and limit-down refer to the ceiling and floor of a pre-designated amount within which a stock can fluctuate during a trading day. Another limit imposed by the Tokyo Stock Exchange and JASDAQ are increments at which stocks can trade. Let's look at some real examples. Rakuten (Jasdaq: 4755), the Japanese "Amazon.com," if you will, closed January 20, 2012, up Y500/share (+0.60%) at Y83,700/share. On that day, Rakuten was limited to a trading range of Y68,200 – Y98,200. Based on its prior close, it's clear that it is allowed to trade up/down as much as Y15,000.

On most days the limit will not be a factor, however, on occasion, say an earnings announcement or revision, analyst action, takeover offer, etc., the limits can result in limited trading as the stock becomes stuck at its limit price. The other limit imposed on Rakuten, based on its share price level, is that it can only trade in Y100 increments. Let's now look at a company that trades at a lower share price, Suzuki (7269), which is Japan's second-largest manufacturer of "mini" (light) autos and third largest of motorbikes, in addition to having strong market share in India's auto market. Suzuki closed January 20th at Y1,669/share. It had a trading limit of Y1,224 – Y2,024, or +/- Y400 based on its prior close of Y1,624. Based on its share price, it can trade in as low as Y1 increments.

See the tables in the following pages of fixed stock price trading ranges and minimum trading increments.

**Share price trading rules/limits per the Tokyo Stock Exchange:**[53]

| Stock price up to JPY/share | +/- JPY trading range |
|---|---|
| 100 | 30 |
| 200 | 50 |
| 500 | 80 |
| 700 | 100 |
| 1,000 | 150 |
| 1,500 | 300 |
| 2,000 | 400 |
| 3,000 | 500 |
| 5,000 | 700 |
| 7,000 | 1,000 |
| 10,000 | 1,500 |

Beyond stock prices of Y10,000/share, the scheme repeats, thus, a stock with a price of Y15,000 up to Y19,990 could trade +/- Y3,000 (see above table where Y1,500 – Y2,000/share stocks can trade in +/- Y300 range). Accordingly, a Y150,000 – Y190,900 stock price can fluctuate by as much as Y30,000. Note that Japanese trading stipulations have no impact on the actual Nasdaq or NYSE physical trading of a company's ADRs (should a company have listed ADRs; this also includes ADRs on the Pink Sheets), which could trade at the lowest decimal pricing offered by one's brokerage and could trade higher or lower than a limit close in Japan – assuming there's no reason for trading to be halted in the U.S. As a reminder, ADR prices are not always a one-for-one conversion with the prevailing foreign exchange rate factored. See Chapter 2 regarding Ordinary-to-ADR ratios.

---

[53] See: http://www.tse.or.jp/rules/stock/sttrading_t.html.

Minimum trading increments per the Tokyo Stock Exchange:

| Stock price up to JPY/share | Minimum trading increment (JPY) |
|---|---|
| 3,000 | 1 |
| 5,000 | 5 |
| 30,000 | 10 |
| 50,000 | 50 |
| 300,000 | 100 |
| 500,000 | 500 |
| 3,000,000 | 1,000 |
| 5,000,000 | 5,000 |
| 30,000,000 | 10,000 |
| 50,000,000 | 50,000 |
| 50,000,000+ | 100,000 |

## Analyst coverage

Just as there are so-called "orphan" stocks in the U.S., there is an equivalent in Japan. While analyst coverage is deep and robust for the largest of companies, it can be very thin to non-existent the smaller the capitalization. Value investors know that in many cases the best valuations are found amongst the smallest of capitalizations, which are by default among the most neglected stocks. As of August 2011 analyst coverage in Japan was reportedly 31% of the then listed 3,639 companies. A Japanese research firm, Belle Investment Research, notes by comparison that coverage in the U.S. is around 25%, granted of a much larger universe.[54] The "emerging" markets of Japan, however, such as Mothers and JASDAQ, only have coverage of around 10%. And the coverage ratio of TOPIX 2 is most certainly closer to 10% than 30%.

In November 2006, a *Nikkei Financial* article citing an IFIS Japan survey said analyst coverage (defined as having at least one analyst) was 57.5% of TOPIX 1, meaning that even amongst larger-caps there were some 42.5% without coverage. TOPIX 2 at that time had 16% coverage. Similarly light coverage extends to ADRs covered by American analysts. The 2006 *BusinessWeek* article I referenced early in the book ("The Toyota Enigma"), noted Toyota only had two analysts following it in the U.S.[55] Beside a global company like Toyota somehow not being known to many money managers in the U.S., maybe part of the issue is that analysts tend to have too much of a home bias. Another matter for U.S. analyst coverage of Japanese ADRs – and possibly being *the* underlying explanation for under-coverage – is that many Japanese companies have large cash holdings and little or no debt, meaning retained earnings allow them to fund investments internally; while those in need of capital still frequently borrow directly from banks as opposed to the debt market. And for many companies, rather than issue debt (despite very attractive rates in Japan), companies may simply issue equity disregarding the dilutive effects to insider and outside shareholders alike, as shares authorized to be issued always allow for fairly easy secondary issuances.

Belle Investment Research cites Y50 billion ($500 million at yen-dollar parity) and up as the minimum analyst coverage threshold, which as of August 2011 included some 700 companies. A real stretch for coverage would include capitalizations of Y20 billion-plus ($200 million), of which there were 500 companies (having up to a Y50 billion capitalization). It is also important to understand that the ratings themselves typically reflect analysts' forecast of

---

[54] "上場企業が克服すべきハード," http://www.belletk.com/page9.php?post=73
[55] See http://www.businessweek.com/magazine/content/06_28/b3992057.htm.

a company's performance for the next half-year to full-year as measured against the TOPIX.[56] For example:

> Daiwa uses a rating system of 1 – 5, with '1' being its highest rating reflecting a forecast for +15% outperformance vs. the TOPIX over the next six months. A '2' estimates 5%-15% outperformance; '3' estimates a performance range of -5% to +5%; a '4' estimates -5% to -15% underperformance, and a '5' estimates underperformance of more than 15%. Nomura had a similar system but has consolidated to three ratings, 1 – 3, and uses a half-year horizon, in which a '1' reflects 15%+ outperformance, a '2,' +5% to +15%, and a '3,' underperformance of more than 5%. Mitsubishi UFJ uses a similar system though with a one-year time frame. Western securities analysts typically use buy/outperform/overweight, hold/equal-weight/neutral, and sell/underperform/underweight. Citigroup (formerly Nikko Citi) employs a 12 to 18 month horizon and a 1 – 3 rating system, and it incorporates risk ratings: 'L," for low risk in terms of earnings outlook and volatility, 'M,' for medium risk, 'H,' for high risk, and an 'S' for speculative stocks, which it sees as having the highest risk and volatility.

In terms of some exceptional analyst ratings (most buys and most sells), let's review a few such stocks here. Stocks with ten or more "buy" ratings, all of which are TOPIX 1st Section listings as of mid-January 2012:

- Mitsubishi Electric (6503)
- Nidec (6594)
- Canon (7751)
- Marubeni (8002)

---

[56] Investors without access to robust subscription data such as Bloomberg, FactSet, or Nikkei NEEDS, can lookup ratings free of charge and with relative ease even in Japanese via such a site as: http://www.rating-list.jp/ (stock codes and dates are readable; stock prices reflect the average target and current stock price, and their percent difference; specific stocks can be searched via the small search box on the top-right using a company's 4-digit code).

- Mitsui & Co. (8031)
- Inpex (1605)
- DeNA (2432)
- Komatsu (6301)
- Hitachi (6501)
- Toshiba (6502)
- Nissan (7201)
- Sumitomo Corp. (8053)
- Unicharm (8113)

As for "sell" ratings, two stocks stand out: Advantest (6857) a struggling maker of semiconductor test equipment had a least nine "sell" ratings at calendar year-end 2011, and Renesas Electronics (6723), an unprofitable and debt-burdened chipmaker, had at least six. Finally, the euphemistic "hold" rating top-list is quite deep, having nearly 90 companies with more than six "hold" ratings as of year-end 2011. NEC (6701) led the pack with at least 11 such ratings. Among those with 9 – 10 "holds" that may be recognizable amongst Western investors include: Lawson (2651), Konica Minolta (4902), Kirin Holdings (2503), Takeda Pharma (4502), and Shiseido (4911).

As this chapter comes to a close, consider the comments contained in a January 16, 2012, opinion piece from the *Nikkei's* editors, entitled (when translated into English), "Number of gems increasing in Japanese stock market."[57] One of the subheadings is, "Professional Japanese stock analysts decreasing." The editor relates words from a market participant that says things are getting so bad that people don't even want to short Japanese stocks anymore. The typical pre-Christmas travel to Japan by overseas fund

---

[57] "日本市場に 「お宝銘柄」 が増えている," Jan. 16, 2012. http://www.nikkei.com/money/column/teiryu.aspx?g=DGXNMSFK1302I_130120 12000000

managers to share ideas and set strategy was virtually non-existent in 2011. Japan has basically fallen off investors' radars. Rather than in years past where overseas investors looked at Asia as 'Japan' and 'Asia ex-Japan', these days it's increasingly 'China' and 'Asia (including Japan) ex-China'. Japanese investments are similarly, increasingly being handled by 'Asia' fund managers. This in turn, has caused Japan-specialist sell-side analysts to see their numbers thin. Thus, coverage of stocks has been on the decline, meaning ever fewer professionals are evaluating stocks based on fundamental value.

# CHAPTER 5

# THE JAPANESE STOCK MARKET: NUTS AND BOLTS PART II

## Dividends in Japan

Japanese dividends – unlike dividends in the U.S., where they are most often paid quarterly – are with a few exceptions paid biannually. Usually companies will set a target payout at fiscal-year end; most companies' fiscal year ends in March. Subsequently such companies' "interim" (mid or half-year) dividend will be paid typically in late September and a year-end payment will be made in late March. Companies can and do change the amounts to be paid during the fiscal year. Revisions are usually made in tandem with quarterly financial results announcements that reflect out/underperformance allowing for or necessitating such a revision. Company boards set a dividend payment amount that is voted on by shareowners at annual meetings. I have long been of the opinion that Japanese stocks would have much broader appeal if companies would only pay out dividends on a quarterly basis. While there may be merit to a biannual system (such as it being easier to make adjustments for any unexpected changes in cash flows) and there certainly is tradition, there is clearly pent up demand for yield in Japan, and it would also accommodate overseas investors accustomed to quarterly payouts.

At long last, in 2006 with Japan's "new Company Law," companies were allowed to amend their corporate charters and payout dividends at will, subject to board approval. A Nomura Securities market strategist commented in May 2006 that quarterly dividends would attract more stable shareholders.[58] Several companies almost immediately stepped forth to both amend their charters and institute quarterly payments (see discussion below). The strategy behind targeting stable shareholders is to try and establish a larger and longer-term (holding period) shareholder base (remember the earlier section of how Japanese investors tend to focus more on technical market developments and trade frequently), which incidentally ought to foster loyalty, an invaluable intangible for a company that faces cyclical markets, and also helpful should any activists appear on the shareholder register.

In May 2006, Honda (Tokyo: 7267) (ADR: HMC), after a fifth-straight year of record earnings announced it would split its stock for the first time in 23 years and it would begin to pay dividends quarterly. The intention behind the stock split was of course to make shares more affordable on a per share basis to individual investors. Five years earlier Honda had reduced its minimum trading unit of 1,000 shares to 100 shares; however, in May 2006 at Y8,000 per share, investors were required to pay Y8 million (for reference at Y100/$1, it would cost $80,000) in order to make an investment. There were and are ways around such a big outlay, but more on that and minimum trading units following this section. As for its plan to pay dividends quarterly, Honda commented at the time: "We wanted to respond to the needs of investors who wish to receive their dividends as soon as possible." At that time, Honda had 43,000 shareholders. As of spring 2011, it had over 202,000.[59]

Honda was the first major company with a large shareholder base to announce a quarterly payout. It went on to raise its dividend several times in succession, continued to pay quarterly dividends during the Global Financial Crisis (even as its share price fell by half from its 2006-2007 peak, and as two of the Big-3 U.S. auto were bailed out by the government). In 2011 its

---

[58] "Firms adapt to new corporate law." *The Nikkei Weekly*. May 8, 2006.
[59] Year 2006 mentions per "Honda Motor Planning Stock Split." *The Nikkei Weekly*. May 1, 2006.

quarterly per share payout was only four cents per share off its peak, and Honda's ADRs actually hit an all-time high in early 2011 ironically despite the pain of the strong yen, which actually boosted the value of its ADRs. While there is no question that Honda's shares/ADRs have been volatile, as have most stocks, long-term shareholders have been rewarded by the company's commitment to quarterly dividends and a willingness to move the needle on payout per share.

On its Investor Relations website, Honda describes its goal of returning profits to shareholders as follows:

> "The Company strives to carry out its operations from a global perspective and increase its corporate value. With respect to redistribution, the Company considers redistribution of profits to its shareholders to be one of the most important management issues, and its basic policy for dividends is to make distributions after taking into account its long-term consolidated earnings performance. The Company will also acquire its own shares at the optimal timing with the aim of improving efficiency in capital structure. The present goal, however, is to increase the shareholders return ratio (i.e. the ratio of the total of the dividend payment and the repurchase of company shares to consolidated net income) to approximately 30%."

On the same IR page, Honda provides recent payout data, changes (+/-), expectations, and also historical data from 2003.[60] Many Japanese companies publish their guidelines or targets for payouts.

*****

I would like to share my activist investment experience with Internet Initiative Japan (IIJI) (3774). I published the following article May 25, 2011, and remain a shareowner at the time of publishing this book.

---

[60] See: http://world.honda.com/investors/policy/returningprofits/.

Internet Initiative Japan (IIJI) is a leading internet connectivity and IT services company in Japan. It trades under relative obscurity in both the U.S., where it has traded as an ADR since 1999, and in Tokyo, despite its listing on the TOPIX-1, Japan's "big board." Nevertheless, IIJ is a solid company, and is very well-positioned to take advantage of opportunities in the cloud and in modernizing Japan's IT systems. Furthermore, it has a strong balance sheet, remained profitable during the financial crisis, and is forecasting solid growth in the coming year to five-year period. Its networks were largely unaffected by the March earthquake and tsunami, and accordingly, the financial impact of the disaster was limited as of the two week-plus post-disaster period reflected in its fiscal Q4.

Readers should know that I have held a varying number of IIJ shares since 2006. Notably, in early 2010, I began to engage the company's board of directors, including its founding Chairman and CEO, Koichi Suzuki. The result of around a half year of back-and-forth is that the company has hiked its dividend four times in the past year; from ¥2,000/share --> ¥3,000/share, a 50% aggregate increase.

While I didn't get the buyback(s) and simultaneous stock splits I pushed for, suffice it to say the dividend increases are welcome. I suspect the company will continue to increase its dividend again, as it has a strong balance sheet, good operating cash flows, and is growing its profits. In addition, I imagine that I will once again push for the simultaneous stock splits; IIJ trades at over $3,000/share in Tokyo; under $9/share in the U.S. I will also push for opportunistic buybacks, such as the smallish one the company completed at the trough of the financial crisis – and one it should have done during the aftermath of the March 11 triple-disaster.

Concerning IIJ being well-positioned in cloud computing in Japan, it turns out that the company has been a pioneer in getting Japan connected to the web since day-one, and continues to build networks for leading companies and the government. Furthermore, in recent years, the company is providing cutting edge mobile high-speed connectivity and network access (including specifically for the Apple iPad), media streaming, and full-service outsourcing, which includes data warehousing and cloud computing.

IIJ does face competition, including from the likes of giants NTT (NTT) and KDDI (KDDIF.PK), but IIJ has done quite well for itself via longstanding relationships with corporate and government clients. The fact that it is a fraction of the size of said giants has allowed it to be far more flexible and a vanguard of new technologies. In fact, NTT and an affiliate own approximately 30% of IIJ, and IIJ and NTT are clients of one another. The large stake held by NTT is not ideal, but such cross-shareholdings are still fairly common in Japan. Note that IIJ purchased AT&T Japan last year, effectively acquiring 1,600 corporate customers. It has said it plans to integrate and cross-sell, something which has already positively impacted IIJ's revenues and profits. IIJ also has a green initiative in its mobile data stations housed in eco-friendly containers.

Following are comments the company made at the end of its fiscal year in March about its prospects regarding cloud computing – don't mind the rigid translation as clearly the company wrote the message first in Japanese and provided an English copy:

- [We] anticipate a paradigm shift in our market brought by cloud computing. We expect to take this business chance aiming for our business to dramatically scale-up to the level such as doubled in the coming five years, with our every effort.

- The usage of cloud computing in Japan which is expected to increase within 3 to 5 years will be a great business opportunity for us. We have 15 years of experience providing outsourcing services, pioneering technological skills to develop network services with our own operated network – facilities throughout Japan and strong relationships with over 6,500 blue chip customers.

IIJ expects fiscal 2011 (ending March 2012) cloud computing-related revenue to be ¥3 billion ($37M), up from ¥0.6 billion ($7M) in 2010. Within five years, IIJ apparently expects such revenues to be around ¥6 billion ($73M). This will make up a small percent of overall revenues, ¥82.4 billion ($1B) in 2010 and ¥100 billion ($1.22B) forecast in 2011, but represents rapid-growth with real potential to drive future earnings.

I think the five-year outlook may prove conservative given long-delayed IT investments across corporate and public-sector Japan. Note that for fiscal 2011, IIJ says it does not expect to see another decrease in systems integration revenue like in 2010, when there was a year-over-year ¥5 billion scale down of one contract. A closer look at IIJ will show that systems integration, or SI as IIJ calls it, has been what has held back faster revenue and profit growth. Keep in mind that IIJ has no illusions concerning the slow-growth Japanese economy, one which has seen companies and other entities delay capital spending. But the company has benefited from recurring revenues amongst its several thousand customers, and has reportedly been adding smaller-sized customers, not to mention the big win of AT&T Japan.

IIJ's fiscal 2011 outlook consists of a 21.3% increase in revenues to ¥100 billion ($1.22B), 52.1% increase in operating income to ¥6.3 billion ($77M) and a 6.1% increase in net income to ¥3.4 billion ($41.5M). Growth rates over the past year were similar (double-digits; net income was up much more sharply following the recessionary 2008-2009 period). Despite sustained high growth, IIJ's P/E multiple remains relatively attractive in the high-teens, a peak ratio has been around 30; trough in the low-teens.

More important to me, as a "value" investor, is the company's 22% of assets in cash and equivalents and a similar amount in "other" and long-term investments, most of which are in securities. Long-term debt, in the form of capital leases, is minimal and manageable. Short-term notes payable can be out-sized since IIJ on occasion uses bank financing such as in its ~$100M acquisition of AT&T Japan. Its cost of debt financing is miniscule.

Of course, no investment is without risks. I have identified several potential ones, including currency, natural disasters, continued delayed capital spending in Japan and persistent "low" margins. But I don't believe any of them can meaningfully, and over the long term, stop IIJ from achieving ever more top and bottom-line growth.

IIJ today is not as cheap per share as it was when I most recently bought at $2 and $5 (in early '09 and '10). But in light of such things as its AT&T Japan acquisition, its side ATM business which is turning profitable, the four dividend hikes, its strong balance sheet, the huge upside it is poised to experience when its systems integration division's contribution is back at pre-crash levels, its founder CEO/Chairman who owns 6% of the company, and of course its high-growth opportunities in the cloud, I think its current valuation is attractive.

I intend to remain a shareholder for the foreseeable future and thus won't get into technical trading factors in this article. While it's nice to see a higher share price, I'm in for the long haul, and I look to buy on pullbacks, pending available capital. Truth be told, I would love to own 3% or more of this company's shares outstanding (which affords favorable legal standing as a shareholder in Japan) and pursue more "friendly" activism with management and the board. Perhaps someone reading this article shares a similar interest or knows someone who might be interested.

*****

Nomura Holdings (Tokyo: 8604) (ADR: NMR) was another Japanese blue chip that began paying dividends in 2006. However, it reverted to biannual payments in 2009, due to fallout from the Global Financial Crisis, no doubt needing to conserve capital. As of November 2011, Nomura has not returned to a quarterly payout.

Beside Honda and Nomura, I do not see that any other companies among those with prominent ADR listings introduced a quarterly dividend payout. The non-payers include the likes of Toyota, who one would presume would have wanted to match Honda's efforts, Nissan, which actually had some of the highest profit margins pre-financial crisis, and the consumer electronics manufacturers such as Sony, Panasonic, and Canon. That is truly a shame since there is most certainly strong demand amongst Japanese investors, from pension funds to individuals, for literally anything that yields more than the near-zero interest rates on savings deposits.

Several companies, not with exchange-listed ADRs, initially said they would introduce quarterly dividends and may have even revised their corporate charters to do so, but they in fact have not (yet) began paying out quarterly. Among those are household names in Japan such as Lion (Tokyo: 4912), a top-seller of toothpaste and the third-largest of toiletries; Hoya

(Tokyo: 7741), a leading global manufacturer of advanced optics used in semiconductors, LCD panels, medical devices, imaging, and eyeglasses; and Aeon Mall (Tokyo: 8905), Japan's leading shopping mall developer (a listed entity of Aeon, Tokyo: 8267). Lesser-known companies that haven't include Sugi Holdings (Tokyo: 7649), a pharmaceutical company, Hiday Hidaka (Tokyo: 7611), a chain restaurant operator, and Riso Kyoiku (Tokyo: 4714), an operator of cram-schools.

Two lesser-known companies that *have* delivered on quarterly-dividends are (1) Hogy Medical (Tokyo: 3593), a manufacturer of consumable medical products and medical equipment, which has paid quarterly since 2009 and also issues *yutaiken* (gifts or gifts certificates that some Japanese companies pay to shareowners meeting certain requirements). Hogy offers those owning 100 or more shares the choice of an original calendar, two surgical masks, one museum pass, or a Y1,000 gift card, which combined with an Y80/share most recent annual payout, makes for total shareholder return of Y9,000, or 2.9%, against a recent stock price of Y3,075 or Y307,500 for 100 shares. Not bad compared to the alternative of near-zero rates on savings; and (2) even more attractive on a yield-basis is Sumida Corp. (Tokyo: 6817), a manufacturer of electronic components, which began paying a dividend in 2008 and has since maintained a quarterly payout. Its stock price was at a 52-week low in November 2011, reflecting its reliance on overseas sales at a time when the yen is the strongest it has ever been; its annual payout of Y25 equates to a dividend yield of 4.8%.

Dividend-on-equity (DOE) is an interesting ratio some Japanese companies publish. In short, it's the company's dividend per share divided by its book value per share. DOE can also be calculated by multiplying ROE and dividend payout ratio. Published DOE minimums or targets often range from 1% to 5%. It may feel somewhat unconventional for Western investors to review DOE given the custom of measuring yield against market value. In fact, DOE could be a bit of a tease in Japan with all the high shareholder equity ratios and correspondingly high net cash balances. Such circumstances combined with a company that's been profitable raises concern over potential better utilization of excess cash. Regarding excess cash, acknowledging the difficulties of realizing synergies from mergers, in most cases I prefer dividends (hikes and/or special dividends, though special dividends in Japan are often smallish compared to outsized ones common in the U.S.) and stock repurchases, though similar to the U.S., Japanese companies are also guilty of procyclical buybacks. In the very least let's agree that transparency with dividend payouts is a positive. Differing capital structures necessitates firm-by-firm due diligence, something value investors have already accepted as part of their modus operandi.

The Dividend Focus 100 Index, which was mentioned in Chapter 2, is a specialized stock index created by the Tokyo Stock Exchange in March 2010. Constituents are chosen based on estimated dividend yield and market capitalization (higher market caps are favored, but the index does include higher-capitalized stocks within the small-cap universe). The index is comprised of 90 stocks and 10 REITs. The most recent constituent listing of January 12, 2012, as published by the TSE, had a forward dividend yield of 3.79%. This is a very respectable yield, easily exceeding those of any government bond duration and many corporate issues. As a bonus, one will not find only the usual large cap suspects among constituents. Rather, how about Coca-Cola West (2579), Japan's largest Coca-Cola bottler. As of January 24, 2012, intra-day, it trades at a mere 0.58x book, 17.2x trailing earnings, and has a dividend yield of 3.06%. Another Coca-Cola play, Mikuni Coca-Cola Bottling (2572), which serves three prefectures (provinces or states) surrounding Tokyo, trades at 0.51x book, 12.7x trailing earnings, and has a dividend yield of 3.52%. Mikuni carries no long-term debt; Coca-Cola West does only because of an acquisition it made to diversify its business, somewhat similar to PepsiCo's strategy. Another component, The Pack Corp. (3950), is a leading manufacturer of paper and plastic shopping bags. It trades at 0.69x book, 7.4x trailing earnings, and has a 3.51% dividend yield. Lots of investment candidates in the Focus 100 Dividend Index; definitely worth a review of constituents.[61]

---

[61] Component list, http://www.tse.or.jp/english/market/topix/data/focus.html; Component list PDF as of Jan. 12, 2012, http://www.tse.or.jp/english/market/topix/data/b7gje60000008gcs-att/201201focus100-e.pdf.

# Minimum Trading Units

According to a report by *The Japan Times*, Japan's minimum trading unit system came to life in 1982, due to *sokaiya* (corporate racketeers from crime syndicates) that gained access to annual shareholder meetings via owning just one share.[62] The *sokaiya* attempted to extort funds from companies by threatening to disrupt shareholder meetings. The answer to try and thwart the *sokaiya* was (1) to introduce minimum trading units that would require a denomination of 1 (often at a multi-thousand dollar per share price), 10, 50, 100, 500, 1,000, or 3,000 shares, which vastly increased the cost of gaining entry to annual meetings, and (2) for companies to hold their annual meetings on the same day, thus explaining to this day a high concentration of shareholder meetings at the end of June. These days the concentration can be an obstacle to activist investors. Nevertheless, the Tokyo Stock Exchange reports continued de-concentration of meeting days in recent years: 41.2% on the peak day of June 29, 2011, compared to 84.1% in 2000, and an all-time concentration peak of 96.2% in 1995 (the concentration level was 70.1% in 1983 and reached 90% by 1988). In 2011, following June 29th, other concentrated days were June 24th (17.5%), June 28th (14%), and June 23rd (9.5%).[63]

As mentioned above, Honda split its stock in 2006 for the first time in 23 years. Prior to the split, at Y8,000 per share and a 100 minimum trading unit, it would cost Y800,000 to purchase its shares. At foreign exchange parity (Y100/$1) that would be $8,000, not an impossible sum, but not exactly money just anyone can easily come up with for an investment let alone try and repeat that in building a portfolio. Imagine if Honda in 2001 had not reduced its minimum trading unit from a 1,000; purchasing its shares pre-split

---

[62] "TSE studies simplifying minimum trade rules," *The Japan Times*, Feb. 4, 2006. http://www.japantimes.co.jp/text/nb20060204a2.html
[63] TSE shareholder meeting concentration data/chart, http://www.tse.or.jp/listing/sokai/shuchu/b7gje600000059q3-att/b7gje60000007s5o.pdf; TSE 2011 shareholder meeting schedule data, http://www.tse.or.jp/listing/sokai/shuchu/b7gje600000059q3-att/b7gje6000001m8og.pdf; TSE shareholder meeting data index page, http://www.tse.or.jp/listing/sokai/shuchu/index.html.

would have cost Y8 million, or $80,000, an amount among U.S.-listed stocks only eclipsed by Warren Buffett's Berkshire Hathaway, which these days trades above $100,000/share (A-shares, BRK.A); B-shares (BRK.B), reflecting a ratio of 1,500:1, trade in the low $70.00s.

Honda's 1:2 stock split in 2006 took its share purchase price (Y4,000/sh x 100 share minimum) to approximately Y400,000 yen ($4,000), a full Y100,000 under the Tokyo Stock Exchange's proposed Y500,000 threshold it recommended in order to attract more investors. This seems far more reasonable since in the U.S. it would be equivalent to buying 100 shares of a $40 stock. Nevertheless, it could still preclude an individual seeking to dollar-cost average and/or one who has a smaller amount of capital to invest. All is not lost for smaller Japanese investors, as some securities firms have obliged to allow trading of so-called mini share lots at 1/10th the required lot, which would allow for example, one to buy 100 shares of a company with a 1,000 share minimum (10 shares of a 100 minimum, or 1 share of a 10 minimum). Shortcomings of mini shares include not being able to place limit orders, not receiving voting rights, and not being eligible for *yutaiken*. Dividends and stock splits are applicable. The "mini" innovation also includes overseas equities and non-equity products. A December 2010 *Nikkei Weekly* article about so-called "micro-investing" mentions the average minimum amount to invest in a stock at the Nikkei's peak in 1989 was around Y1.58 million (over $20,000 at around Y77/$1) or more than seven-times the present at Y220,000 ($2,850).[64]

Similar to the likely positive reaction if more companies paid quarterly dividends, reducing and/or eliminating minimum trading units would bode well for broader and deeper market participation. Serious Japanese value investors actually regard undervalued stocks with high per share prices and/or large minimum trading units to be that much more attractive; of course these conditions could be cited, at least partially, as the cause of their undervaluation. In light of declining trading volumes in Tokyo since the Global Financial Crisis, it seems the Tokyo Stock Exchange could enact a termination of minimum trading units – it would obviously be in the

---

[64] "Micro-investing makes markets more accessible," *The Nikkei Weekly*, Dec. 20, 2010.

Exchange's best interest to see volume increase. Note that there is a particular dearth in trading among stocks listed outside the TOPIX 1st Section, the number of which slightly exceeds TOPIX 1 listings. Osaka and the regional exchanges would almost certainly follow the TSE's lead on any enhancements.

The Nagoya Stock Exchange is the third largest in Japan; it had 96 sole listings and 231 dual listings as of February 2012.[65] The Fukuoka Stock Exchange had 128 listings of which 36 were sole listings, as of February 2012.[66] The Sapporo Securities Exchange reported having 73 listings, 18 of which were sole listings, as of January 2012.[67] Trading on the Nagoya Exchange has been in sharp decline over the past decade. Average daily turnover for the entire exchange was only ¥300 million ($3 million at exchange parity) in 2011, more than 90% off its level in 2002. On both the Fukuoka and Sapporo Exchanges trading is very thin and many stocks go untraded each session. Illiquid trading may limit opportunities for investors, but with a similar line of thinking to neglected stocks with high per share prices and/or large minimum trading units, value investors may find hidden gems listed on the regional exchanges.

A March 2010 article in *The Nikkei Weekly* reported that about 15% of stocks listed on Japan's three emerging markets were untraded more than half of each month, and the rate of such neglected stocks has been on the rise.[68] Beside companies with minimum trading lots that require unnecessarily high purchase costs, the article says companies' floats may be limited due to founders and other large holders owning more than half of shares outstanding; in some cases with little expectation of them reducing their holdings. No doubt there are some companies where the misguided thinking

---

[65] See: http://www.nse.or.jp/e/ for English language information, including links to a variety of market statistics.
[66] The Fukuoka Exchange maintains an English website at http://www.fse.or.jp/english/index.php.
[67] The Sapporo Exchange does not have English language information beyond a short PDF pamphlet. Listing information per: http://www.sse.or.jp/listing/list.html. Home page: http://www.sse.or.jp/index.html.
[68] "Trading on markets for start-ups slows to a crawl," *The Nikkei Weekly*, Mar. 15, 2010.

is that the higher the quoted stock price, the more prestige for the company. Apparently underwriters may even be supportive of high-priced quotes as it makes their job selling an IPO easier.

After an IPO, there may be companies that have suffered declines in their high-quoted stock prices, which discourages any selling among both insiders and minority shareholders; consequently a stock becomes that much more illiquid. Such a lack of liquidity once again may pose a problem, especially for larger investors (but a number of such untraded stocks could be too small for inclusion depending on portfolio size anyway), but there may be some great overlooked companies. Know that many of the leading stock indexes in Japan factor in liquidity when selecting constituents. A coveted TOPIX 1st Section listing could come into play, too, for the more successful companies on the emerging markets. Ahead of their 2012/2013 planned merger both the Osaka Securities Exchange (JASDAQ) and TSE (Mothers) have announced revised listing/delisting conditions.

While one certainly runs the risk of buying stocks that will remain obscure, the point is to buy at significant margins of safety, levels at which many neglected stocks already trade; to buy stocks that pay dividends with viability to increase them; to thusly focus on total return since companies can also repurchase shares; and to keep open the possibility of a merger, spinoff, or activism as possible means to unlock value. Martin Whitman's "resource conversion" approach (see Chapter 6) is particularly appropriate for Japanese stocks.

A last note on minimum trading units and why the TSE should simply eliminate them – in two of the following cases, the culprit was not a 100 or 1,000 minimum trading unit but conversely unnecessarily high share prices of several thousand dollars a piece that are a by product of the minimum trading unit system.[69] The Exchange took some hits (verbal and monetary) in 2005 and 2006 when it ran into technological problems, one of them involving an

---

[69] Portions of this section based on an entry concerning "technology problems" at the Tokyo Stock Exchange on Wikipedia:
http://en.wikipedia.org/wiki/Tokyo_Stock_Exchange#Technology_problems. Most recently, due to technological problems (unrelated to minimum trading units), the TSE had to halt trading in 241 stocks for 4 ½ hours on February 1, 2012.

erroneous trade order, which was a mirror image of a similar trade input incorrectly in 2001 (curiously, both instances happened in December). One matter was on November 1, 2005, when a bug in a newly installed trading system by Fujitsu forced the Exchange to suspend trading for all but 90 minutes. Then, on December 8, 2005, came the erroneous trade, one in which a Mizuho trader intended to sell shares of J-Com at Y600,000, but mistakenly sold 600,000 shares at Y1! The net loss was reportedly $347 million. In December 2001, a UBS Warburg trader sold 610,000 shares of Dentsu at Y1 on its first day of trading, instead of selling one share at Y610,000; UBS Warburg reportedly lost £71 million. Following the Exchange's problems, a Nomura strategist told *The Japan Times* in 2006 that minimum trading units "are confusing even to professionals" and that "the order mistakes would not have happened if there had been a single trading unit [NB: referring to the ability to trade any number of shares, i.e. no minimum unit]."[70] The Exchange's unwillingness and/or inability to cancel erroneous orders is also a problem.

## Share repurchases

Believe it or not, share repurchases have been allowed in Japan only since 1994 (in Germany since 1998, the UK since 1981, and even earlier in the U.S. although they weren't significant in the aggregate until the 1980s). Prior to that they were not only illegal but also would have resulted in a taxable event for all shareholders; the tax was repealed in 1995. Regulators had long been concerned with the possibility of share price manipulation. Meanwhile, although the ability to buyback shares opened the door for companies to award employees with stock options, they are used to a significantly lesser extent (in terms of breadth of usage and size of awards) in Japan compared to the U.S. This is good news for investors since there is less, essentially nominal, risk of dilution. I believe, however, if more executives and key employees were compensated with a reasonable amount of options that such an incentive would be a net positive for all concerned.

---

[70] "TSE studies simplifying minimum trade rules," *The Japan Times*, Feb. 4, 2006. http://www.japantimes.co.jp/text/nb20060204a2.html.

Another favorable development for investors in Japanese stocks is that stock buybacks mean a lot less smoke and mirrors, as they sometimes entail in the U.S., and accordingly, much better transparency. For starters, Japanese companies announce a buyback that becomes effective on a soon forthcoming date and likewise expire typically within a month to as much as a year of commencement. Companies provide a reason for initiating a buyback, the number of shares to be repurchased (and what percentage the shares equate to shares outstanding), and the aggregate price to be paid. Following a buyback, notice is provided of the exact number of shares repurchased, at what aggregate price, the latest count for shares outstanding and treasury shares, as well as the original terms of the buyback.

By comparison, repurchases in the U.S. are often announced with a quarterly earnings release, at which time the board is said to have approved a certain amount to be spent over a specified period. Henceforth, there are usually no formal updates made except for a brief reference in quarterly earnings announcements and corresponding changes to financial statements. It is not immediately clear when or ultimately whether shares will be repurchased. Most dissatisfying is to learn of the pro-cyclicality of repurchases in which increasingly higher amounts are spent as earnings are increasing, which means the repurchases are occurring at ever-higher per share prices. Japanese companies exhibit similar tendencies, although there is a tremendous opportunity to repurchase counter-cyclically with so many net-cash and low-debt companies trading at or below book value. Buybacks in these conditions (i.e. low valuations) provide the most "bang for the buck."

In many cases, investors should easily be able to locate past and current share repurchase information. This will almost certainly be the case for companies with ADRs, those with a large overseas shareholder base, and those with large (or a large percentage of) overseas sales. NTT DoCoMo (9437) (DCM) maintains a subpage on its website (within its Investor Relations' pages) dedicated to share repurchase information. Details of past repurchases extend back to 2002. Nidec (6594) (NJ) includes share repurchase information back to 2008, which is contained on a page comprised of various company stock and bond details. Kikkoman (2801), which does not have sponsored ADRs, but has double-digit foreign share ownership, and obviously its soy and other sauces are well known outside of Japan, maintains a page with various announcements, including stock repurchases. The shortcut to uncovering share and company-related information is to locate a company's Investor Relations website. More often than not there will be some amount of information available in English. As mentioned earlier in the book, a lack of information could suggest possible hidden value to non-Japanese investors, although it could also indicate a lack of interest in, or concern for, overseas investors; either case may represent an opportunity, but the latter possibly a more challenging one ceteris paribus to realize value.

## Parent and subsidiary stock listings; cross-shareholdings

The Japanese stock market could be consolidated in a major way if parent companies were to wholly-acquire their listed subsidiaries. A unique practice exists in Japan where it is not uncommon for parent companies to list select subsidiaries. A 2010 report of the market's status as of year-end 2009, showed that there were 256 parent companies with 526 listed subsidiaries, accounting for 6.9% and 14.3%, respectively, of the listed Japanese stock universe (based on the number of listed companies).[71] Since an ownership threshold of 33% was used, there are many more such listings at lower levels of equity ownership. Regardless of the ownership level, anytime two companies own equity in each other they are referred to as cross-shareholdings.

As for market capitalization, the 526 listed subsidiaries comprised 9% of the market's aggregate capitalization, and only about 20% of their parent companies' aggregate capitalization. Combined, these parent-subsidiary companies equate to roughly 55% of the market's total capitalization. Unsurprisingly, a large majority of parent companies are 1st Section listings, while subsidiary listings were more balanced: 41% 1st Section, 25% 2nd Section, and 34% emerging market. Half or more of these subsidiary listings could be neglected (i.e. thin trading and analyst coverage). An interesting fact

---

[71] "株式市場における親子上場の存在感とその功," NLI Research Institute of Japan. http://www.nli-research.co.jp/report/report/2010/11/repo1011-3.pdf

is that subsidiary listings have been an important component of domestic IPOs, where prior to the 2008 financial crisis they often accounted for around 15% of new listings each year.

Reasons for a parent to list a subsidiary sound similar to those provided in the U.S. when companies undertake spinoffs. For example, besides generating cash proceeds to the parent, a spinoff will afford the subsidiary's management both more prestige, and autonomy in decision-making. Interestingly, there may be some older-fashioned thinking in Japan, where there is prestige for a parent company to have a large number of listed subsidiaries. A sometimes-favorable arrangement for parent companies is when equity ownership in the subsidiary remains high and the profits flow back to the parent. Note however, that some investors argue or complain the parent is in effect overcharging its subsidiary, which takes profits away from outside minority shareholders; which may explain why some companies have listed subsidiaries, since if they were wholly-owned, the parent would not want to hurt margins (and by extension stock market valuation) by overcharging.

Effissimo Capital Management is an example of a hedge fund known for its ability to scrutinize company filings and expose related transactions damaging to outside minority shareholders. Note the argument that it's not the listing structure itself that creates potential exploitation of subsidiaries by parents, but rather (whether a company is public or private) a more important factor is whether there is a controlling shareholder. To that argument one can of course add the variable of the quality of management. Some Japanese parent companies have found that they would rather be the beneficiary of all a listed subsidiary's profits rather than share with outside minority investors – this suggests in these cases there's no opportunistic pricing between related parties. For example, Hitachi wholly acquired five listed subsidiaries in July 2007, reportedly for this very reason of not wanting to let precious profits trickle to outside shareholders.[72] Profitability is a good problem to have; obviously the parent-subsidiary listing arrangement sours when there are losses. In the case of cross-shareholding relationships in general, losses are

---

[72] "日立、上場子会社5社を完全子会社へ," Jul. 27, 2007.
http://jp.reuters.com/article/topNews/idJPJAPAN-10224220090727

particularly hard to swallow if a counterpart is not exactly related to one's core business.

The above scenarios are where outside investors come into play, especially value and activist investors. If a listed subsidiary is rather thinly traded, trades at less than book value, and otherwise is a profitable company, investors clearly see an opportunity for either the parent to wholly acquire the company, sell it, or watch the company possibly become a takeover target. Spinoffs are not a viable option because they would be disadvantageous tax-wise to common stock holders. This partially explains the conglomerate discount in Japan; they exist, too, in the U.S. for example, but not for this reason. Nevertheless, similar to the eventual repeal of taxes on share repurchases in 1995 in Japan, it may simply be a matter of time before the tax law concerning spinoffs is revised and companies then willingly explore possibilities. As for non-subsidiary equity investments, and especially ones that are in businesses unrelated to core operations, the gut reaction among investors is to want the company to offload them when they trade lower and must be marked down; ideally this would happen before any markdown or at least not have to happen at bargain basement prices.

While bull markets will result in higher valuations on the balance sheet, bear markets can be painful with losses (balance sheet markdowns and income statement losses) mounting for non-operating reasons. The 2008/2009 financial crisis became increasingly messy as selling begat selling and the value of cross-shareholdings sank in tandem. In a November 2008 interview with *The Economist*, a portion of which was not published, I argued that despite the heavy collateral damage suffered from cross-shareholdings, at that point such investments would ultimately serve as a solid foundation for the eventual bottoming of the market – there would be no more sellers. During the market selloff Japanese analysts among others found the negative impact of cross-shareholdings to be ironic, since in the years preceding the crash cross-shareholdings saw somewhat of a resurgence for the purpose of keeping away unwanted suitors, but lower stock prices stemming from cross-shareholding losses had in effect made companies cheaper to would-be acquirers. Though in hindsight, it turns out that there would be very little deal making due to the gravity of the global crash. In fact, in the aftermath, it was the Japanese that went on to make foreign acquisitions in the tailwind of record yen strength.

Among Japan's most prominent parent-subsidiary listings include:[73]

- NTT (9432) owns over 63% NTT DoCoMo (9437) as of Sept. 30, 2011. NTT's market cap of Feb. 2, 2012, is Y5.048 trillion; DoCoMo's is Y5.958 trillion, greater than its parent's! NTT's stake in DoCoMo is worth Y3.75 trillion and equates to over 74% of NTT's own market value. The absurdity of NTT's under-valuation, standalone or as a conglomerate cannot be explained in words.

- Softbank (9984) owns 35.5% stake of Yahoo! Japan (4689) as of June 22, 2011. Softbank's market cap as of Feb. 2, 2012, is Y2.47 trillion; Yahoo!'s is Y1.406 trillion. Softbank's 35.5% of Yahoo! Japan is worth Y500 billion and equates to 20% of Softbank's own market value.

- Canon (7751) owns just over 50% Canon Marketing Japan (8060). Canon's market cap as of Feb. 2, 2012, is Y4.375 trillion; Canon Marketing's is Y144 billion. Canon's 50% stake in Canon Marketing is worth Y72 billion or less than 2% of Canon's own market value. Canon Marketing's equity is clearly insignificant to Canon's market value, but it serves as a good example of a listing that may be better wholly acquired. While not neglected (as it is traded on 1st Section of the TSE and has decent daily volume in the hundreds of thousands of shares), it trades at a mere 0.52x book value, carries a very nominal amount of debt, and earns very low returns on assets and equity.

Cross-shareholding is a system commonly associated with Japan given its once widespread existence and controversial resurgence after the year 2000 with the arrival of foreign activist hedge funds and even some maverick Japanese fund managers. The shareholdings are considered as being non-

---

[73] "親子上場," Wikipedia Japan. NB: ticker codes, stake %s, and other details added to above paragraph by the author.

trading, long-term holdings and are carried on the balance sheet as such. Irrespective of shareholding intent, a down market will inflict pain on holding values. The Toyota Group is a good example of integrated cross-shareholdings; while snack maker Ezaki Glico's (2206) cross-shareholdings were deemed to have "no apparent synergies" by activist fund Steel Partners Japan.[74] Nomura Securities' research arm has studied cross-shareholding and published findings since 1990. During this time, cross-shareholdings (as measured by the market value of listed companies' stock held; excluding the holdings of insurance companies) have come down from a peak of as much as 30% in 1991, to a study period low at just over 11% at the end of 2010.[75] The downtrend post-2008 is likely to continue, incrementally, to a point until there simply won't be many changes since some tie-ups are unlikely to be undone under any circumstances.

The unwinding of holdings at an NTT would certainly be huge news and have an outsized impact on the percentage of cross-shareholdings. Surrounding any selling by NTT there would likely be downward pressure on the broader market, which is one argument by those not necessarily against cross-shareholdings, since widespread untying of holdings would surely overwhelm demand for shares. Near term, it is more plausible that we will see the Japanese government selling off stakes of its large holdings in the likes of NTT and Japan Tobacco. This could upset supply/demand of shares, but will likely be viewed favorably by the market with the understanding that the government needs to raise funds. Value and activist investors may find great investment opportunities by identifying undervalued companies that have equity holdings unrelated to their core businesses that can be sold. Effecting a sale is far easier said than done, but it can be an additional positive to a company that already looks attractive based on fundamental and any other analyses.

---

[74] Re. Ezaki Glico and Steel, see "Steel Partners Calls on Ezaki Glico to Address Losses from Cross-Shareholdings," Bloomberg, Oct. 22, 2008. http://www.bloomberg.com/apps/news?pid=newsarchive&sid=adh14oq9JMuM.
[75] "上場会社の株式持ち合い比率11.1%　過去最低を更新," Jun. 28, 2011. http://www.j-cast.com/2011/06/28099707.html

## Kagome, a Japanese favorite

The best way to approach the Japanese stock market is not how most Japanese (institutions and investors alike) approach it. For many of them are textbook traders, relying upon candlestick charts and technical analysis. Despite the deep undervaluation of domestic equities, on the surface value investing appears to take a backseat in Japan. To be fair, similar to the U.S., media reporting and investor interest appear to center around the hot stocks and stories. My experience has been that Japanese value investors take a very simple approach, perhaps by virtue of having such a universe of undervalued stocks, where they look to buy already cheap stocks (i.e. trading for less than book value) or ones that have sold-off. They like to buy "on sale" and then collect dividends and also *yutaiken* or the equivalent of gifts or gift certificates typically for a company's products. For illustrative purposes, let's look at Kagome (Tokyo: 2811), a well-known maker of ketchup, sauces and ingredients, which has *yutaiken* as explained below. As you'll see, a stock too popular with retail investors can leave something to be desired in terms of attractive valuation. Note that *yutaiken* is not applicable to investors based outside of Japan.

> For holders of between 100 and 999 shares, the shareholder will receive Y1,000 ($13) worth of Kagome products twice a year, in May and November. For holders of 1,000 or more shares, they will receive Y3,000 ($39) worth of Kagome products. As will be discussed below, Kagome was trading at Y1,500 a share in mid-November 2011, meaning establishing a 100-share position would cost Y150,000 ($1,948). The annual *yutaiken* of Y2,000 and an annual dividend of Y1,500, makes for a total (Japanese individual investor) shareholder return of 2.3%. Not an amount to go crazy over, but that's 2.2x% more than savings accounts yield, and it is a good mix of beloved products and cash.

Kagome is perennially among the most favorite stocks of Japanese individual investors – more on their favorites later when I discuss Nomura's monthly survey. Kagome's popularity is evidenced by its 60-plus trailing twelve month P/E ratio as of intra-day November 18, 2011 – its Y1,500 share price is a mere 50 yen off its year-to-date high set in late January, despite the broader market facing various serious domestic and external pressures pushing it to year-low levels. The 60 P/E fell to only around 50 when the stock hit its low of Y1,230 after the March 11th disaster. Again, that reflects how much Kagome is liked, but barring even greater future sell-offs, its sky-high P/E precludes value investors from nibbling. Kagome has a market capitalization of Y149.425 billion yen ($1.94 billion). Still, the relative undervaluation of Japanese stocks is somewhat evident in Kagome: it has a 61.4% shareholder's equity ratio and trades at 1.68-times book value. Somewhat surprisingly, its dividend yield is only 1% – throw in biannual product gift baskets and the return is sweetened to over 2%. Nevertheless, reported ROE for the past year totals only 2.8% and ROA, only 1.8%; returns over the two years prior are similarly low, by +/- 10%.

Kagome became a favorite stock among Japanese investors by design. With its products already widely-liked, and as its cross-shareholdings were winding down early in the new millennium, in addition to *yutaiken*, a July 2004 *Nikkei Weekly* article describes how it embarked on a strategy to lure more retail investors by way of: reducing its minimum trading unit, spicing up its annual shareholder meetings by turning them into consumer focus sessions, and hosting annual buffet parties.[76] In 2001, the company reportedly set a goal of having 100,000 individual shareholders. At that time, and in the few years prior, Kagome had roughly 6,500 individual shareholders. The growth thereafter is indicative of its marketing success: over 44,000 individual shareholders in its fiscal year ended March 2002, 67,000+ in 2003, 76,000+ in 2004, close to 88,000 in 2005, nearly 138,000 in 2006, when the number then stabilized until exceeding 147,000 in 2009, almost 151,000 in 2010, and just short of 171,000 as of its fiscal year ended March 2011.[77]

Meantime, Kagome's stock, which hit a decade low of around Y700/share in late 2002, went on to experience growth mirroring its increase in individual shareholders: Kagome hit Y1,000 in 2003/2004, Y1,200 in 2005, as high as Y1,800 in 2006 (it ended the year at around Y1,600, more than double its 2002 low), advanced beyond Y2,000 in 2007 (a triple within five

---

[76] "Firms luring fickle individual investors via special perks," *The Nikkei Weekly*, Jul. 5, 2004.
[77] Kagome historical shareholder count, http://www.kagome.co.jp/company/ir/stock/holder.html.

years), before falling to around Y1,400 in 2008, to rally back to Y1,800 in 2009, having since pulled back and trading around the Y1,500 level (meaning Kagome is still more than a double over the past decade). Although Kagome's expenses for its new annual meeting format quadrupled to Y400 million ($3.7 million at that time) in 2004, it seems too have paid off nicely. As of March 2011 individual shareholders owned over 61% of the company. The 2004 *Nikkei Weekly* article quoted Kagome's president saying that its shareholders buy about 10-times as many Kagome products as non-shareholder consumers.

## Nomura's *Individual Investor Survey*

Unfortunately, the *yutaiken* will be irrelevant to non-Japan-based investors, and could be regarded as an unnecessary expense for such investors, but in fact, companies that pay both a dividend and *yutaiken* can be viewed as having management that are focused on shareholders and quite possibly as ones that have the balance sheet and hopefully the cash flows to support such payments. Among all the big name Japanese companies, such as Toyota in autos, Sony in consumer electronics, and Mitsubishi UFJ in banking, Kagome finds itself among these giants in Nomura's monthly survey of individual investors (in the section concerning "most-watched" stocks).[78] Nomura's *Individual Investor Survey* is published monthly, usually near the start of the month and contains some potentially insightful information, including: the responses to a variety of questions by the first 1,000 respondents concerning their expectations for the market's return over the next three months, what is most likely to impact the market, the most and least appealing investment sectors, foreign exchange outlook, most-watched stocks, and a spot question.[79]

---

[78] Nomura's surveys can be found amongst its news releases at http://www.nomuraholdings.com/news/nr/.

[79] The February 2012 spot question is revealing with regards to dividends and excess capital allocation expectations. The highest response rate for required dividend yield was 26.8% of respondents at a yield of 2% to 3%, followed by 21.2% at 3%-plus, and 19.9% at 4%-plus. The average dividend yield demanded was 2.77%, compared to

In the May 2011 Nomura *Individual Investor Survey*, the first one published post-earthquake/tsunami (March 11, 2011), it is interesting to see that longtime constituent Kagome actually dropped off the list of most-watched stocks.[80] An unsurprising new addition was Kajima (Tokyo: 1812), a large construction company; and moving up in the ranking was Komatsu (Tokyo: 6301), a leading manufacturer of industrial equipment including construction machines and vehicles. Among other noticeable new entrants are Mitsubishi Heavy Industries (Tokyo: 7011) and Chubu Electric Power (Tokyo: 9502). The notorious Tokyo Electric Power (Tokyo: 9501), "Tepco," owner-operator of the stricken nuclear facility in Fukushima, remained a top-5 most-watched stock, though the number of people selecting it as their most-watched pick was largely unchanged. On one hand there was still ambiguity over Tepco's ability to resolve the problems with the damaged nuclear reactors, and on the other there were no doubt individuals speculating on a possible recovery in stock price.

Back to the overall list of most-watched stocks, many of the names will be recognizable to non-Japanese investors and most if not all will be household-type names to Japanese. Still, despite some resemblance to the top-holdings of benchmark indices, and thus the "popularity" (and cyclicality) associated with some of these stocks, there are opportunities for value investors. The November 2011 top-10 most watched companies:

| Company | Code | P/E | P/B | Dividend |
|---|---|---|---|---|
| Toyota | 7203 | 18.8 | 0.77 | 2.04% |
| Takeda Pharma | 4502 | 10.2 | 1.27 | 5.62% |
| Softbank | 9984 | 15.0 | 3.54 | 0.19% |

TOPIX 1st Section's year-end 2011 yield of 2.33%. Regarding shareholder distributions, an overwhelming number favored cash dividends, followed by *yutaiken*, with share buybacks and stock splits being least interesting.

[80] May 2011 survey: http://www.nomuraholdings.com/news/nr/nsc/20110520/20110520.pdf.

| Company | Code | P/E | P/B | Dividend |
|---|---|---|---|---|
| NTT DoCoMo | 9437 | 11.5 | 1.12 | 3.82% |
| Komatsu | 6301 | 12.4 | 1.98 | 1.97% |
| Aeon | 8267 | 13.4 | 0.90 | 2.00% |
| McDonald's JP | 2702 | 35.0 | 1.78 | 1.45% |
| Mizuho Fin Grp | 8411 | 4.8 | 0.58 | 6.06% |
| Panasonic | 6752 | 19.2 | 0.62 | 1.46% |
| Sony | 6758 | - | 0.55 | 1.92% |

*As of November 18, 2011, market close, per Yahoo! Finance Japan. P/E is trailing twelve month.*

Each of the above except Aeon (a supermarket operator and property developer) and McDonald's Japan is not only down for the year, but is trading at/near its year low – in line with the broader market. A number of them are among Japan's biggest companies by market capitalization, and all of them have market caps in excess of $1 billion. That would certainly be the case in the U.S. as well, where the most-watched and widest-held stocks are those with multi-billion dollar capitalizations. The most-watched list can be good for idea generation, maybe more so for those outside the top-10. A contrarian take may also be useful. Longtime favorite Nintendo (7974) fell off the list in summer 2011 as its stock continued to face unabated selling pressure (see next chapter for a detailed look at Nintendo). Nintendo shares would go on to fall by roughly 50%, but have started to rally from February 2012, when it also happened to reappear on the survey's most-watched list.

# Top Companies of 1980 vs. 2010

A key difference between Japan and the U.S. is captured in a slide (entitled, "Revitalizing Japan's Capital Market") from an April 2011 presentation created by the Tokyo Stock Exchange to promote its new exchange designed for professional investors with targeted listings for venture-type companies.[81] The slide lists the top-20 companies sorted by market cap at the end of 2010 and 1980 for both Japan and the U.S. The 1980 listing for the U.S. only included NYSE-listed companies; the 2010 one includes both NYSE and Nasdaq companies. Similar to the above most-watched list, Aeon and McDonald's Japan were the exception here, too, in terms of not making the list at all. To be fair, no U.S. supermarket operators (unless we count Wal-Mart) or fast food chains made the top list, either. Some of the highlights:

- Japan had 8 newcomers to the 2010 list; the U.S. had double that, 16

- Of the 8 in Japan, only 1 was a "venture" company: Softbank

- Of the 16 in the U.S., 5 were "venture" companies, including: Apple, Microsoft, Oracle, Google, and Intel

- At the end of 1980, there were 6 banks in Japan's list; 3 in 2010

- At the end of 1980, there were 0 banks in U.S. list; 4 in 2010

- At the end of 1980, 14 of 20 in the U.S. were oil co's; 2 in 2010

---

[81] "Japan Society Corporate Program: Revitalizing Japan's Capital Market and Entrepreneurship after the Quake." Apr. 14, 2011. By Tetsutaro Muraki, Tokyo AIM, Inc.

- At the end of 2010, there were 5 consumer-type companies in the U.S. (Wal-Mart, P&G, J&J, Coca-Cola, and Pfizer).

- At the end of 2010, there was only 1 consumer-type company in Japan (Takeda Pharma)

- U.S. computer soft/hardware companies include: Apple, Google, IBM, Intel, Microsoft, and Oracle. While the Japan list includes more of a hardware than software focus unless counting video games and music/movies: Canon, Nintendo, Panasonic, and Sony. In 1980, Canon and Nintendo would not have made the top-20, but Hitachi and NEC did.

Let's now look at some American equivalents of the most-watched list from Nomura's *Individual Investor* November 2011 survey, and do a simple comparison of valuations as of the market's close on November 18, 2011.

| Company | Ticker | P/E | P/B | Dividend |
| --- | --- | --- | --- | --- |
| General Motors | GM | 4.7 | 0.99 | 0.00% |
| Ford | F | 6.1 | 6.46 | 0.00% |
| Gilead | GILD | 11.7 | 4.90 | 0.00% |
| AT&T | T | 14.5 | 1.49 | 6.00% |
| Deere | DE | 12.2 | 4.13 | 2.20% |
| Kroger | KR | 11.6 | 2.51 | 2.10% |
| McDonald's | MCD | 18.2 | 7.08 | 3.00% |
| Bank of America | BAC | - | 0.28 | 0.70% |

Comparing the two tables shows the relative undervaluation of Japanese stocks as evidenced by price-to-book ratios, with the lone exceptions being General Motors, whose P/B of 0.99 is the lowest non-bank value among the American stocks listed (though it's higher than Toyota's 0.77), and Bank of

America's P/B of 0.28, which believe it or not is less than half of Mizuho's (0.58). As has been the case in recent years and still despite Toyota's continued struggles of late, the latter's market cap is more than double either GM or Ford's and it exceeds the latter two combined (Y8.4 trillion or $109 billion vs. GM $34B and Ford $38B), although both have traded as high as double their current levels year-to-date. Lastly, regarding the automakers, there is a stark difference in price-to-book ratios when looking at Ford, which was not bailed out, and the fact that neither U.S. automaker pays a dividend (again, yet). On a price-to-earnings basis, however, Toyota's P/E of 18.8 is more than triple Ford's and GM's. The discrepancy can be partially explained by record-strong yen eating away at Toyota's earnings, while Ford and GM are trading at year-to-date lows.

*****

In April 2006 I compiled the market capitalizations of global auto companies and compared them to Toyota's, which at the time was trading near an all-time high (market cap of $205B with the yen at 117/$ compared to around 77 in November 2011).[82] At that time, Toyota was by far Japan's most valuable company, and in the U.S. there were only seven companies with larger market caps (I noted Exxon (XOM) at $390B, GE (GE) at $350B, and Microsoft (MSFT) at $280B). Toyota was then on its way to becoming the third-largest auto manufacturer in the U.S. and the largest in the world, based on unit sales volume. Most interesting is that its market cap equated to 43% of the world's combined listed automakers (including Honda, which had a 12.4% share, DaimlerChrysler 11.9%, Nissan 10.8%, Volkswagen 6.0%, Volvo 3.9%, Ford 2.9%, Fiat 2.7%, PACCAR 2.5%, GM 2.4%, and Tata Motors 1.6%). Hard and fast contrarians may have avoided Toyota shares due to their inordinate capitalization compared to the auto industry at large. Value investors, however, would have likely found a number of reasons to remain optimistic. It turns out that Toyota had a little more gas left for a run: from April 2006, Toyota went on to gain another 20% or so before peaking in late 2006, early 2007.

Fast forward to November 2011, and it's a drastically different composition. Compared to 43% of the pie in April 2006, Toyota has slipped

---

[82] "Toyota's Dominance Shows in Share of Global Auto Market-Cap Pie," Seeking Alpha (dot-com), Apr. 19, 2006. http://seekingalpha.com/article/9182-toyota-s-dominance-shows-in-share-of-global-auto-market-cap-pie

to just below 26%, as its market capitalization has fallen by nearly $98 billion (-47%). Honda has been much more stable by comparison, at 12.2% vs. 12.4% previously, as its market cap has fallen by $8.1 billion (-14%). Otherwise, the most notable change is the 84% surge in Volkswagen's market cap to $53.3 billion, $1.5 billion ahead of Honda, and now ahead of both Daimler and Nissan. Both Ford and GM have seen significant increases in market cap, 171% and 193%, respectively. Volvo, PACCAR, and Tata, have also grown, at 23%, 15%, and 29%, respectively. Despite the sizable declines in capitalization for Japan's Big-3, Daimler (-21%), and Fiat (-50%), they have been offset by the aforementioned gains, and thus, the current capitalization of all the above auto manufacturers of $425 billion is only about 14% off the $484 billion mark in 2006.

Consider how challenging it can be in the shoes of a value investor. During Toyota's big run between 2003 and 2007, when its shares more than tripled, its price-to-earnings ratio was on average never more than about 13.5, which was to be the highest it reached before shares peaked in early 2007 and went on to shed nearly half their value as of November 2011. Toyota never traded much beyond twice book value; in 2003 it was trading at/near book value. Dividends grew with the tremendous growth in profits, such that Toyota's dividend yield actually increased 33% between 2003 and 2007. The question is after an impressive four-year run whether investors should have took some profits, completely liquidated, or held on for more gains. What about newer or prospective investors?

The Value Investment Institute published what amounts to a case study on key Toyota Group affiliate (and cross-shareholding), Toyota Industries (6201), a longtime shareholding of Martin Whitman's Third Avenue Value Fund. Long story short, Whitman began buying Industries in 1998 and detailed the position in a shareholder letter in 2000 – for simplicity's sake let's say he began accumulating at around Y2,000/share. After the Nikkei bottomed in 2003, Industries like many stocks recovered and went on to grow many fold; it topped Y6,000 in early 2007. With substantial unrealized profits, Whitman continued to buy, believing Industries was still undervalued given its 5.5% stake in Toyota and the market's mispricing of assets and undistributed earnings. However, early 2007 was to be the peak and by late 2008, Industries had fallen below his original purchase price of Y2,000/share.

The Value Investment Institute did a fine job of combining Industries' mentions in Third Avenue's shareholder letters with its stock price performance. However, it argues that (1) the investment was a failure in corporate governance; Whitman makes a similar argument, and (2) it was a value trap. I tend to disagree. (1) It's virtually inconceivable that Industries would sell any Toyota shares, but maybe they would have been receptive to somehow unlocking some shareholder value had Whitman and Third Avenue made an overture and tried to explain/convince them. (2) A tripling of share price in roughly three years is hardly a value trap.[83]

*****

It was difficult to find a small enough traditional pharmaceutical concern to compare against the Y2.5 trillion ($32 billion) market cap of Takeda. The closest was Gilead, more a bio-tech, however, at $30B. Otherwise, there is Sanofi at $90B, Merck at $106B, GlaxoSmithKline at $108B, Novartis at $132B, and Pfizer at $150B. Thus explains the much higher price-to-book for Gilead and the lack of a dividend, whereas Takeda is paying a very attractive 5.6% (GSK was closest with a 5.0% yield).

Softbank (Y2.9 trillion or $37.6 billion market cap) does not have a close comparison in the U.S. with Sprint's share price so beaten down. For NTT DoCoMo (Y5.9T market cap), Japan's largest wireless carrier, when combined with NTT (Y5.5T market cap), Japan's largest landline and internet provider, they have a market cap of $147B, which is then more competitive with the integrated AT&T at $170B; Verizon is at the opposite end, at $103B. AT&T trades at nearly a 50% P/E premium, and similarly for book value, but its dividend yield is more than double – and its operating market, while equally as competitive, is much more favorable in terms of population growth.

Deere and Komatsu matched up somewhat closely in terms of market cap, $31B vs. Y1.9T or $25B, and they also traded at fairly similar P/E ratios and dividend yields, but Deere's price-to-book value of over 4 is more than

---

[83] "A Lesson on Japanese Corporate Governance from Third Avenue," June 2011, http://www.valueinstitute.org/imgdir/docs/56363_A_Lesson_in_Corporate_Governance_from_Third_Avenue_(1).pdf.

double Komatsu's. Similar results can be seen between Aeon and Kroger. Kroger's market cap of $13B is $2B more than Aeon's (Y8.4T), and it has a bit higher dividend yield and is cheaper on a P/E basis, but its price-to-book ratio is approaching 3-times that of Aeon (2.5x vs. 0.9x). McDonald's Japan (Y2.8T or $3.6B market cap) vs. the U.S. McD ($95B) is not a fair comparison, although it is indicative of how small a market Japan is. McD Japan trades at twice the P/E of McD USA, but the latter trades at over three-times the book value of the former; McD USA's dividend yield is more than double McD Japan.

The banks and especially the consumer electronics comparisons are not very interesting. Bank valuations are widely depressed in both Japan and the U.S. The notable difference in this case is just how cheap BoA is trading on a book value basis and how much higher Mizuho's dividend is. Meanwhile, Japanese consumer electronics makers are struggling amid intense global competition (i.e. severe margin pressure) and record-high yen. Apple, not listed above, blows away the competition in terms of market cap and a modest P/E, although it controversially does not pay a dividend

## IPOs

Initial public offerings in Japan have declined sharply since 2006. Value investors need not pay much attention to IPOs except in cases post-listing where a profitable or asset-rich company trades lower and may be worthy of review.[84] What Japan has lacked in IPO volume is made up for in size as there was a $1 billion-plus listing in December 2011 by South Korean on-line gaming company Nexon, and in 2010 Dai-Ichi Life Insurance had a $10 billion-plus IPO, the largest in Japan since 1998. In 2012 Japan Airlines could also be poised for a $10 billion plus IPO. And possibly in the offing is the long anticipated listing of the Tokyo Stock Exchange.

---

[84] TOKYO IPO (dot-com) is a free online source of information for those interested in IPOs in Japan. The English language page contains just enough information on current IPOs and offerings over the past two years to whet the appetite; the Japanese language pages are much more robust in content and also contain other market-related information. See http://www.tokyoipo.com/top/iposche/index.php?j_e=E and click companies' hyperlinked names for additional information.

Something of interest to investors is that historically there has been a sharp drop in the number of IPOs in May, when new listings often total no more than half a dozen. Another slow time is early January (due to the New Year holiday and the exchanges being closed). The main reason for the slowdown in May is that the Golden Week holiday, which starts at the end of April and lasts through much of the first week of May, means not only are stock exchanges closed, but it also extends the time required between the approval of a listing and the start of trading. In addition, the financial statements of Japanese companies require the approval of shareholders at an annual meeting held within three months of the fiscal year end. Since these official financial statements must be used for exchange listing applications, a March fiscal year company (which most Japanese companies are) cannot begin the application process until after its June shareholders meeting. Consequently, companies generally avoid scheduling an IPO in May in particular, and this is why there are a large number of IPOs starting in September each year.[85]

An interesting data point in the Tokyo Stock Exchange's inaugural edition of its *TSE Magazine* (December 2011), is that there are around 3,500 listed companies in Japan and amongst those, about 1,500, or 40%, were listed in the past decade.[86]

## Refocus on micro, less macro

A June 2010 report by Bain & Co. (Japan), entitled, "Reenergizing Japan, Inc.'s growth, company by company," makes a case for the need and great efficacy for structural change in Japan.[87] Companies ought to be more aggressive in targeting higher growth opportunities (i.e. in neighboring high-growth Asian economies), accordingly target higher market share in such segments, and in turn prune their operating divisions and subsidiaries as needed, says Bain. No sacred cows. Doing so, Bain estimates, would result in increasing annual sales growth to 5% (from 2%), EBIT margins to 7% (from

---

[85] "May IPO Market Summary and Outlook for June," Tokyo IPO, Jun. 18, 2007. http://www.tokyoipo.com/ipoms/070618ipoms-1
[86] See: http://www.tse.or.jp/english/about/magazine/index.html.
[87] See: http://www.bain.com/publications/articles/reenergizing-japan-incs-growth-company-by-company.aspx.

4.5%), capital efficiencies by 10%, thus allowing for a possible tripling of Japan's market capitalization – equal to its 1989 bubble peak level but without the bubble.

The Bain report is no doubt self-serving in some respects since a consultancy only stands to gain from claiming change will result in gains. Nevertheless, there is evident truth in the report. Among the most compelling arguments is Japan's failure to sell more products and services to neighboring Asian economies, most of which have higher economic growth rates and feature opportunities to sell across a broader spectrum, not just the high-end or luxury segment Japan has typically focused on too heavily. Said focus has resulted in a multi-year if not decade-plus of market share deterioration. That margins have also come down goes without saying with heightened competition coming from the likes of South Korea, Taiwan, and increasingly mainland China. And as much as Japan has prided itself on operational excellence (i.e. cost-cutting) and financial optimization (i.e. debt reduction and/or no-debt encumbrance), Bain says these two methods happen to both be the least disruptive (i.e. not requiring massive job cuts) and unfortunately not effective enough in overtaking global leaders.

Bain calls for Japanese companies to utilize their often overlooked undervalued or underutilized "hidden assets" (such as untapped customer insights, undervalued business platforms, and underexploited capabilities). Examples of success stories in the U.S. include Harman International, IBM, and Apple. An example closer to Japan is South Korea's LG, which Bain says should compel Japanese companies to even revisit dated assets that may be under-appreciated in Japan, but have great value overseas. A success story from within Japan: Suzuki in India. Its profit margin in India was almost 13% in fiscal 2007, three-times the parent company's margins. Finally, part of the massive shake-up needed within Japanese companies entails externally hired CEOs, a rarity in Japan, and also via company executives with atypical career paths, also not so common in the traditional executive suite structure, but both offer possibilities for fresh ideas and serve as agents for change.

# CHAPTER 6

# BULLISH TAKE ON JAPAN

Jim Rogers: "A market I am looking at is Japan; I own the yen. I bought Japanese shares when the tsunami came, I think I am probably going to buy some more. I own the U.S. dollar. It has been terribly beaten down. Everybody is bearish on the U.S dollar including me. It's fundamentally a terribly flawed currency. **But when everybody is bearish on something it is usually a time to own it.**"[88]

## Bearish sentiment abound

Early in the book I covered what amounts to Japan bears' playbook. For the simple reason that very few people are bullish, the contrarian instinct of value investors should take over and allow at least a review of the many attractive investments available. Most readers ought to be familiar with the name Jim Rogers. The commodities guru and inveterate contrarian can often be heard saying things like, "When everybody is bearish on something it is usually a time to own it." I am certainly not advocating investors

---

[88] Excerpt of July 2011 interview of Jim Rogers by Fox Business, http://dealbreaker.com/2011/07/answer-the-deficit-talks-the-dollar-tim-geithner/. Emphasis added.

indiscriminately buy individual Japanese stocks or a basket of stocks such as the iShares MSCI Japan ETF (EWJ). Rather, without belaboring the point, I'm saying in light of how much Japan is either despised and/or dismissed by market participants, it warrants a look, and readers already know well there is great value in the "ugly duckling" of the investing world.

Don't confuse bearishness on the Japanese currency or the government with the quality and the attractiveness of companies. The ongoing bet for years by Western money managers and traders against Japanese government bonds (JGBs) is known as the "widow-maker trade." The latest big names to try and profit from a collapse are hedge fund managers Kyle Bass of Hayman Advisors, based in Dallas, Texas, and David Einhorn of Greenlight Capital, based in New York City.

Forbes.com reported in February 2010 that Mr. Bass took his bearishness so far as to finance his home with a five-year loan denominated in yen, betting that a depreciated yen will be cheaper to pay back.[89] Unfortunately for Mr. Bass, and despite the specter of collapse post-triple-disaster (March 11, 2011), as of late-August 2011, at a conversion rate of ¥77/$1 compared to one of between ¥90 and ¥95 in early 2010, he would have to pay at least 14% more at this point. Maybe he will be proven right over the next couple years. In any case, he made a fortune off his shorting of sub-prime mortgages ($700 million return from a $110 million investment) and the yen mortgage is probably not meaningful to his overall wealth. On the topic of sub-prime and how it compares to what he sees in Japan, Mr. Bass commented, "Japan is the most asymmetric opportunity I have ever seen. Way better than sub-prime." He purchased options for $6 million that expose him to $12 billion worth of 10-year JGBs, in which case if the interest rate rises from the low-1% level to 4%, he stands to earn $125 million.

---

[89] "The Global Debt Bomb," Forbes (dot-com), Jan. 21, 2010, http://www.forbes.com/forbes/2010/0208/debt-recession-worldwide-finances-global-debt-bomb.html. For more information on the "widow-maker" trade, see "Japan's Struggles to Leave Debt's Door," *Barron's*, July, 30, 2011. http://online.barrons.com/article/SB50001424052702304719804576468254158312620.html#articleTabs_panel_article%3D1

The five-year $/JP¥ chart below shows the sharp drop in the value of the dollar against the yen. At the same time Mr. Bass was making headlines about his JGB short – February 2010 – BusinessInsider.com published a story, which included a chart from an exhibit of a Morgan Stanley report that polled investors on their favorite currency short. The yen garnered nearly 50% of the votes, followed by the euro at around 25%, the pound at about 15%, the Australian dollar at 5%, and so on.[90] The moral of this story is simple: avoid following the crowd; be cautious if you do. Time will tell if Bass, Einhorn, and any others are proven right, and if they are, they will be lauded as heroes. And if not, well, no sweat in Bass' case since he's really just leveraged $6 million, which like his yen mortgage is immaterial to his fund's assets. Meanwhile, who knows if these guys are sleeping well at night; I'll leave the big macro bets to them. Some of the material discussed in Chapter 4 should have Bass and company worried.

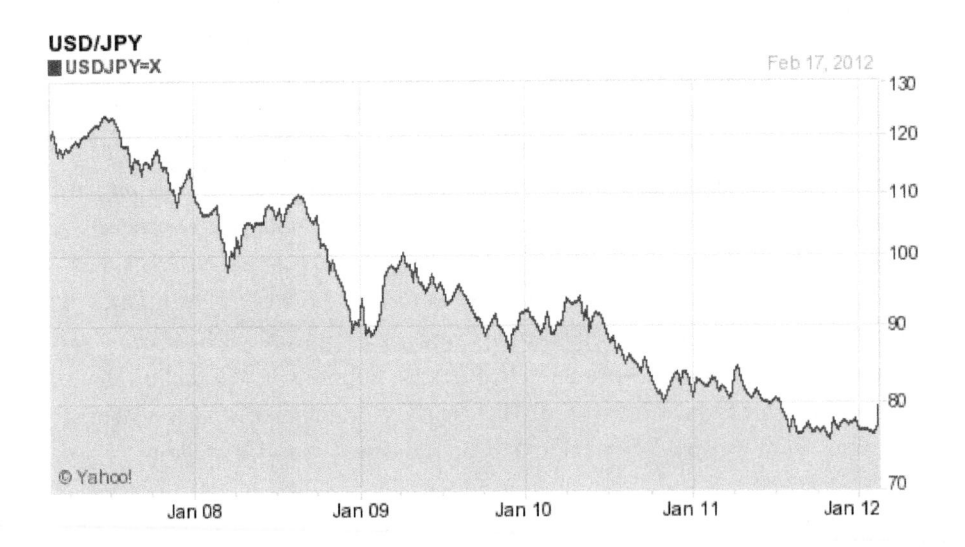

---

[90] "Kyle Bass is so Bearish on Japan, He Financed His Home in Yen," Business Insider, Jan. 21, 2010. http://www.businessinsider.com/kyle-bass-is-so-bearish-on-japan-he-financed-his-home-in-yen-2010-1

Another representative example of widespread bearishness on Japan is the following October 2011 admission by Bloomberg columnist William Pesek, who has covered Japan for the past ten years and tends to be far more candid than sensationalist:

> "When I travel and speak overseas, there is a troubling lack of interest in Japan. Audiences are at full attention when talk turns to China, India or Thailand. Mention Japan, and out come the BlackBerrys."[91]

There is seemingly no end to the widespread disinterest in Japan and Japanese stocks.

Overall, the lack of presence of value-oriented investors in Japan represents an opportunity in one respect since there are so many companies that appear to be undervalued based on traditional metrics. The difficulty is how that value will be realized. And the challenge for value investors is that we all tend to find our own favorites and it is not often that more than a couple large value shops (big enough to require a public disclosing of their stake) are in the same stock at the same time. However, it is certainly the case that once there is a large enough presence of value investors (and eventually and more broadly, growth and momentum-type investors), valuation gaps will narrow and someday close. For the sake of those who have money invested in Japan or who might after reading this book, we hope that *value* investors become more prevalent, but since stocks are so cheap already, a broad bull rally may occur anytime due to relative undervaluation attracting capital regardless of deep absolute undervaluation merit.

So, firstly, why does the Japanese market, despite its tantalizingly vast selection of undervalued companies lack more Japanese value investors?

Many investors who were burned in the now 20-plus year old Nikkei crash in 1989 have remained wary as have those too young then to have participated but that have witnessed the effects of the crash either first-hand, say in their family, or by way of the media. Know that Japanese are not promoters or cheerleaders, for a lack of a better word, of wealth like we are in the U.S. (e.g. *Forbes'* lists; Japan's way of publicizing wealth is the news' coverage of the nation's conspicuous list of highest tax payers, which is

---

[91] "More Money Than Brains Leads to Olympus Shock," Bloomberg, Oct. 20, 2011. http://www.bloomberg.com/news/2011-10-20/more-money-than-brains-leads-to-olympus-shock-commentary-by-william-pesek.html

another way of singling out the nation's highest earners), and there is not much of an equity culture, either. Meaning it is nowhere near as ingrained as it is in the U.S. that the stock market is a key pillar to generating wealth. Then it may not be a surprise that the Japanese by way of their investment preferences demonstrate a bias against their own stocks when they do invest, perhaps for the preceding reasons, and thus are often more eager to invest their capital in what is perceived to be higher-growth and or higher-yielding overseas securities. Institutional investors have obliged by providing and actively marketing such funds (as discussed earlier in the book). Just as there is an abundance of perceived sexier overseas funds, the media (print, TV, and web) tend to heavily favor a trading mentality, by referencing technical trading levels, candlestick charts, and promoting near-term price target-based trades instead of longer-term holding periods. Finally, there is no Warren Buffett-like figure in Japan (although Buffett is fairly well known amongst investors and the Japanese seemed to enjoy his first-ever visit in November 2011), thus there is nobody that commands attention and respect pounding the table about the attractive valuations and spelling it out in simple, commonsensical terms.

*****

Beside a subsidiary's ownership of a Japanese company (Iscar – Tungaloy), Warren Buffett's Berkshire Hathaway is not known for having ever invested in Japan (although a 2006 article in the *Nikkei Financial* newspaper reportedly said he had bought and already sold three Japanese stocks in which he had taken small positions). The oldest comments of his that I could find concerning Japanese stocks are from an October 1998 speech he gave (specifically, the Q&A portion, when he was asked his thoughts about Japan) at the University of Florida School of Business, in which he said despite a cost of capital of only 1% (on debt that would not mature for ten years) he found "… very few wonderful businesses in Japan."[92] He cited companies' low returns on equity and said that lousy businesses yield lousy results even if you buy them cheap. However, he did note friend and fellow successful value investor, Walter Schloss (since deceased, whom was mentioned several times in the first chapter of this

---

[92] Warren Buffett lecture at the University of Florida School of Business, Oct. 15, 1998, transcript via http://www.intelligentinvestorclub.com/downloads/Warren-Buffett-Florida-Speech.pdf.

book), who was a so-called "cigar butt" investor, taking advantage of quantitatively (valuation) cheap stocks that have "one puff left." Buffett says this is inelegant. Perhaps it is, but it is another approach to value investing, that can work quite well.

Buffett noted the then low returns on equity and the similar situation in the 1980s despite the booming economy and market. "Incredible market without incredible companies," said Buffett, adding that "they were incredible in terms of doing a lot of business," but not in ROE. Unable to disregard the significance of a 1% cost of capital, he finished his answer to a student's question by saying that he would keep looking for opportunities. He mentioned that "so far (we have) done nothing" in Japan. Fast forward to May 2006, and in a *Nikkei Financial* (newspaper) article, it was reported that should Buffett be a buyer of Japanese stocks, two possibilities would be Kao (4452), the "P&G of Japan," though it faces tough domestic and overseas competition from P&G, and Sony Financial Holdings (8729). At present, 2011/2012, I would argue that there are plenty of incredible opportunities in Japan and whether a company qualifies as "incredible" per Buffett's standards or not depends on how long one is willing to remain a shareowner. Shuhei Abe, head of asset manager SPARX Group (8739) and one of the largest hedge funds in Asia, has previously commented that Japan is a better place to use a Buffett-style investment approach given how much more inefficient the market is.[93]

- ♦ Kao, Japan's leader in toiletries and second-largest cosmetics company, in 2006 had an ROE of over 16%, however, in the past three years (fiscal year-ended in March) its ROE has been nowhere near as impressive: 2010: 8.5%, 2009: 7.3%, and 2008: 11.5%. Sales barely grew in 2010 and declined somewhat in 2009. Earnings increased in 2010, but are down over 27% from 2008. Kao is paying down the billions (of dollars) of debt it took on to acquire cosmetics

---

[93] "Buffett Ideas Lift Japan Fund of ex-Soros Adviser Abe," Jun. 14, 2006. http://www.bloomberg.com/apps/news?pid=newsarchive&sid=aBlCYokbw4qk&refer=japan. Abe worked with George Soros in the 1980s, first riding the boom in Japanese equities and then trying to short the bubble, but they were apparently two years early on their big short. Abe is said to be very fond of Buffett; the article mentions his "Buffett Club" of two-hour mandatory morning meetings each Friday with his analysts.

maker Kanebo (in 2006), but unless earnings improve drastically, it will be a while before earnings are a multiple of long-term debt like they were pre-acquisition. A sluggish domestic market has compelled Kao/Kanebo to more urgently (in scope and scale) grow overseas sales. As of December 20, 2011, Kao shares at Y2,029/share, were trading at 23.1x trailing earnings and 1.93x book, with a 2.86% dividend yield. Not particularly cheap; maybe revisit if shares get cheaper and its earnings improve as it continues to pay down debt (granted it could seemingly take on more debt to finance an overseas acquisition).

- Sony Financial was partially spun off by Sony (6758), which retained majority control. It is primarily a life insurance company with other lines of insurance and financial offerings including online banking and foreign exchange trading. Sony Financial's ROE in the fiscal year-ended March 2011 was 14.8%, compared to 20.3% in 2010, and 13.2% in 2009; FYE'11 revenues increased 14% compared to FYE'09. These returns are more interesting than Kao's, especially since Sony Financial is trading around half its 2007 IPO spinoff price, and has lost around one-third of its value (as of December 20, 2011) over the past six months. Accordingly, Sony Financial's outlook and financial statement's deserve further review.

In Buffett's 1998 speech Q&A he said if he were investing in Japan (and he was intrigued by the 1% hurdle) he wouldn't want to get involved in any currency risk, so it would be a yen-denominated investment, such as Japanese real estate or stocks. It is this "1%" that got many an investor in trouble in 2008, when the financial crisis hit full steam in September, and yen carry trades began to unwind – closing these trades proved increasingly expensive as the yen strengthened. With the yen even stronger now in 2011, going into 2012, and acknowledging it could get stronger still, it nevertheless seems there is fairly broad agreement of a higher likelihood for yen weakness as opposed to strength, longer-term. So the matter of hedging is always present when investing outside of one's own currency. Buying ordinary Japanese shares in yen will eventually require one to convert yen back into dollars. Buying Japanese ADRs in dollars will subject one's holdings (values) to fluctuations in the yen-dollar exchange rate. There is no one best (or one-size-fits-all) solution for currency exposure. My feeling is that hedging comes at both a monetary and opportunity cost; and the potential gains of astute value investors will be very outsized, much higher than the broader market's, thus it's not the end of the world by any means if some points are lost on forex. Keep in mind that forex has an impact especially on Japanese companies that derive a high percentage of sales overseas, that have overseas operations, and amongst domestic companies that serve as suppliers of exporters.

*****

The $130 billion Japan Pension Fund Association (PFA) is an interesting case study. Per a March 2011 interview with *The Wall Street Journal*, it allocates 25% of its assets to overseas equities, 15% to domestic equities, and the remaining approximate 60% to domestic and foreign bonds.[94] While income is crucial to a pension fund, its obligatory patronage of Japanese government bonds is excusable, but its allocation to domestic equities versus overseas equities is most disturbing. Following the 2008 financial crisis and subsequently as Japanese stocks have lagged the global rally through year-end 2011, the PFA's allocation was ostensibly wise. However, it is missing tremendous opportunities to accumulate shares of domestic stocks trading at substantial discounts and attractive dividend yields.

The PFA was a pioneer in activist investing in Japan amongst pension funds and it stands to reap significant psychological and real benefits from a Japanese market that trades even at book value let alone one that might trade at a modest premium. A somewhat unfortunate development is that it no longer requires companies have an ROE of 8% or better in the past three years to receive support for director election votes – it is now using a less definitive hurdle of "significantly poor" ROE – though it says its focus on performance has not changed. I mostly agree with CIO Daisuke Hamaguchi's claim that the 8% floor was a "superficial target" based on Anglo management style. Yes, Japan is different, as he says, but the bottom-line is

---

[94] The WSJ article is dated March 11, 2011, highly unfortunate timing given the triple-disaster, for such a revealing article about one of the most important investors in Japan. "Japan Pension Fund Seeks Risk."
http://online.wsj.com/article/SB10001424052748704629104576191612132844484.html

that ROE is comparatively low not all due to lower earnings but more so because of large amounts of equity. There's no need to meddle in ordinary business decision-making but there is reason to be concerned about capital structure and distribution.[95]

Fact: there is tremendous value in Japan right under the noses of institutional investors. In the WSJ interview Hamaguchi declared that more risk taking is needed due to Japan being a low return environment. So he is turning to private equity and hedge funds as a possible solution to capture more alpha instead of trying to match market returns (i.e. beta). Private equity done right can generate tremendous upside for both investors (general and limited partners; and to a lesser extent the public equity holders prior to being taken private) and the acquired company, though there are dubious measures taken that can damage a firm and negatively impact society, such as taking on substantial debt, sometimes in order to pay a special dividend to the partners, and also the job losses and factory closings as extreme cost-cutting measures may be undertaken. Without getting sidetracked here, simply think for a moment: if individual and institutional investors favor overseas securities, and domestic-focused hedge funds are very few in number, outside of overseas investors being sellers, by default downside risk due to domestic selling is seemingly limited while upside is of an unlimited nature since there are many trillions of dollars (of net cash) available to invest.

## Valuation

It may come as a surprise that the Nikkei 225 Stock Average's year-end 2011 close of 8,455 is its lowest since 1982 – nearly a 30-year low! Its lowest close otherwise was around 6,995 in late October 2008; in early March 2009, it closed as low as around 7,020, after having rallied back to the 9,000 level at the start of the new year. The N225's low following the March 11th triple-disaster came in the week after at about 8,230. It had been trading at around

---

[95] See "Pension Fund Association Guidelines for the Exercise of Shareholder Voting Rights," http://www.pfa.or.jp/jigyo/shisan/gava_giketsuken/files/gov_e20101228.pdf.

10,500 prior to; post-disaster it recouped the 10,000-level in July, but it was mostly downhill into the end of the year.

## 5-year chart of the Nikkei 225 Stock Average to Dec. 30, 2011

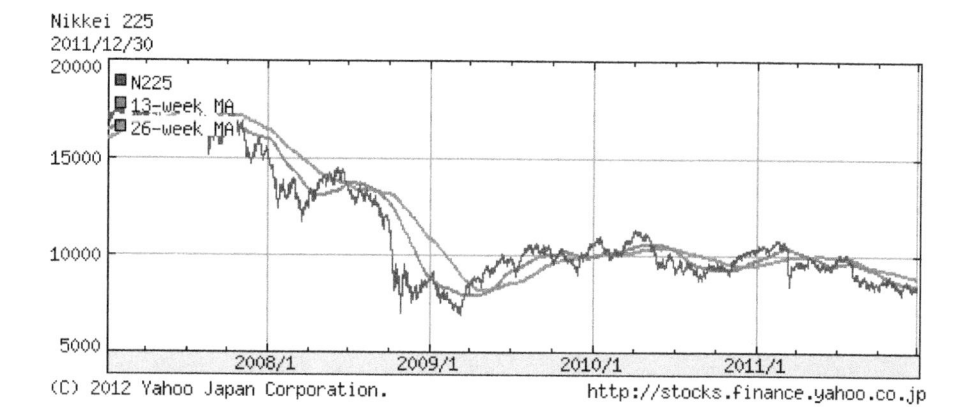

To get a sense of how undervalued Japan is to other markets, let's first look at market-wide price-to-book ratios as of year-end 2011:[96]

| Country | Median price-to-book |
| --- | --- |
| China | 2.13 |
| France | 0.97 |
| Germany | 1.27 |
| India | 0.56 |
| **Japan** | **0.67** |
| UK | 1.25 |
| U.S. | 1.46 |

---

[96] The data used in this section is from New York University professor Aswath Damodaran's website, which has a very robust collection of market data. Each January for the past decade he has uploaded spreadsheets of individual company data by country. Beside this data, he also provides a variety of data sets based on financial metrics and more. See:
http://pages.stern.nyu.edu/~adamodar/New_Home_Page/data.html.

India looks cheap, but when setting a minimum of a $25 million market cap, the median P/B value almost doubles to 1.07. At a minimum of $100 million, it increases to 1.5. In Japan, the median P/B of companies with less than a $100 million market cap is 0.58. From $100 million to $1 billion it increases to 0.73, well below book value. And for companies at $1 billion-plus, P/B rises to 0.90, still a discount to book value. In the U.S., companies under a $100 million market cap have a median P/B of 0.73, which more than doubles to 1.56 for companies with capitalizations between $100 million and $1 billion. Beyond $1 billion the median P/B increases slightly to 1.61. There are a large number of companies in both Japan and the U.S. that have both negligible market caps and P/B values. Otherwise, small capitalizations can comprise a large portion of listed companies in a market such as India's. China has far fewer such listings, but companies have median P/B values in excess of 2.0 throughout all capitalizations.

On a price-to-sales basis, Japanese companies with market caps of up to $100 million traded at a median value of 0.25-times sales; at $100 million to $1 billion, they traded at 0.43-times sales; and at $1 billion-plus they traded at a still amazingly cheap level of 0.59-times. By comparison, in the U.S., companies with market caps of up to $100 million traded at 0.49-times sales; at $100 million to $1 billion, they traded at 1.17-times sales, and above $1 billion they traded at 1.8-times sales. Thus, in both countries there is naturally more of a premium the higher the capitalization. However, while companies in the U.S. do in fact trade at a premium, Japanese companies in the aggregate trade at a heavy discount. Companies in the UK also trade a premium, higher at the $100M-$1B level, but much cheaper (closer to book value) at the $1B-plus level. Note that companies in France and Germany trade at around 0.8-times sales at both capitalization ranges; Chinese companies, by the way, trade at between 2.0 and 3.0-times sales.

As of December 30, 2011, various benchmarks of the Japanese stock market had the following valuations:[97]

---

[97] Valuations per *Nikkei Shimbun* (dot-com): http://www.nikkei.com/markets/kabu/japanidx.aspx.

**Book value:**

Nikkei 225 Stock Average:   0.93
Nikkei 300:   0.95
Nikkei 500:   0.94
TOPIX - 1st Section   0.92
TOPIX - 2nd Section   0.63
JASDAQ   1.12

**Price-to-earnings (Forward P/E):**[98]

Nikkei 225   14.7 (14.8)
Nikkei 300   15.4 (14.9)
Nikkei 500   15.6 (15.2)
TOPIX - 1   15.5 (15.0)
TOPIX - 2   15.8 (12.0)
JASDAQ   17.3 (14.2)

**Market Capitalization:**

TOPIX -1   Y255.2 trillion ($3.33T)
TOPIX -2   Y32.4 trillion ($422B)
JASDAQ   Y84.7 trillion ($1.1T)
*Japanese GDP (real, nominal)*[99]   *$4.3T, $5.5T*

---

[98] P/Es drop meaningfully, of course, when backing out excess cash.
[99] GDP data accessed via Wikipedia:
http://en.wikipedia.org/wiki/List_of_countries_by_GDP_%28PPP%29 and
http://en.wikipedia.org/wiki/List_of_countries_by_GDP_%28nominal%29

As of year-end 2011, oil services/equipment companies and trading companies are among the most attractive in terms of offering ROEs in excess of 10% and having P/B values of less than 1.0 (14.3%/0.65 and 14.27%/0.73, respectively). The highest ROEs by far are unsurprisingly found in internet software and services companies, 27%, with a P/B of just over 3.0. Beside high-ROEs, another approach is to identify industries with a high number of companies with ROEs of less than 10 and P/B values below 1.0. There are seven of them including: Engineering, Trading companies, Auto Parts, Electronics, Computer Services, Food Processing, and Business Services. There are almost enough regional banks for an eighth candidate (0.5 P/B, 5.5% ROE). The idea behind these is the potential for consolidation. Mergers and acquisitions will remain an area of interest since there are so many viable takeover candidates that should a consolidation boom occur it will almost certainly play out over a fairly long period of time.

*****

"Has Nintendo Bottomed?" I published the following on January 5, 2012:

It is not uncommon for a value investor to buy shares in a company only to see them become cheaper in the early stages of a holding period. I said this was likely going to be the case back in June when I initially wrote about being bullish on Nintendo (NTDOY.PK) following its ugly stock price decline over the past couple years as it hits a cyclical low. After a nice little advance into early July, Nintendo's stock has since been mostly downhill again, which has provided investors opportunities to buy cheaper a world-class company now trading only 20% above book value. Nintendo carries no long-term debt; its cash and short-term investments equal to over 57% of its market cap. And recent news of holiday sales suggests 3DS worries were overdone.

Nintendo closed at Y10,990 (+3.7%) ($17.84 ADR equivalent at Y77/$1) Wednesday in Japan in the market's first day of trading in 2012, following a solid first day of trading for its ADRs on heavier than normal volume. Wednesday trading in the U.S., however, saw a more than halving of volume, although its ADRs closed up 2.1% to $17.88. Most value investors should care less about volume and day-to-day pricing. I'm mentioning this for the sake that after such a horrendous year (or string of years) there may be prior Nintendo investors coming back to the stock. In my June article I commented on the likelihood of belated, albeit obligatory, analyst downgrades. There indeed were some then and there have been a couple more as recent as last month.

<u>December ratings:</u>

- Daiwa cut Nintendo a notch to a '3' rating meaning it expects a +/- 5% return vs. the TOPIX over the next six months and it lowered its price target to Y11,000 from Y15,000.

- Merrill maintained a 'neutral' rating and lowered its price target to Y12,000 from Y14,000.

More important than any new downgrades, I am aware of there being just one upgrade in the past year-plus (Macquarie in early November to "outperform" from "neutral," PT to Y14,200 from Y11,400), thus, on one hand, yes it may still be a bit early to buy, but on the other, it is ever more reason to be bullish. Note that Mizuho and SMBC both maintained their existing "buy" (or equivalent) ratings on Nintendo in late October and both have price targets of Y18,000, among the highest (60%+ recent price levels).

The biggest problem with Nintendo is the (relatively) strong yen against the weak dollar and a euro that just broke the Y100 level. Foreign exchange weighs far heavier than any concerns ahead of the Wii U launch, previously over slow post-launch 3DS sales and the price cut to the 3DS, or a lack of games. The average Y/US$ exchange rate in Nintendo's fiscal year ended March 2011 was 85.72; it was as high as 92 in Q1. Compare that to a recent 77, which matches its full year forecast (which was 80 prior to revision when it announced FQ2 results), meaning should sales (the holidays in particular) be better than expected, Nintendo may beat expectations in the U.S. Reports thus far have been overwhelmingly positive.

The yen/euro's average in Nintendo's last fiscal year was 113.12 and was as high as 117 in Q1; compare that to the recent breaking of the 100-level. This may prove problematic since Nintendo's forecast is for a rate of 106 for its full fiscal year (adjusted from 115 previously). Interestingly, given all the reported troubles in Europe, Nintendo's sales in the EU in the first two quarters this fiscal were not far behind their prior fiscal year level. However, in the U.S. sales were running at half the prior fiscal. Nevertheless, Black Friday and winter holiday sales reports suggest respectable sales were achieved in the U.S. (and Japan for that matter). Recent headlines mention the 3DS hitting the 4 million unit sales mark in both the US. and Japan in 2011; Wii unit sales in 2011 in the U.S. totaling more than 4.5 million; a couple of million unit game software sales for the 3DS; and conveniently, a struggling Sony Vita (SNE) (JP: 6758) post-launch week. Nintendo's Wii and DS family installed base now exceeds 90 million.

For the record, along with its fiscal Q2 earnings reported in October, Nintendo downward revised its full year earnings outlook to -Y20 billion from Y20 billion previously (Y156.40/share) and compared to Y76 billion (Y607/share) in its prior fiscal year. With the dollar right at where Nintendo expected and the euro (only?) 6% stronger than forecast, could we be in for a surprise when it announces fiscal third quarter earnings on January 26 (scheduled release date)? Should we even bother with surprises at this stage, ahead of a critical console launch next year? I suppose some positive press and momentum wouldn't hurt! The big picture, however, is Q4 earnings next spring in which we will get our first look at Nintendo's outlook factoring in expected sales of the Wii U.

Finally, know that shareholders of record as of March 31 will receive Nintendo's annual dividend, which was unfortunately previously cut to Y100; it was Y310 in the prior fiscal year. I don't think we will see an upward revised dividend this fiscal almost no matter how strong sales and any recovery in profits there may be. Nintendo is typically on the conservative side and though it has made appropriate upward revisions the past, I think the economic uncertainty at home and in the U.S. and EU will make Nintendo play it safe forecast-wise. Regarding Nintendo's dividend I will say that it obviously was not fun having it cut to zero for its current fiscal year interim payout and for its fiscal year-end payout to be cut to Y100. Yes, it makes sense in terms of its consecutive years of $1 billion-plus forex impairments, but there is a disconnect with its massive cash hoard. As I said in my June article, I am not exactly ready to begin any activism until things are more settled (i.e. forex, domestic/global economy, domestic/geo-politics, natural disasters ...). Meantime, I intend to increase my position in Nintendo.

*****

# Trillions upon trillions of assets

As of September 30, 2011, the Bank of Japan estimated Japanese citizens had Y1,471 trillion of assets or approximately $19 trillion.[100] That equates to roughly $150,000 per person. The relative strength of the yen obviously makes the dollar amount higher than it would if the yen and dollar were at parity, in which their assets would total around $15 trillion, still a substantial sum. Nevertheless, Merrill Lynch – Capgemini report in their annual wealth survey that Japan had over 1.7 million millionaires in 2010, second-most behind the U.S. at 3.1 million, and ahead of Germany at 924 thousand, China at 535 thousand, and the UK at 454 thousand.[101] Less than 4% of Japanese individuals' assets, or Y56.1 trillion ($730 billion) are directly invested in equities (3.8%), while just over 3% are invested in the equivalent of mutual funds, but that may not amount to as high a figure in terms of actually being invested in domestic equities given the abundance of funds investing in overseas equities and domestic/international debt securities. Consider that the TOPIX 1st Section had an aggregate market capitalization of Y246.3 trillion, $3.15 trillion as of November 28, 2011; JASDAQ-listed companies were worth $1 trillion. Individual investors' direct equity investments accounted for roughly 18% of the market's total capitalization. And note that 52% of individuals' assets (Y765.7 trillion or $9.95 trillion) are held in cash-type deposits. If a mere 1% of cash assets (Y7.7 trillion or $100 billion) were diverted to stocks, it would equate to 2.4% of the TOPIX 1st Section and JASDAQ's combined total capitalization. Should 10% be reallocated to stocks it would be almost a quarter of total capitalization!

Following equities, individuals' largest assets are insurance reserves, nearly Y220 trillion or $2.9 trillion (15%) and pension reserves of about Y202 trillion or $2.6 trillion (almost 14%). Direct investments in JGBs amounted to Y29.5 trillion or $383 billion, or 2% of assets. In terms of liabilities, consumer credit was less than 2% of assets, about Y25 trillion or $324 billion. Housing (i.e. mortgages) totaled Y158 trillion or $2 trillion, or about 10.5% of assets. No wonder there has long been a desire by overseas asset managers to enter and expand in the Japanese market. Making an entry may be easier than ever, but successful expansion appears to be proving challenging due to a variety of reasons such as high risk aversion (meaning little in the way of alternative asset investing) and the prolonged bear market in equities combined with a trader's mentality amongst investors (and of course brokers) instead of one of buy-and-hold.

---

[100] Bank of Japan statistics, http://www.BOJ.or.jp/en/statistics/sj/index.htm/.
[101] http://en.wikipedia.org/wiki/Millionaire#Number_of_millionaires_by_country

*****

The following should help investors better understand why Japan's stock market struggled in the first of the two lost decades. Know that in the first half of the 1990s banks had no choice but to be net sellers of equities since they had to raise liquidity to shore up their impaired balance sheets ravaged by nonperforming loans. At the same time, life insurance companies would have liked to have been selling into the painful bear market, but they held so much stock that selling would have not only hurt their balance sheets but also would have pushed prices even lower. Thus, insurers had little ability or reason to buy stocks. Retail investors were licking their own wounds, and badly scarred by the end of the bubble in real estate and stock prices. Therefore, Japanese investors at large did not emerge as net buyers of stocks even as they became cheaper and cheaper (note that companies were not permitted by law to buyback their own shares until 2004 and it was not meaningful tax-wise for shareholders until 2005).

Capping any rallies was selling by domestic investors, insurers in particular. Otherwise a lot of domestic money sat on the sidelines, much as it does today. Partially absorbing the years of selling were overseas investors. American and European investment funds accumulated shares based on fundamentals and some funds would eventually reap substantial returns. The presence of overseas investors continued to grow and today they equate for a quarter to a third of the market as measured by the value of their holdings (compared to around 5% in 1990), and they account for as much as two-thirds of daily trading. In conclusion, it essentially took until around the market's bottom in 2003 for circumstances to have normalized for all stripes of domestic investors. Most of the selling of legacy holdings were complete, institutional balance sheets were improving, and valuations were increasingly compelling as global growth prospects would help lessen P/E ratios.

*****

# Earnings and Dividend Yield

Earnings yield is simply the P/E ratio inverted and reflected as a percentage. Thus, a $10 stock that has earned $1/share over the past year has a P/E of 10 and has an earnings yield of 10%. From time to time investors will see analysts, strategists, and other investors pointing out the irrationality of selling equities yielding (on an earnings basis) 5% or 10%, to hold money in cash accounts yielding next to nothing (in Japan for individuals) or no better than 1% or 2% in the case of holding Japanese government bonds. Leaving individuals even worse off over the long term is that should they have selected quality, undervalued stocks there may have been dividend hikes (and possibly even *yutaiken*), which makes selling them for the alternative of cash all the more dubious.

A closely watched metric is the dividend yield of equities versus the yield of the 10-year Japanese Government Bond. The problem is that these days, post-2008, equity dividend yields are easily outpacing the yields on 10-year government bonds in Japan. *These days* are hardly normal ones; some claim they are the *new normal* in some respects, while others see zero interest rates, high unemployment, and the plethora of other problems in the public and private sector, as being a harbinger of even worse times ahead. Longtime Japan watcher, Jonathan Allum (now with Mizuho, based in London), is often cited in *Barron's* regarding his views on Japanese stocks, and it is not uncommon to see him referencing the impending cross of dividend yields exceeding JGBs or the existence of such a state, with either case being a signal to buy Japanese stocks. Unfortunately his longtime signal has lost its affect for now, though given broad undervaluation, it may plainly be a screaming buy indicator.

On the surface, the dividend argument is a sound one and should have natural merit. However, domestic investors have basically continued to favor overseas equities, bonds, REITs, and currency deposits. How odd for there to be such an overseas bias despite attractive domestic dividend yields as it's no secret that all walks of Japanese investors are starved for yield. The negligible yields in savings and other fixed-term deposit accounts, thanks to the Bank of Japan's ongoing battle with a deflationary economy, have created such a craving for yield. Nevertheless, we know how the grass can look greener on the other side and that is there is always a place, or securities, with higher yields. Look beyond the surface and Japanese investors have largely missed to-date an opportunity to pick up cheap shares yielding more than JGBs and much more than cash deposits. Investors (especially value investors) ought to be thankful for this situation since we now have a great opportunity to witness in the least a narrowing of the discounted valuations.

Mr. Allum himself in a June 2011 story in *Barron's* ("A Zen-like Gain in Store for Japanese Stocks") says Japanese stocks are worth the effort if one knows when to get in and out, and knows where to place bets.[102] Not easy, but possible, says Allum. He calls Japan a typical mean-reverting market, which favors value investors and disadvantages momentum investors. Readers of this book will recognize these circumstances. There is great value in cyclical stocks, just as much as the average undervalued stock in Japan, but one has to run carefully with the herd in such cases. The same *Barron's* piece notes that Japan essentially tracks other developed markets. The best play: "market weight," says *Barron's*.

Using Allum's favorite yardstick (dividend vs. JGB yield), which is *not* mentioned in that particular *Barron's* article, attractive dividend yields (and of course overall valuations) and the economy's cyclical bottom(ing) make Japan very compelling to value investors. As of mid-October 2011, the Nikkei 225 has a current (and expected forward) yield of about 2.1%. By comparison, the 10-year JGB is hovering around 1.0%. This is one of the widest spreads in recent history (in Japan), possibly the widest in the past half-century. It really makes one wonder again and again how investors can (but are) – especially the Japanese – ignoring this. The smaller the capitalization, the greater the dividend/JGB yield disparity. Both the JASDAQ and the TOPIX 2nd section have current yields of about 2.45%, and forward ones of 2.40%.

---

[102] See: http://online.barrons.com/article/SB50001424053111904210704576357672577406948.html.

# Explaining Japanese Companies' Low ROE

Typical articles covering Japanese stocks mention the fact that returns on equity (ROE) are significantly lower in Japan than in the U.S. or EU. It is true, very much so, that ROEs are lower in Japan: ROEs in excess of 10% are somewhat rare and such companies often trade at a premium to companies with subpar ROEs. Quite simply buying these higher-ROE stocks at/near cyclical or market lows and selling once P/Es hit cyclical highs (or far exceed the market's P/E) would be very similar to the buying growth at a reasonable price (GARP) strategy. While GARP and the PEG ratio may have merit, the broader market in Japan is so undervalued and may have such hidden value that investors would be missing out on a lot by not rolling up their sleeves and hunting for traditional, deep value. Now, let's find out why ROEs are low in Japan:

1. <u>Over-capitalization:</u> a random review of Japanese stocks will surely result in a number that have unnecessarily high shareholders' equity ratios, which in short means there is little leverage employed. With such little debt, naturally, returns on equity are going to be lower than those at leveraged companies ceteris paribus. Other factors at play may include low profitability, which of course leads to low ROE regardless of the equity base; lack of distributions to shareholders, thus sustaining a higher-than-necessary equity base; and tying up of significant assets that have low or negligible yields in such holdings as cash, government bonds, and real estate. There also may be equity investments as cross-shareholdings. Any, or a combination, of the above is possible, although its often a combination of factors. A low ROE that is due to low or no debt may be preferable to a company that has a higher ROE but a heavy debt level. A company with a low ROE due to soft earnings, but one that also has a high shareholders' equity ratio can certainly be of interest for its lack of liabilities and potential to improve returns or distribute excess capital to shareholders.

2. <u>Depreciation:</u> Over-investment typically leads to over-capacity, which results in lower margins.[103] Simultaneously, investment incurs depreciation

---

[103] A helpful book on the reasons for, and impact of, over capacity and production is Robert Brenner's *The Boom and the Bubble: The U.S. in the World Economy* (2003).

costs, which are heavier in Japan than in the U.S., which decreases profits. Double whammy: constraints on margins and reported profits! However, depreciation is a non-cash charge meaning it pays to review the cash flow statement (operating cash flows), something all value investors should be doing; but one must not simply disregard depreciation due to the need to factor in so-called "maintenance" capital expenditures (against the tradition of embracing capex in Japan).

A study by economist Andrew Smithers (of advisory Smithers & Co.) showed that depreciation as a percentage of after-tax profits in Japan totaled 194%, while the corresponding figure in the U.S. was only 60%.[104] The period of study reflected the fiscal year (for Japan) ended March 30, 2011, and included Tokyo Stock Exchange-listed companies and S&P 500 components. Previously, Smithers has noted the upside potential for Japanese stocks given their large but falling level of depreciation, as capital spending has declined. Prior to the 2008 crash, the normalized level of depreciation as a percentage of profits was 65% in Japan, compared to less than 50% in the U.S., according to Smithers.

What's often forgotten about depreciation is that despite it being profit-zapping, it in fact means less corporate taxes owed, so it is actually not so bad after all. Another point of view (see also Smithers' below) is that capex necessarily keeps people employed (explaining Japan's comparatively low unemployment rate) and it (and R&D spending) results in such things as Japan's prolific filing and receipt of quality patents, second behind the U.S.

*****

Andrew Smithers, typical of the best market watchers, is very consistent in his thinking and writing. He had the following to say in a late-September 2009 article published in *Nikkei Veritas*: "I have regularly pointed out in previous articles, that the major economic imbalance in Japan has been

---

[104] "Your new safe havens are in Japan," FT Alphaville, Sept. 6, 2011. http://ftalphaville.ft.com/blog/2011/09/06/669791/

between investment and consumption.[105] Japan has invested too much and consumed too little. The only purpose of investment is to generate growth and, although Japan has invested much more than other mature economies, it has grown more slowly. Much of the money spent on investment has therefore simply been wasted. An increase in consumption at the expense of investment should therefore allow the economy to grow just as fast as before. This is a highly desirable outcome which will result in an increase in the wellbeing of the Japanese people."

Smithers argues that a reduction in domestic investment – a necessity under circumstances of a declining or aging population – will in turn result in less depreciation charges, allowing companies to pay higher wages (without hurting margins), thus of course, fueling much needed consumption. As he recognizes, the domestic market is saturated in many areas, and the fierce competition has severely eroded profits. The need for differentiation, not necessarily diversification (which has too often led to corporate bloat and lack of focus), is one that has been evident since at least 2000.[106] One note on wages: as baby boomers retire, not only should unemployment ease as there will be more openings for the un-/underemployed younger age groups, but companies will save on compensation and could even increase their typically low salaries to younger employees.

*****

In Martin Whitman's *The Aggressive Conservative Investor* (1979), he makes the following important observations about return-on-equity and investment. In summary, a high ROE most of the time means a small net asset value (NAV), and may indicate a proprietary position (i.e. a moat) and suggest sustained earning power, however it may also attract competition, which will reduce margins. A low ROE could mean overvalued assets and/or inefficient management, or it could indicate significant unused resources that can serve as a margin of safety and be used to expand earning power. Whitman also

---

[105] See: "A New Era for Japan," http://www.smithers.co.uk/news_article.php?id=82&o=30.
[106] See Michael Porter, Hiroka Takeuchi and Mariko Sakakibara in *Can Japan Compete* (Perseus, 2000).

points out that analysts place heavy importance on ROE and ROI but dismiss the importance of book value. Ironically, book value is essential in ROE and ROI analysis.

Value investors in Japan must always be vigilant and opportunistic for quality (of the moat variety as opposed to one-hit wonder types), high-ROE stocks that have hit cyclical lows or that are being sold indiscriminately for whatever reason. The lower-ROE stocks with low price-to-book ratios must be carefully analyzed on three bases: (1) quality of assets, (2) earnings potential, and (3) management's concern for, or commitment to, shareowners. And for companies themselves, some have probably realized (while others will realize over time) that higher ROEs can be a most beneficial goal since success means both pleasing shareholders and likely keeping at bay any would-be acquirers targeting underperforming companies.

Referring to Whitman again — he has done a great service to investors that take the time to read and think about what he has written — he is a proponent of what he calls "resource conversion," which means that he is not looking to buy a stock with the crowd and sell with the crowd's bullish momentum. Rather, he seeks to extract value by such means as M&A, LBOs/MBOs, turnarounds (and exchange of securities), spinoffs, financing/refinancing, buybacks, and dividends. The philosophy of resource conversion should resonate with those researching and investing in Japanese stocks.

There has been some consolidation in Japan since circa 2000, but there is much more opportunity for further consolidation. There is too much domestic competition, which spills over globally (notably in electronics and autos), and there's redundancy domestically in such products as mobile handsets that beg consolidation and more serious attempts to expand outside Japan. Banking is yet another area that needs another round, or more, of consolidation. Beyond the theme of "consolidation," there is a great need for parent companies to wholly-acquire key listed subsidiaries and to divest non-core listed subsidiaries. There are also a large number of smaller-sized companies whose equity is controlled by founders' large stakes, many of whom are at or nearing retirement age and may not have a successor from within their family. Lastly, there are also attractive targets for LBOs and

MBOs. Realization of the above catalysts for realizing value is more a matter of when, not if. Some of the largest private equity firms are already in Japan, and while the volume of activity has been light, there is no indication of PE firms throwing in the towel.

To conclude, in light of all the low ROEs on the surface, potential investment targets can be judged based on price-to-earnings (P/E) multiplied by price-to-book (P/B) of a certain limit, say no more than 25. What this means is an investor could find stocks trading at 50-times earnings and 0.5-times book, which may suggest an asset-rich company that is turning around. One could also find a company trading at 8-times earnings and 3-times book, suggesting a neglected company possibly with good margins. If one were to ignore high P/E stocks at large, one will miss those trading at low price-to-book values. If one dismisses high price-to-book stocks, one could miss hidden gems that trade conversely at low P/Es. Increased profitability is the most pure way to boost ROE, but Japanese companies' capital structures and investments in subsidiaries allow for ample opportunity to make returns to investors more attractive.

## Impact of faster-growing Asian economies, especially China

In Chapter 2 when discussing the Tokyo Stock Exchange and its various indexes I mentioned the TOPIX "Active in Asia" index, which was launched in October 2011. Often overlooked when assessing Japan's economy and its prospects is its proximity to China and the rest of Asia (many countries are growing at much higher rates than Japan and other advanced economies). Since 2009 China has overtaken the U.S. as Japan's largest trading partner and it has also surpassed Japan to become the world's second-largest economy. GDP per capita presents a different picture of course, but China's sustained high growth is not something to be feared. Instead it should be cheered, since it means greater trade opportunities and such things as tourism-related demand (the Japanese government has already been easing Chinese tourist visa requirements; and Chinese tourists are reported to be much bigger spenders than Western tourists).[107] Let's review the "Active in Asia" index's components:

Note that some companies have listed ADRs, while others may have unsponsored ones. MC refers to market capitalization, in yen, followed by U.S. dollars. P/B refers to price-to-book value, which uses the prevailing stock price and most-recent fiscal year (trailing twelve month) financial data. P/E is the price-to-earnings ratio; based on the same fiscal-year-end figure.

| Company | Code | MC JPY | MC $ | P/B | P/E | ROE |
|---|---|---|---|---|---|---|
| Inpex | 1605 | 1.765T | $22.6B | 0.86 | 11.8 | 7.6% |
| Toray | 3402 | 900.6B | $11.6B | 1.46 | 15.2 | 10.9% |
| FUJIFILM | 4901 | 955.1B | $12.2B | 0.53 | 14.1 | 3.7% |
| Asahi Glass | 5201 | 776.1B | $9.9B | 0.88 | 6.2 | 15.8% |
| Nippon Steel | 5401 | 1.300T | $16.7B | 0.66 | 12.9 | 5.0% |
| Sumitomo Metal Mining | 5713 | 573.5B | $7.3B | 0.85 | 6.6 | 13.8% |
| Sumitomo Electric Ind. | 5802 | 655.0B | $8.4B | 0.70 | 9.3 | 7.6% |
| SMC | 6273 | 872.5B | $11.2B | 1.53 | 17.4 | 9.1% |
| Komatsu | 6301 | 1.875T | $24.0B | 1.93 | 12.1 | 17.2% |
| Daikin Ind. | 6367 | 625.2B | $8.0B | 1.29 | 31.3 | 4.0% |
| Hitachi | 6501 | 1.876T | $24.0B | 1.29 | 7.9 | 17.5% |
| Toshiba | 6502 | 1.407T | $18.0B | 1.75 | 10.2 | 16.6% |

[107] "Chinese Tourists Return to Japan in Big Numbers," *The Wall Street Journal*, Jan. 30, 2012. http://online.wsj.com/article/SB10001424052970204740904577190352257661174.html

| Company | Code | MC JPY | MC $ | P/B | P/E | ROE |
|---|---|---|---|---|---|---|
| Nidec | 6594 | 960.4B | $12.3B | 2.68 | 17.6 | 15.1% |
| Omron | 6645 | 385.7B | $4.9B | 1.16 | 13.3 | 8.7% |
| Panasonic | 6752 | 1.675T | $21.5B | 0.62 | 19.1 | 2.8% |
| TDK | 6762 | 440.6B | $5.6B | 0.88 | 9.7 | 8.4% |
| Fanuc | 6954 | 2.912T | $37.3B | 2.57 | 19.8 | 14.1% |
| Rohm | 6963 | 390.1B | $5.0B | 0.59 | 39.1 | 1.4% |
| Murata Manuf. | 6981 | 916.8B | $11.7B | 1.07 | 16.3 | 6.6% |
| Nitto Denko | 6988 | 509.1B | $6.5B | 1.15 | 8.7 | 13.9% |
| Honda Motor | 7267 | 4.162T | $53.3B | 0.96 | 7.8 | 12.2% |
| Suzuki Motor | 7269 | 882.5B | $11.3B | 0.94 | 19.5 | 4.7% |
| Yamaha Motor | 7272 | 349.1B | $4.5B | 1.13 | 18.0 | 7.5% |
| Canon | 7751 | 4.548T | $58.3B | 1.57 | 17.1 | 9.3% |
| Tokyo Electron | 8035 | 715.2B | $9.2B | 1.22 | 9.9 | 13.3% |
| *Average* | - | 1.297T | $16.6B | 1.21 | 14.8 | 9.9% |

*Constituent list per Tokyo Stock Exchange website, published on September 22, 2011.*[108] *Market capitalization (including US$ conversion) and metrics recorded intra-day December 15, 2011.*

Note that Asahi Glass (5201) appears both in the TSE's "Active in Asia" index as well as its Dividend Focus 100 index; its divided yield was 3.96% as of December 15, 2011. It is the only company to appear in both indexes.

---

[108] See the TSE's "Active in Asia Index" webpage: http://www.tse.or.jp/english/market/topix/data/asia.html.

Rohm had a dividend yield of 3.79%, Canon 3.51%, Sumitomo Metal Mining, 3.24%, and Nitto Denko 3.07%. Otherwise a majority of companies' dividend yields were between 1 and 2%.

Among companies with an ROE greater than 10%, they had shareholder equity ratios of: Toray 37.8%, Asahi Glass 45.8%, Sumitomo Metal Mining 59.9%, Komatsu 43.0%, Hitachi 15.7%, Toshiba 16.1%, Nidec 47.5%, **Fanuc 87.9%,** Nitto Denko 63.9%, Honda 38.5%, and Tokyo Electron 70.8%. Fanuc and Tokyo Electron are very impressive compared to the leveraged likes of conglomerates Hitachi and Toshiba. Fanuc's returns on equity for fiscal years (March end) 2010, 4.5%, and 2009, 11.1%. Tokyo Electron's, however, were unimpressive: -1.75% in 2010 and 1.4% in 2009.

Let's look at one-year charts of the above group (ROE > 10%). As you can see, beside Toray and Fanuc, all are trading at 52-week lows. Most are likely at 2 - 2 ½ year lows similar to the broader market; many are well off all-time highs or most-recent highs in the bull market ended in roughly 2007.

**Toray (3402)** and **Asahi Glass (5201)** year-to-date December 15, 2011:

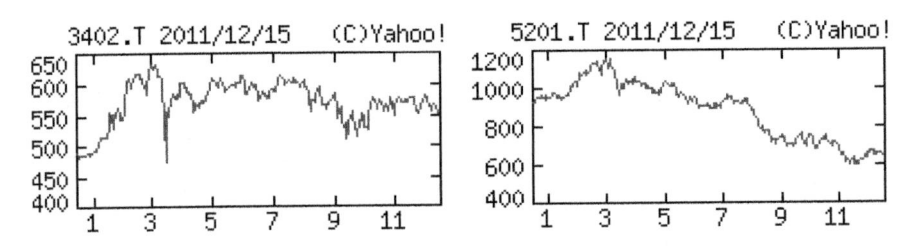

**Sumitomo Metal Mining (5713)** and **Komatsu (6301)**

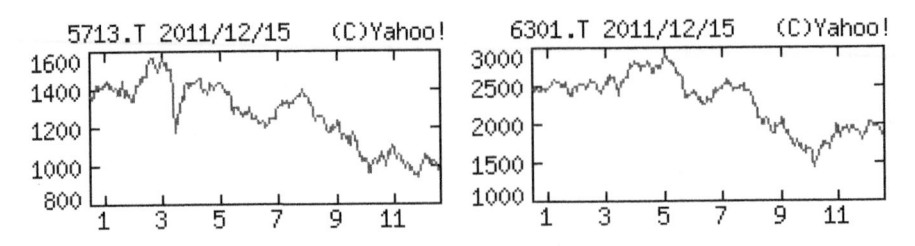

**Hitachi (6501)** and **Toshiba (6502)**

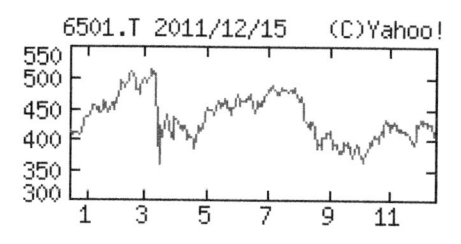

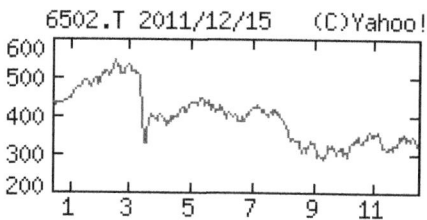

**Nidec (6594)** and **Fanuc (6954)**

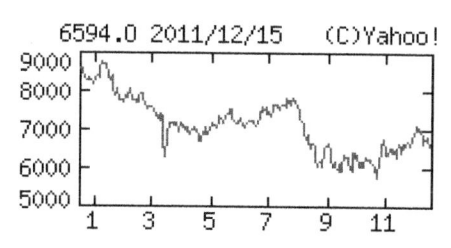

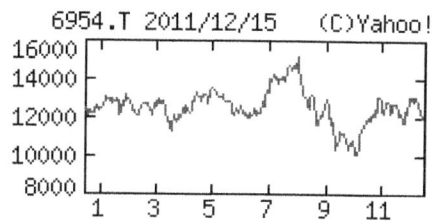

**Nitto Denko (6988)** and **Honda (7267)**

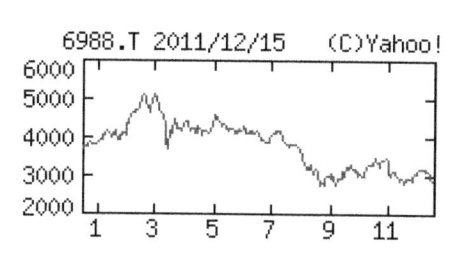

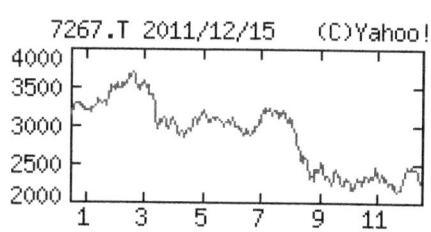

**Tokyo Electron (8035)**

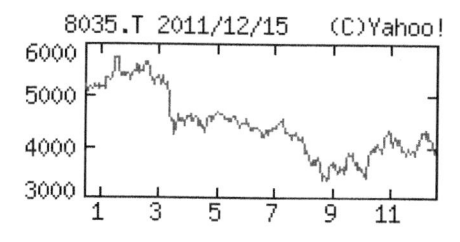

Other companies with high shareholder equity ratios include: Rohm 87.7%, Murata Manufacturing 83.1%, SMC 74.8%, Inpex 74.5%, and Tokyo Electron 70.8%. It goes without saying that the above charts and ratios are snapshots, for reference purposes, hopefully serving as examples of the cheapness of stocks and their broadly depressed prices.

## Companies sitting on valuable real estate

Somewhat similar in the thinking behind the periodic attraction of cyclical exporter stocks, investors (domestic and non-Japanese) in Japanese securities have demonstrated varying degrees of interest in the real estate value of listed companies. As you will see from the stock charts below, when Japan's export engine is strong and there is broad, solid demand for Japanese stocks, property-related stocks including those that sit on significant land but are not organized as REITs (I have provided three examples below) can increase many fold in a hurry. Of course, as the charts show, prices revert and sometime all the way back to pre-boom levels.

There are at least a couple dozen or so non-REIT listed companies in total that investors commonly associate with having *tremendous* land value; and the potential for any company to have real estate assets means it's a good idea to check, especially if based in a metropolitan area. Land value as reported on the balance sheet may be a fraction of market value or what an acquirer would pay, however, part of the problem is that the land may never be sold and thus proceeds to shareholders never realized. Buying at as low a price-to-book value as possible is critical; catching a favorable growth cycle could yield handsome returns. The big questions are how greedy to be on the upside, and should Japan finally normalize (i.e. truly exit deflation and achieve higher GDP along with an increase in births) do these stocks have such a vicious price reversion? Investors interested in companies with possible undervalued land (beside distinct property-related companies) should focus in particular on companies involved in hotels, leisure, retail, transportation, and warehousing.

Note the prices, values, and ratios that follow are as of the market close February 17, 2012; as reported on a consolidated basis. P/B and P/E based on trailing financials. 10-year stock charts.

**Tokyo Theatres** (T1: 9633), Y116 pps, Y9.259B MC, 0.77x P/B, 47.9x P/E, 0.86% dividend yield, FYE March 2011 1.54% ROE, 0.56% ROA

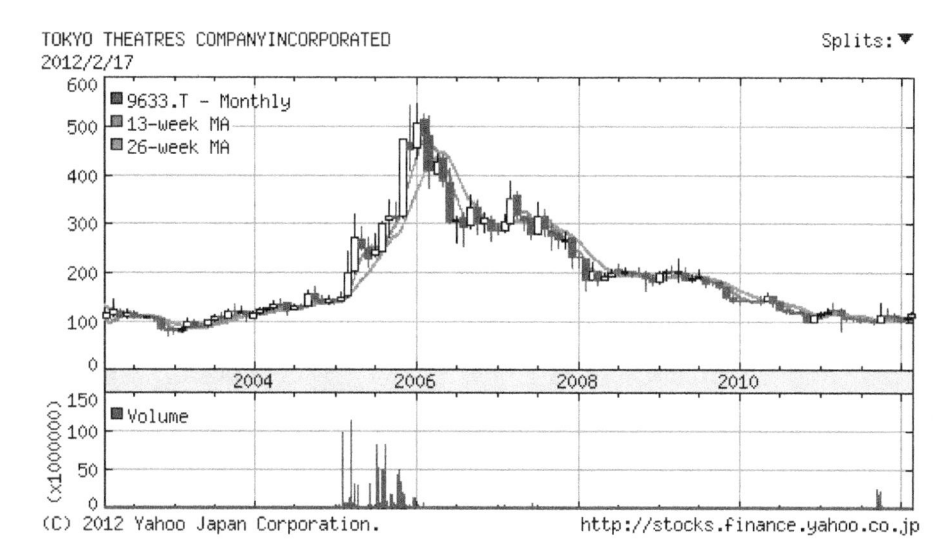

**Yomiuri Land** (T1: 9671), Y256 pps, Y21.38B MC, 1.12 P/B, 17.4 P/E, 1.95% dividend yield, FYE March 2011 6.68% ROE, 2.18% ROA

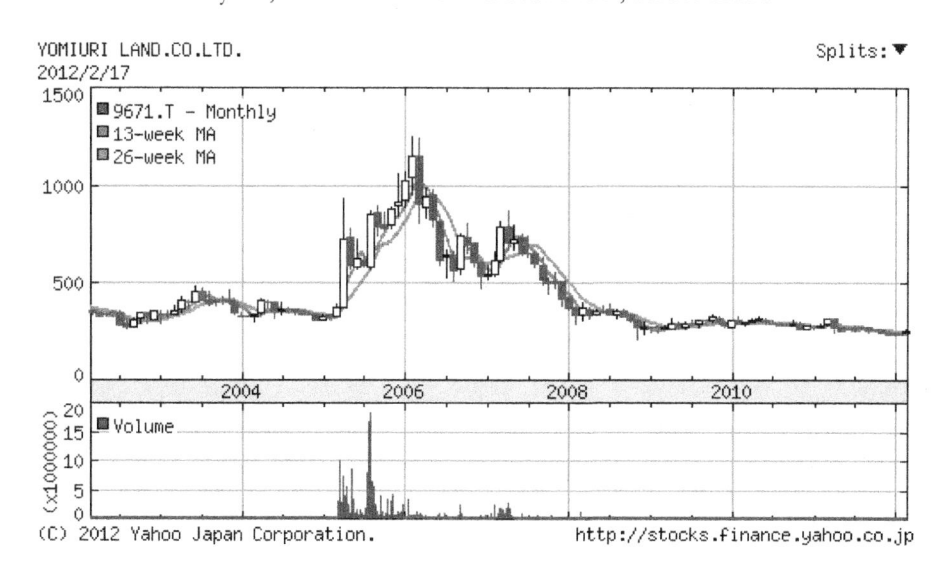

**Tokyotokeiba** (T1: 9672), Y122 pps, Y35.09B MC, 0.69 P/B, 19.4 P/E, 2.46% dividend yield, FYE December 2010 3.56% ROE, 2.91% ROA

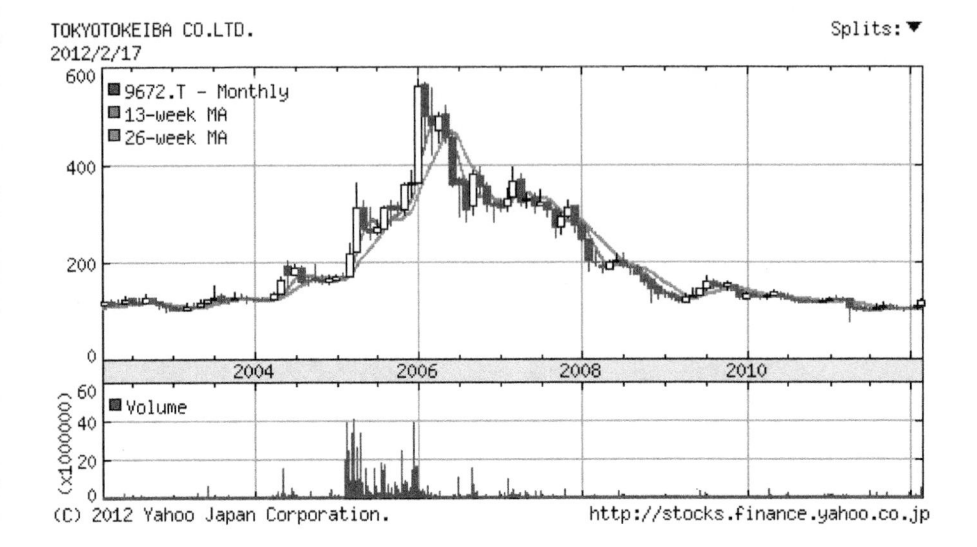

# CHAPTER 7

# THERE'S ALWAYS SOMETHING TO DO

"There's always something to do. You just need to look harder, be creative and a little flexible." – Irving Kahn, value investor, b. 1905. "There's always something to do," is the title of a biography of late value investor Peter Cundill (1938 – 2011).

## Substantial Shareholders

Per Japan's Company Law, investors taking a 5% or greater stake in a listed company must disclose such a position within five business days. Disclosure is made public via EDINET, which stands for Electronic Disclosure for Investors NETwork – the equivalent of EDGAR in the U.S. Mandatory electronic disclosure (excluding the large or substantial shareholding report) went into effect June 1, 2004; the large shareholding report did not until April 1, 2007.[109] Note that the large shareholding report

---

[109] At the time of publishing, these filings are not yet available in English via the Tokyo Stock Exchange's new English language disclosure page: https://www.release.tdnet.info/index_e.html. See http://www.tse.or.jp/english/listing/co_announce/index.html for details about English disclosure. Meantime, use Strike Co.'s STPEDIA database of filings: http://stpedia-ma.com/taiho/index.php?cmd=search&hoyucode=E08950. At the

is also commonly referred to as the 5% rule. It is tracked by a number of websites and obviously news of such an investment in a closely watched stock will be big news on the market. Otherwise, the filings are a great resource for investors to see what value (or growth) shops are buying. Overseas investors' buys (in particular) and sells are watched and can be news when involving a more mainstream stock, but those of the value orientation tend to be less newsworthy stocks. Nevertheless, as I show in the next section, overseas investor ownership is closely watched in Japan.

*****

In its inaugural edition, the Tokyo Stock Exchange's December 2011, *TSE Magazine*, includes mention that the Exchange intends to publish reports of Mothers-listed companies – those are the smaller-capitalized and often thinly-traded issues regarded mostly as new and/or growth-oriented companies – in English, with the first 60 coming by March 2012.[110] The TSE says they will be accessible via its homepage and that it aims to distribute them overseas. I think this is all a move in the right direction, the magazine, the English reports, and the ability to review select filings in English. However, certain fundamental conditions and realities exist that probably make Mothers companies unattractive to most value investors, and certainly to traders: lack of liquidity and an often expensive (absolute terms) stock price per share – obviously the latter is a factor in the former. This does not mean value investors should shun such listings, but rather, regard any otherwise attractive companies as being even more so with the possibility of a stock split. The Exchange could do more to encourage lower per share prices, too.

*****

---

site, substitute the E08950 code for another EDINET code from the pages that follow. Alternatively, in the other search box one can input a company's 4-digit code to see its large shareholder filings rather than a fund's.

[110] *TSE Magazine*: http://www.tse.or.jp/english/about/magazine/index.html.

The 5% rule requires disclosure whether the shares are held solely, for example by a single individual or a hedge fund; or jointly, say via any number of mutual funds of the same fund family.[111] Subsequent disclosure is required whenever the position changes by 1% or more. Filers must include the number of shares transacted, price per share, the purpose of holdings shares, and the source of investment capital. Select investors may receive exemption to ease their filing burden (for example, large asset management companies), which instead requires them to file within 15 days whenever a position exceeds 5% and for changes of greater than 1% in the first instance; subsequent changes of 2.5% or more requires disclosure by the 15th of the following month.

Following is a list, in alphabetical order, of prominent domestic and overseas investors with their accompanying EDINET registrant code in parentheses.

アライアンス・バーンスタイン・エル・ピー (E06241)
Alliance Bernstein LP

あすかアセットマネジメント (E24292)
Asuka Asset Management

ブラックロック・ジャパン (E09096)
BlackRock Japan

ブランデス・インベストメント・パートナーズ (E06133)
Brandes Investment Partners

ブリランス　キャピタル　マネージメント (E23176)
Brillance Capital Management Pte. -- Singapore

キャピタル・リサーチ・アンド・マネージメント (E06267)
Capital Research and Management Company

---

[111] As for insider transactions, activity is far less brisk in Japan than in the U.S., so much so that there is no real merit to an insider-focused strategy beyond ad hoc situations.

中央三井アセット信託銀行 (E06123)
Chuo Mitsui Asset Trust & Banking Company

クレディ・スイス証券 (E11027)
Credit Suisse Securities

クレディ・スイス・セキュリティーズ(ヨーロッパ) (E11028)
Credit Suisse Securities (Europe) Ltd.

ダルトン・インベストメンツ・エルエルシー (E08827)
Dalton Investments, LLC

ドイツ銀行ロンドン支店 (E09106)
Deutsche Bank – London

エフィッシモ　キャピタル　マネージメント (E11852)
Effissimo Capital Management Pte Ltd.

フィデリティ投信 (E12481)
Fidelity Trust

エフエムアール エルエルシー (E12208)
FMR LLC

ゴールドマン・サックス・インターナショナル (E05875)
Goldman Sachs International

ゴールドマン・サックス証券 (E11198)
Goldman Sachs Securities

ハリス・アソシエイツ・エル・ピー (E07786)
Harris Associates L.P.

いちごアセットマネジメント・インターナショナル (E11469)
Ichigo Asset Management International Pte. Ltd.

インベスコ投信投資顧問 (E06479)
Invesco Asset Management (Japan)

ＪＰモルガン・アセット・マネジメント (E06264)
JPMorgan Asset Management

ラザード・アセット・マネジメント・エルエルシー (E11648)
Lazard Asset Management LLC

三菱東京ＵＦＪ銀行 (E03533)
Mitsubishi Tokyo UFJ Bank

三菱ＵＦＪセキュリティーズインターナショナル (E05881)
Mitsubishi UFJ Securities International PLC

三井住友銀行 (E03537)
Mitsui Sumitomo Bank

みずほ銀行 (E03540)
Mizuho Bank

みずほコーポレート銀行 (E03532)
Mizuho Corporate Bank

みずほ信託銀行 (E03628)
Mizuho Trust & Banking Co.

モルガン・スタンレーＭＵＦＧ証券 (E10802)
Morgan Stanley MUFG Securities

日本生命保険 (E06125)
Nippon Life Insurance Company

野村證券 (E03810)
Nomura Securities

オービス・インベストメント・マネジメント (E09810)
Orbis Investment Management BVI Limited

プロスペクト・アセット・マネジメント・インク (E09912)
Prospect Asset Management Inc.

ルネッサンス・テクノロジーズ・エルエルシー (E21784)
Renaissance Technologies LLC

シュローダー証券投信投資顧問 (E06132)
Schroders Securities Investment Advisors

シルチェスター・インターナショナル・インベスターズ (E24872)
Silchester International Investors LLP

シンプレクス・アセット・マネジメント (E10670)
Simplex Asset Management

サウスイースタン　アセット　マネージメント　インク (E06251)
Southeastern Asset Management

スパークス・アセット・マネジメント (E11161)
SPARX Asset Management

タイヨウ・ファンド・マネッジメント・カンパニー (E09183)
Taiyo Fund Management Company, LLC

タイヨウ・パール・ジー・ピー・エル・ティー・ディー (E12249)
Taiyo Pearl, GP Ltd.

テンプルトン・グローバル・アドバイザーズ・リミテッド (E06462)
Templeton Global Advisers Limited

テンプルトン・インベストメント・カウンセル (E06461)
Templeton Investment Counsel, LLC

ザ・エスエフピー・バリュー・リアライゼーション・マスター・ファンド・リミテッド (E08950)
The SFP Value Realization Master Fund Limited

サード・アベニュー・マネージメント・エルエルシー (E10342)
Third Avenue Management, LLC

タワー投資顧問 (E06234)
Tower Investment Advisors

## Effissimo Capital

From the above list, let's first review Effissimo Capital Management, a Singapore-based hedge fund, and perhaps one of the most savvy and shrewd among all value/activists in Japan.[112]

In August 2011, Effissimo agreed to sell its large stakes in two longtime attractive value plays, Tachihi Enterprise (8821) and New Tachikawa Aircraft (5996), for $1 billion (ostensibly realizing a respectable return on investment; see stake purchase history and chart below) as part of a merger and MBO. The two companies have sizable, valuable landholdings on the outskirts of Tokyo that date back to the days of when the land (Tachikawa Airfield) and manufacturing operations were controlled by the Imperial Army. Focusing strictly on value, the companies actually aren't overly pricey at their takeout prices, trading at 1.25 and 1.5-times book value; both are profitable, and long-term debt is highly negligible in one instance and non-existent on the other. The takeout premiums were 47% for Tachihi and 67% for New Tachikawa, based on their three-month average closing prices.

Effissimo first disclosed its position in Tachihi, 5.23%, on August 20, 2007. It disclosed a 6.83% stake in New Tachikawa Aircraft on July 31, 2007. It began increasing its stake in both that September, to 6.23% and 10.62%, respectively (it disclosed two increases in New Tachikawa during September). Effissimo went on to incrementally add its position over the remainder of 2007, during 2008 and 2009, and essentially made its last meaningful additions by early 2010 (it last reported respective 17% and 22% stakes). The 10-year chart below shows New Tachikawa (5996) in red, Tachihi (8821) in blue, the Nikkei 225 in green, and the TOPIX in black.

---

[112] Effissimo was founded by former members of Yoshiaki Murakami's fund, MAC Asset Management. A successful, albeit controversial activist fund, MAC and Murakami's run ended in 2006 when he became ensnared in an alleged insider trading suit and eventually received a jail sentence.

```
TACHIHI ENTERPRISE CO.LTD.
2011/12/15
```

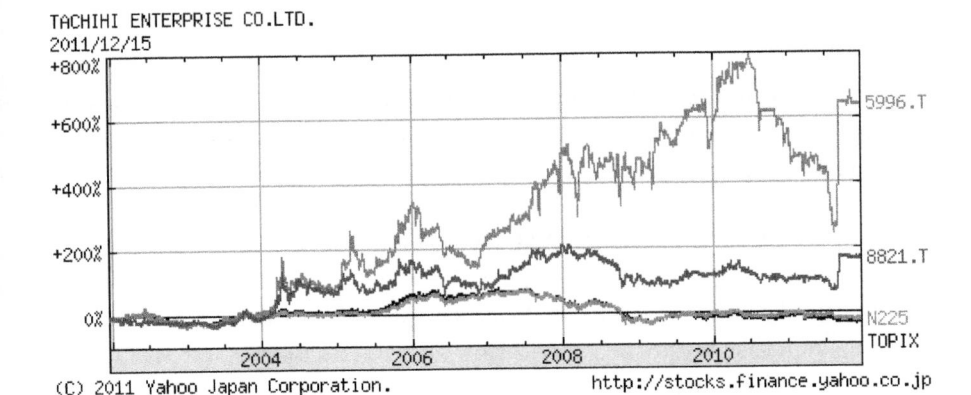

*Chart showing Tachihi Enterprise Co. Ltd. (5996.T), 8821.T, N225, and TOPIX from 2004 to 2010, with percentage change on y-axis ranging from 0% to +800%.*

(C) 2011 Yahoo Japan Corporation.    http://stocks.finance.yahoo.co.jp

A review of large shareholder filings shows that beside Effissimo, the only other asset management firm to disclose a 5%-plus position in New Tachikawa was Schroders, which initially disclosed that it had established a 9.2% stake in June 2006, however it then gradually reduced its stake over the next five years to below 5%. There were no other 5%-plus positions in Tachihi since 2006.

Interesting to note that both Tachihi and New Tachikawa were TOPIX 2nd Section constituents; deemed by the market to be inferior to 1st Section (NYSE "big board" equivalent). Another point is the longtime cross-shareholding relationship in which New Tachikawa most recently owned over 39% of Tachihi, and Tachihi owned just below 25% of New Tachikawa. In addition, listed IHI (7013), a leading heavy machinery manufacturer and TOPIX 1st Section constituent, owned 10.8% of New Tachikawa and 10% of Tachihi. IHI's predecessor originally established the Tachikawa aircraft concern that was taken over by the Imperial Army.[113]

---

[113] See Tachikawa Aircraft Company Wikipedia entry:
http://en.wikipedia.org/wiki/Tachikawa_Aircraft_Company_Ltd.

# SFP Value

Let's now take a look at The SFP Value Realization Master Fund. It claims some "firsts" in Japan among hedge funds and has been involved in two takeovers resulting in premiums in excess of 100% (though after a review of its cost basis the story for SFP is not as good as the fund makes it out to be, granted more recent investors would have done very well, indeed). In a December 5, 2011, press release that reads quite self-congratulatory, SFP touted its facilitation of a management buyout (MBO) of Sanjo Machine Works (6437; see 10-year chart below). Sanjo, a leading manufacturer of tobacco production equipment, automobile engine parts, and general machinery and dies, is to be taken over by the company's president for Y468/share, which represents a 135% premium to its prior close of Y199 (139% compared to its 6-month average). The press release notes this is one of the largest premiums ever in Japan and it's the second 100%-plus premium SFP has realized in the past year. It previously sold its 9% stake in Aloka Corp., a global leader in ultrasound equipment to Hitachi Medical for a 119% premium. SFP calls its investment style "engaged investing."[114]

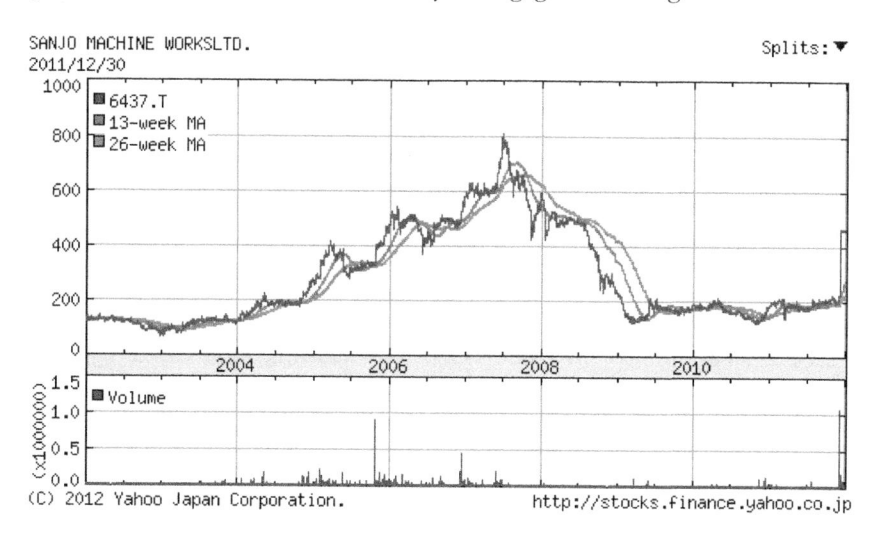

---

[114] "Symphony Financial Partners Co., Ltd. Sells Stake of Portfolio Company at 135% Premium," Enhanced Online News, Dec. 5, 2011. http://eon.businesswire.com/news/eon/20111205005975/en

Sanjo Machine Works, a TOPIX 2nd Section constituent, has a market capitalization of just over Y7 billion ($91 million) at its takeover price. Despite the takeover premium, it trades at only 0.64 times book (Y733/share book value vs. Y468/share market value), although its trailing P/E is a more lofty 31. Sanjo has low returns on equity and assets, but this may be a classic case of simply being over-capitalized, as its shareholders' equity ratio is greater than 70%; it reports no long-term debt. The gap between book and market value may raise doubt whether shareholders are being taken out at too low of a price or whether the premium is a generous one after 2 ½ years of a floundering stock price – Sanjo traded as low as Y128 in 2011, in the aftermath of the March 11th disaster; Think about how low its book vs. market value was at that time! At Y468/share, over 65% of Sanjo's market value effectively consists of cash and cash equivalents.

A cursory review of SFP's historical purchases of Sanjo show that it likely initially acquired its stake in winter 2006/2007 and expanded it from around 10% to almost 16% in spring 2007, the latter time being right around when 5%-plus stake disclosures became mandatory electronically. By September 2007 SFP had amassed a position of 17.7%. Sanjo traded at the Y500-level in December 2006 and roughly between Y600 and Y800 during January to October 2007. SFP would go on to increase its stake to over 20% by January 2009, but Sanjo's stock price had by then fallen to the Y200-level. Over the next year and half, SFP would lower its stake to about 15.7%, all at prices at around the Y200-level. Subsequently, SFP would go on to increase its stake at similar prices to above 23% through October 2011, ahead of the MBO announcement. Back of the envelope calculations suggest that overall SFP lost money on Sanjo, possibly around 8% assuming it had originally purchased its stakes in 2007 at Y600. Thus, in conclusion, while the 135% announced premium is a big deal, and shareholders of the past couple years would have done very well, the MBO may not have been as lucrative a deal for SFP as the press release suggests.

As for SFP's aforementioned investment in Aloka (which was taken over by Hitachi Medical for a 119% premium), it is not as easy to readily determine what kind of returns SFP may have realized. What's clear is that during 2011, SFP has had two investments taken over at considerable premiums to then recent trading levels. Such large premiums, despite any shortfall compared to book value, may satisfy most shareholders, especially recent ones poised to see most of the upside, longtime holders seeking a liquid exit (i.e. not having to sell into a market for thinly traded shares), as well as the fact that few would be bold enough to declare a 100%-plus premium insufficient. That being said, after taking a look at SFP's current holdings, I will discuss Scott Callon of Ichigo Asset Management, who successfully intervened blocking a takeover of Tokyo Kohtetsu at a premium of only 6% when it was trading at book value. SFP's reported holdings as of year-end 2011 include:

**Zuiko** (OSE2: 6279), 11.45% stake (increased by 1% on both Nov. 30, and Jun. 30, 2011, +0.3% on Mar. 14, 2011; first electronic large shareholder filing appears to be June 4, 2007 +1% to 7.1% stake). Leading manufacturer of equipment used to produce sanitary products, esp. feminine care. Reports no long-term debt; shareholders' equity ratio > 70%, and an ROE over the past three years of 4% - 8%. Trades at 0.65-times book and 8.4-times trailing earnings. 2.29% dividend yield. 10-year stock chart:

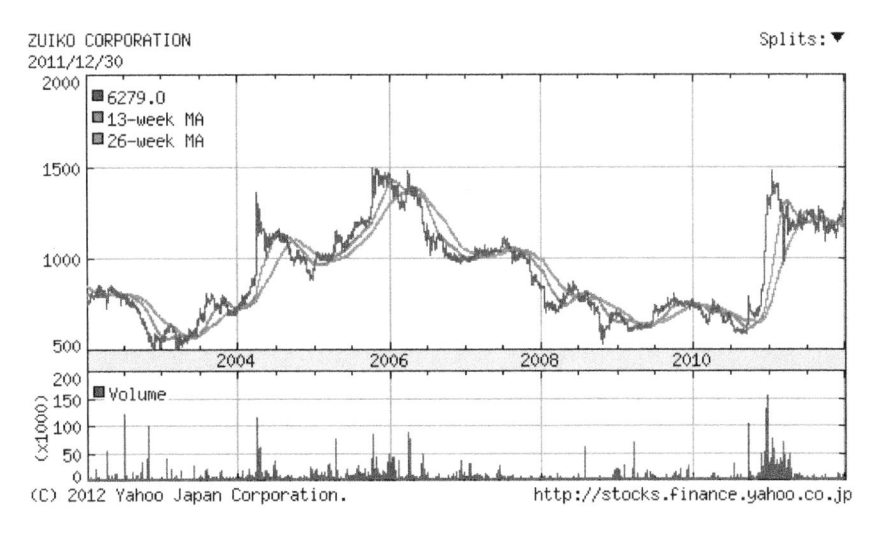

**Nagawa** (Jasdaq: 9663), 12.66% stake (increased by 1% on May 19, 2011, +1.3% Mar. 14, 2011; SFP appears to have established initial stake of 5% per April 2007 filing). Leading manufacturer of unit houses for construction sites, etc., also leases construction machinery; notice the spike in its shares following the March 11th disaster. Reports no long-term debt, shareholders' equity ratio > 85%, and an ROE over the past three years of 0.7% - 2.3%.

Trades at 0.5-times book and 42.1-times trailing earnings. 2.16% dividend yield. 10-year stock chart:

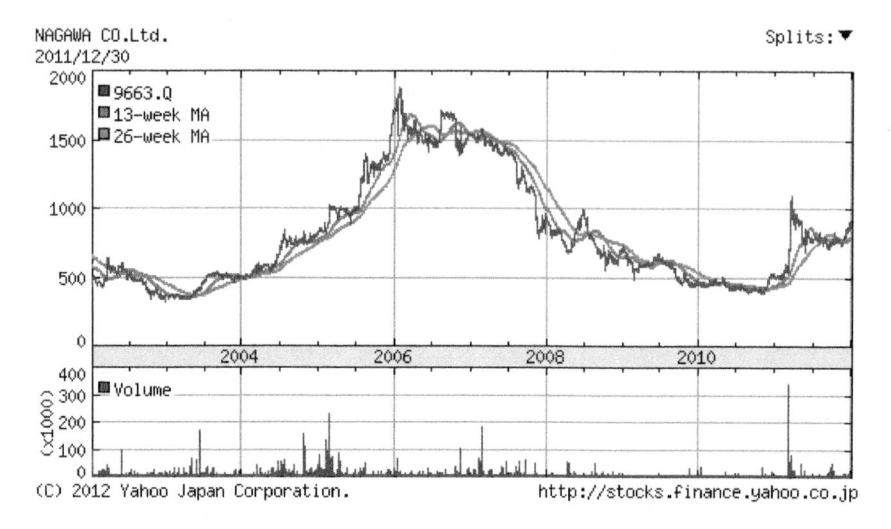

**Infomart** (Mothers: 2492), 6.09% stake (increased by 1% on Apr. 18, 2011; position apparently established at 5.05% per April 13, 2011 filing). A food industry-focused network application service provider. Reports no long-term debt, shareholders' equity ratio > 75%, and an ROE over the past two years of 14.9% and 17.7%. Trades at 2-times book and 14-times trailing earnings. 4.66% dividend yield. All-time stock chart:

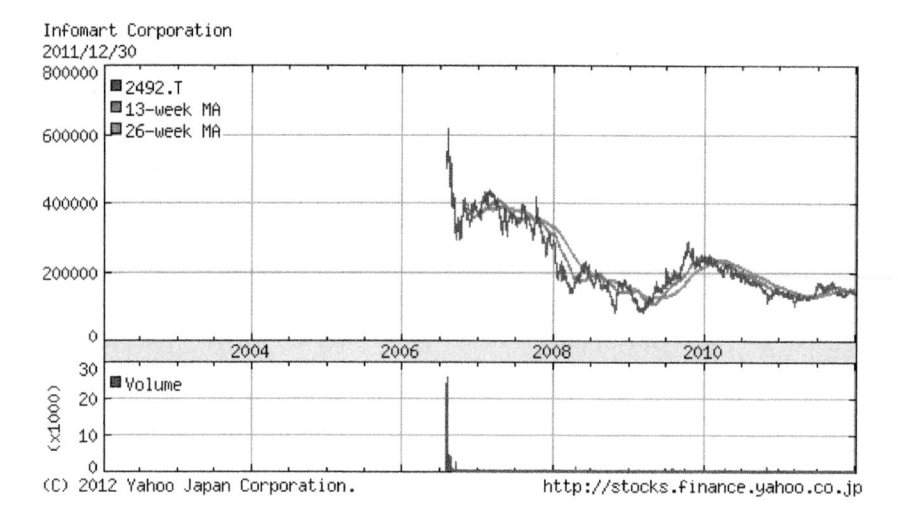

## *Ichigo Ichie*: One lifetime, one encounter

Ichigo Group Holdings is an interesting story for Japan-focused value investors and activists. Scott Callon, the founder of Ichigo Asset Management (at the time with AUM of $25 million; he was previously with Morgan Stanley Japan as head of equities), is of particular interest.[115] He made headlines following the October 2006 announced merger of Osaka Steel (5449) and Tokyo Kohtetsu (Jasdaq: 5448), the latter a much smaller steel company, for a 6% premium to Tokyo Kohtetsu's market value reflecting practically nothing for control or the possible cost savings from synergies (in Callon's opinion). In fact, Tokyo Kohtetsu traded at only 6-times earnings (less than half that of bigger TSE-listed steelmakers), it also traded at its reported book value, and had an ROE in the high-20s, which all suggested a worthiness of a much higher premium. Callon, whom had identified Tokyo Kohtetsu as an investment target prior to the announced merger and launching of his fund, but had not yet taken a position, would build an 11% position and seek a much higher premium in the neighborhood of 30%.

Callon initiated the first ever shareholder-initiated proxy solicitation in Japan and was successful against sizable corporate backing of both companies (Mitsui owned over 29% of Tokyo Kohtetsu and Nippon Steel owned 61% of Osaka Steel), not to mention a close business relationship between Mitsui and Nippon. Ichigo rallied very respectable support amongst individual shareholders (23% supporting votes), which in the aggregate with Ichigo's votes (11%) and institutions (8%) totaled 42%, exceeding the 33% minimum needed to vote down the merger. That Mitsui would be willing to accept such a small premium is disappointing, but perhaps understandable with the various business connections. Tokyo Kohtetsu claimed the 6% premium it was offered was reasonable based on fairness opinions from leading Japanese investment banks.[116] It also claimed potential merits from cost savings and warned it would face harsher competition from imports. The longer story of

---

[115] "What does 'Ichigo' mean?" Ichigo Asset Management website: http://www.ichigoasset.com/en/what-ichigo.html.

[116] Never trust an investment bank's fairness opinion, whether in Japan or the U.S., although investors' options may be limited without ownership of a meaningful number of shares or an ability to ready a class action.

how Callon became compelled to not only take a position in Tokyo Kohtetsu but to take action to effect a larger premium (or at least to prevent a takeover at such a low premium) stems from he being moved very much by the outcry against the deal on Tokyo Kohtetsu's message board on Yahoo! Japan Finance. Callon is fluent in Japanese and is a multi-decade resident of Japan. The tactics he used as well as the positive response from individual shareholders, is one all value investors can appreciate.[117]

These days, Callon appears to be more involved in Japanese real estate as a part of the Ichigo Group, which is listed on the JASDAQ under code 2337. Meanwhile, outside of listed real estate-related companies, Ichigo Asset Management most recently reported 5%-plus holdings include Autobacs (9832), 10.2% as of November 17, 2011, and NishiMatsuya Chain (7545), 10.5% as of October 17, 2011. On August 2nd, it reported the following holdings: Uchida Yoko (8057) 5.33%, Nikki (6042) 23.2%, Aiphone (6718) 10.68%, Chiyoda Integre (6915) 24.17%, HappiNet (7552) 9.72%, Ohashi Technica (7628) 7.88%, Chiyoda (8185) 11.99%, Nanao (6737) 7.16%, Toba (7472) 14.93%, and Aica Kogyo (4206) 6.93%. As for Tokyo Kohtetsu, it turns out that while there was an advance of around 30% in its share price in 2007 during Ichigo's proxy activities, subsequently it has not been able to recoup such a level after a sharp decline in 2008, though it has advanced well beyond its trough. Pre-2006 merger announcement Tokyo Kohtetsu was trading at book value; as of calendar year-end 2011 it is trading at 0.65-times book. Then it was trading at 6-times earnings, now it is at nearly 11-times, since profits are down, but it has remained profitable despite the difficult economic backdrop. Callon contended then and reiterated his belief in a May 2011 interview with *The Manual of Ideas*, that Tokyo Kohtetsu is Japan's best small steel company.[118] Like Tokyo Kohtetsu, all of the above companies

---

[117] Among the various coverage of Callon, Ichigo, and Tokyo Kohtetsu, see: "Ichigo's Scott Callon Leads Japan's First Successful Shareholder Revolt," Japan Society New York speech, May 3, 2007, http://www.japansociety.org/ichigos_scott_callon_leads_japans_first_successful_shareholder_r.

[118] Interview with Scott Callon, *Manual of Ideas*, May 2011. http://manualofideas.com/files/content/the-manual-of-ideas_interview_with_scott-callon_2011.pdf.

trade for less than book value, some as low as around half-book (one, Uchida Yoko at 0.35). All except Uchida Yoko were profitable over the past year.

**Tokyo Kohtetsu 10-year chart as of December 30, 2011:**

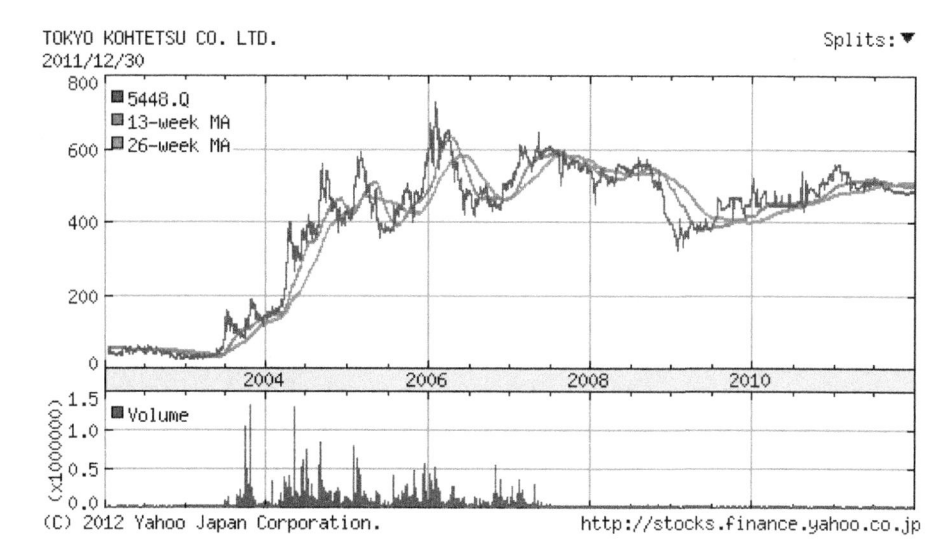

In the above-mentioned *Manual of Ideas* interview, Callon made a number of points that should resonate with value investors and also some that are crucial for those interested, or already investing, in Japan. One was that he is not in the diversification business, as his fund has only about ten major positions. A cursory review of 2011 stock performance suggests a down year overall for his portfolio, but that doesn't mean Ichigo is down based on its cost basis, nor does it portend disaster. Despite value investors' longer term holding periods, during which there invariably will be periods of underperformance, the financial media and other value investors will publicize and in the worst case exhibit unflattering and unnecessary schadenfreude.[119] Anyhow, in Callon's case, he is among the few that specialize only in Japan (Effissimo, Prospect and Taiyo are select others),

---

[119] Bruce Berkowitz of the Fairholme Fund (FAIRX) is practically an object of ridicule at present (year-end 2011) given some serious declines in his highly-concentrated portfolio.

primarily in small-caps, and he says, "... we expect to be only a small part of our clients' highly diversified portfolios and thus we concentrate only on what we consider to be our very best ideas." Another point of Callon's is that Ichigo has a value fundamentalist approach focused on asset value and operating value (targeting companies trading around or below tangible book value). Ichigo doesn't try to guess what the market is or will be doing, though similar to Martin Whitman's thinking, Callon does not say other approaches to investing are wrong, and adds that the market is big enough to accommodate a variety of approaches.

Another point concerns *The Manual of Ideas* referencing Buffett's 1998 University of Florida speech in which he said Japanese companies' ROE were unattractive. Callon's reply was that Japan's "ROE challenge is really about the E, not the R." As discussed earlier, since many Japanese companies have retained so much of their earnings, the returns are not so much the problem as the large equity bases are since they "dilute" (in Callon's words) the earnings. A bonus to value investors looking at Japan is the large amount of cash held on balance sheets (i.e. in terms of liquidity; "cash is king.") The challenge remains of how or how best to unlock value.

## "Overseas" Investors in Japan

As mentioned in the prior section, foreign ownership of Japanese stocks is fairly closely watched. There are a variety of rankings published most frequently on a monthly, quarterly, or annual basis. Investors in Japan are aware just how important a role overseas investors play as they are responsible for as much as two-thirds of trading and have held as much as around 30% of Japanese equity in recent years. Thus, among popular stock picking strategies is to try and determine which companies would be of interest to foreign investors, and another is to buy on the coattails of foreign buying. On the contrary, foreign ownership is hardly a topic of interest in the U.S. barring a few exceptions such as when so-called "oil money" is doing the buying (e.g. Saudi Prince Alwaleed or GCC sovereign wealth funds) or the U.S. government intervenes to block deals, such as China's CNOOC attempt to acquire Unocal.

## Top-20 Japanese stocks based on % of overseas shareholders:[120]

| Company | Code | Foreign owned | Largest shareholder |
|---|---|---|---|
| Levi Strauss Japan | 9836 | 83.90% | 83.59% |
| Shaklee Global Grp | 8205 | 82.05% | 38.87% |
| Oracle Corp. Japan | 4716 | 81.27% | 74.72% |
| Ichigo Group Hldg | 2337 | 80.53% | 70.31% |
| Chugai Pharma. | 4519 | 75.67% | 59.89% |
| Goodman Japan | 8992 | 72.43% | 51.57% |
| Japan Asia Group | 3751 | 71.57% | 39.33% |
| MonotaRo | 3064 | 69.55% | 47.40% |
| Trend Micro | 4704 | 68.67% | 13.13% |
| Aozora Bank | 8304 | 68.58% | 49.78% |
| PGM Holdings | 2466 | 67.80% | 64.21% |
| MK Capital Mgmt | 2478 | 67.53% | 19.31% |
| Nissan Motor | 7201 | 67.50% | 43.40% |
| LITE-ON Japan | 2703 | 67.45% | 49.49% |
| Asahi Tec | 5606 | 64.69% | 62.41% |
| Osaka Sec. Exchg. | 8697 | 62.97% | 5.02% |
| Shinsei Bank | 8303 | 62.47% | 16.60% |
| Showa Shell Petro | 5002 | 61.46% | 33.24% |
| FISCO | 3807 | 61.44% | 54.50% |
| Verite | 9904 | 58.87% | 57.45% |

---

[120] Per *Toyo Keizai* (article published Dec. 13, 2011).
http://www.toyokeizai.net/business/industrial/detail/AC/875b402fa98a08812d024c785d858138/.

Many of the above companies have a large controlling shareholder. This can be either a good or bad arrangement for outside, minority shareholders. A positive take is the possibility that a parent makes a listed subsidiary wholly-owned, resulting in a premium paid to shareholders; though this may not be so ideal to shareholders of the parent if too much or any premium is paid. A negative take is that the controlling shareholder stands as an obstacle to new or increased investments by institutional or other large investors, including de facto thwarting of any possibility of a takeover.

Some of the above companies will be recognizable in terms of who their top shareholders are, such as Levi, Shaklee (RHJ Int'l), Oracle, Nissan (Renault), and Showa Shell. Not so obvious is the case of Goodman Japan (8992), which is controlled by Australia's Macquarie, known for its listed funds in areas such as real estate and infrastructure. Goodman manages a real estate fund focused on distribution centers. Making it obscure even to Japanese investors is its Mothers market listing. Goodman turned a marginal profit in its most recent fiscal year ended March 2011, but came nowhere near to recouping the losses it made in its two prior fiscal years. A cursory review shows that it is trading at a very low price-to-book value and a not too expensive earnings basis, but returns on assets and even equity are quite low.

Oracle Japan (4716) should be of more interest to Japanese investors since it has a dividend yield of 6.3% based on the Y170 per share it has paid annually in recent years, but making this story even more compelling is the Y460 per share total dividend (which includes a special dividend) it paid during its fiscal year ended May 2011. With an ROE of between 26% and 27% over the past three years, at a recent Y2,608/share, it is trading at 15-times trailing earnings and is only about 10% above its 52-week low, which puts it below its post-IT bubble low.

## TSE's Investor Trends

The Tokyo Stock Exchange publishes weekly updates of what it refers to as "investor trends," which include the buying and selling activity of domestic equities by overseas investors. The data sets are fairly robust, broken down by market type (TSE 1, 2, Mothers, regional exchanges, etc.) and type of investor.[121] The Japanese Ministry of Finance also publishes weekly "international transactions in securities."[122] These publications are usually covered by journalists and reported on shortly thereafter. Headlines typically read that foreigners were net buyers or sellers of Japanese stocks. It is not uncommon for foreigners to be buyers when domestic investors are selling and vice versa. Furthermore, it is typically the case that foreigners dominate trading of Japanese stocks at large (since TOPIX 1st Section trading value exceeded the combined trading value of the 2nd Section and Mothers by a factor of over 60). For instance, in the last week of 2011, among brokerages, foreign brokers accounted for 63.1% of the purchase value and 61.8% of the sale value of stocks on the TOPIX 1st Section. Conversely, individual investors played an even bigger role in TOPIX 2nd Section trading, accounting for 71.7% and 75.8%, respectively, during the same week. The same dominance by individuals applies for Mothers as well.

For calendar year 2011, the purchasing and selling value by foreign investors of TOPIX 1st Section stocks amounted to 67.7% and 67.8%, respectively, making them net sellers by a fairly small margin. Domestic individual investors were also net sellers, 19.8% (purchases) vs. 20.0% (sales). On the TOPIX 2nd Section, while domestic individual investors dominated trading by value (68.2% of purchases and 71.3% of sales), foreign investors were actually net buyers (14.9% vs. 13.6%). A similar situation for Mothers: Japanese net sellers, 66.4% vs. 65.9%, compared to foreigners being net buyers at 22.7% vs. 22.4%.[123]

For value investors the above data can be helpful in a general, informational sense, but it is more applicable to momentum and shorter-term traders. News of net foreign buying may become self-fulfilling. What's key then is to know if Japanese investors are participating. The problem is that

---

[121] "Investment Trends by Investor Category," Tokyo Stock Exchange, http://www.tse.or.jp/english/market/data/sector/index.html.
[122] See Ministry of Finance homepage in English: http://www.mof.go.jp/english/.
[123] Trading Value by Investor Type (2011), http://www.tse.or.jp/english/market/data/sector/b7gje60000008yda-att/E_stk2_y11.pdf.

the data is published on a weekly basis, although there are third-party reports of dealings by brokerages on a daily basis. Value investors will be best served identifying undervalued companies either with strong growth prospects and/or possible catalysts for realizing value such as a takeover or more efficient use of excess capital. Presumed confirmation of a bull or bear market should not change the modus operandi much for value investors beside bull markets possibly necessitating closer monitoring for profit-taking opportunities as valuations rise. Bear and sideways markets afford more time to conduct due diligence since there will be less noise when stocks aren't in vogue.

## The "Mysterious China Fund"

2010 proved to be an interesting year for Japanese stocks in terms of a meaningful source of demand. "SSBT OD05 Omnibus China Treaty 808150" appeared on the shareholder registers of a number of Japan's largest companies. Based on research by The Chiba Bank Group ("Chibagin"), there are actually two Chinese funds buying Japanese stocks, whose reported holdings jumped from 13 in 2009 (aggregate holding value of Y155.6 billion or $2 billion) to 85 by the end of September 2010 (aggregate value of Y1.497 trillion or $19 billion). Initially shrouded in mystery, it was soon determined that the esoteric fund may in fact be a fund of China's sovereign wealth fund, administered by State Street Bank and Trust (out of Sydney, Australia).[124]

Chinese government buying of Japanese assets had already been gaining attention as China has been buying JGBs in increasingly larger amounts in order to diversify its foreign exchange reserves, according to an official at China's State Administration of Foreign Exchange.[125] As of spring 2010, China's JGB purchases amounted to a very small portion of outstanding

---

[124] "日本株に食指伸ばす中国マネー 中核ファンド2社は政府系," Big Globe News (Japan) Jan. 5, 2011.
http://news.biglobe.ne.jp/economy/0105/jc_110105_4654658036.html
[125] "China Buys Japan Debt to Diversify," Wall Street Journal, Jul. 7, 2010.
http://online.wsj.com/article/SB10001424052748704535004575349900794159356.html

JGBs, and were also focused primarily on short maturities of one-year or less. While there is some concern on Japan's part about the impact on the yen (at a time of historic relative yen strength while some countries are devaluing their currencies), the buying of equities in particular does not seem to be causing too much concern; again it's more a matter of mystery or curiosity.

As of the fiscal year ended March 2010, the Chinese fund's largest holdings in terms of percentage of a company's shares held included:

> ORIX (8591) 1.96%
> Nitto Denko (6988) 1.87%
> NEC (6701) 1.82%
> Oji Paper (3861) 1.70%
> Hitachi (6501) 1.65%
> Credit Saison (8253) 1.58%
> Sumitomo Trust & Banking (8403) 1.32%
> Kajima (1812) 1.30%
> Taisei Corporation (1801) 1.30%
> Teijin (3401) 1.29%
> Nomura (8604) 1.29%
> Mitsui Sumitomo (8316) 1.28%

Ranked in terms of amount invested (based on known stakes as of March 2010 and stock prices as of July 8, 2010:[126]

> Mitsubishi UFJ (8306) Y76.5 billion
> Mitsui Sumitomo (8316) 48.5 billion
> NTT (9432) 40.9 billion
> Takeda Pharma (4502) 35.6 billion
> Sony (6758) 29.7 billion
> NTT DoCoMo (9437) 27.1 billion
> Hitachi (6501) 25.2 billion
> Mizuho (8411) 24.1 billion
> Softbank (9984) 23.6 billion
> Nomura (8604) 23.4 billion

---

[126] "オムニバス・チャイナ・トリーティーを大追跡謎の"チャイナファンドの正体見たり！" *Nihon Stock Journal*, http://www.nsjournal.jp/column/detail.php?id=217895&dt=2010-07-14

A quick glance at the Chinese fund's largest holdings indicate a preference for large-cap companies, particularly ones in finance (both bank and non-bank). Other standouts include consumer electronics (and telecom) and construction. Two key points are that by all indications the fund's investments are not strategic, but instead reflect portfolio diversification purposes, and there have been no attempts to-date (as of year-end 2011) to take positions of 5% or more, which require disclosure by Japanese law. The reaction by Japanese companies, beside one of viewing the Chinese fund(s) as somewhat of a mystery, has ostensibly been mostly neutral or positive. Take Sony for instance, in which a spokesman was quoted in summer 2010 in Japanese saying the company was not particularly worried (about having a Chinese fund as a top-10 investor). Interestingly, as of year-end 2011, Sony's IR website lists the China fund among its top-10 shareholders (sans "China" in its name) and notes the Omnibus Account is primarily for European and North American shareholders. Separately, an ORIX spokesperson commented in Japanese that in summary, it is not inconceivable that the company has Chinese shareholders since it conducts IR activities overseas, thus in fact the appearance of the Chinese fund on its register could be the result of such activities.

Taizo Nishimuro, former president of Toshiba and former chairman of the Tokyo Stock Exchange, was named an international representative of China's sovereign wealth fund (China Investment Corp., known as CIC), and is the only representative from Japan. In January 2011 the *Nikkei* published a Q&A with Nishimuro, in which he mentioned it was May or June 2010 when a CIC official acknowledged that Japanese stocks were relatively undervalued (compared to other countries). Nishimuro told CIC that he also thought Japanese stocks were undervalued. At that time, CIC was said to be increasing its staff including having some specialize in Japanese stocks. Nishimuro supports CIC's approach to investing in Japan using intermediaries and taking small steps (i.e. passive, smaller-size shareholdings) as opposed to strategic/active larger stakes.[127]

---

[127] "Inflows Of China Money Into Japan Unstoppable: Former Toshiba CEO," *Nikkei* (*Nikkei Veritas* original in Japanese). January 30, 2011.

# CHAPTER 8

# CORPORATE GOVERNANCE IN JAPAN

When discussing shareholder rights in Japan, Scott Callon's (Ichigo Asset Management) first-hand experiences and comments on such should be heeded. Callon told *The Manual of Ideas* in May 2011 that his first key lesson learnt from blocking Tokyo Kohtetsu's merger with Osaka Steel was that Japanese shareholders are willing to stand up for their rights.[128] In a May 2007 speech he made at Japan Society New York, he noted Japanese shareholders' "incredibly strong" legal rights and that "Japan is not a board-level governance regime; it is a shareholder-meeting regime."[129] By that he means shareowners in Japan can effectively call a shareowner meeting at will, as well as add shareowner resolutions to shareowner meeting agendas. A shortcoming, however, is that there is a much higher ownership requirement to submit proposals in Japan (more on that later in this chapter). That said, unlike the pervasive advisory votes in the U.S., resolutions passed in Japan

---

[128] Interview with Scott Callon, *Manual of Ideas*, May 2011. http://manualofideas.com/files/content/the-manual-of-ideas_interview_with_scott-callon_2011.pdf.

[129] "Ichigo's Scott Callon Leads Japan's First Successful Shareholder Revolt," Japan Society New York speech, May 3, 2007. http://www.japansociety.org/ichigos_scott_callon_leads_japans_first_successful_shareholder_r

become policy. And for any readers with experience submitting shareowner proposals in the U.S., imagine not having to face automatic no-action requests and all the savings possible for individual proponents and of company (i.e. shareowner) funds.

In the May 2007 speech that Callon gave in New York, he made a very poignant point about the approach of many Western activist investors in Japan to-date:

> "However, the challenge that some global activists have had is they show up and they propose a big dividend increase, and the shareholders don't vote for it. Because for Japanese shareholders sometimes it is too drastic, and it feels like it is taking hard-earned savings over many, many years, and distributing them to current shareholders at the expense of employees."

## Buffett and Olympus

During Warren Buffett's first visit to Japan in November 2011 (his previously planned trip was postponed in March due to the triple-disaster), at a time when a billion dollar scandal at Japanese blue chip Olympus was a top news story, Buffett had the following comment:[130]

> "The fact that Olympus happens here or Enron happens in the U.S. doesn't affect our attitudes at all."

My thoughts are similar. As bad as the Olympus scandal is (the latest reports, in early November, estimate as much as $1 billion in investment losses spanning as far back as the 1990s that were hidden as fees paid for M&A advice), it does not discourage me from investing in Japan. Heads should roll, and there have been some resignations/firings, but at the same time investors must somehow hold the auditors more accountable. What were the auditors doing? It's the old question of who is auditing the auditors? In addition, in a

---

[130] "Buffett Says Berkshire Could Spend Up to $10 Billion on Deal," Bloomberg, Nov. 21, 2011. http://www.bloomberg.com/news/2011-11-21/buffett-says-berkshire-could-spend-up-to-10-billion-on-next-acquisition.html

time of global capital (investment) flows, we must see respective countries enforce stricter punishment for securities-related fraud. Material monetary fines combined with meaningful jail time may be the best remedy for cleaning up corporate fraud. Therefore, as easy as it is to decry Japan's perceived poor corporate governance, a cursory reflection on the frauds in the U.S. and those happening on U.S. exchanges (including the spate of Chinese companies found to be cooking their books in 2011) suggests we have more a matter of some bad apples exploiting a system that effectively enables fraud due to vague accountability requirements and a lack of meaningful punishment for board directors, auditors, and advisers.

In a November 24, 2011, *New York Times* article about former Olympus CEO Michael Woodford ("First, He Blew The Whistle on Olympus. Next, He Wants to Leads Its Comeback"), the following apt, brief description of Japanese corporate governance and business appears:[131]

> "Truly independent board members are rare in corporate Japan, and foreign ones are even rarer. Cozy cross-shareholding arrangements typically ensure compliant stockholders who tolerate mediocre management, or look the other way in cases of boardroom impropriety. And in a mixture of fact and myth, often lurking in the background of the Japanese business world are tales of corruption and rumored links to the country's infamous organized crime syndicates, the yakuza."

However, if one were to write a brief summary of corporate governance and business in the U.S., perhaps it would go something like this:

> Truly independent board members are rare in corporate America, and minorities (race) are even rarer. Cozy institutional long-only 401(k) or pension fund investment arrangements typically ensure compliant stockholders who tolerate mediocre management, or look

---

[131] See http://www.nytimes.com/2011/11/24/business/michael-woodford-would-like-a-chance-to-redeem-olympus.html?pagewanted=all.

the other way in cases of boardroom impropriety. And in a mixture of fact and myth, often lurking in the background of the American business world are tales of corruption and rumored links to the country's infamous organized crime-enabling syndicates: the auditors, rating agencies, regulators, and sell-side analysts.

It's too easy to dismiss Japan as a backward, corporate governance nightmare when that's often the uninformed opinion that makes it on TV and articles on the web and in print. In fact, I would argue that most activists with experience in Japan would say that despite the hurdles out of the gate – which may include language and cultural differences, as well as differences in management beliefs and conventions – the environment can be far more welcoming, both from a legal rights perspective and in terms of interaction with management. After all, how many management teams or boards in the U.S. have there been that readily agree or acquiesce to an activist investor's demands? In Japan, activists in recent years may not have achieved easy or direct success, but the most controversial of all, the former Steel Partners Japan Fund, even found that although dividend proposals didn't win majority votes, boards still hiked dividends and in some cases quite meaningfully. My personal experience with Internet Initiative Japan (IIJI) (3774) is a great example. As an ADR holder, I learnt that according to Japanese law I was not able to submit a shareowner proposal. As I had already been communicating with the board of directors, I still requested that it consider and action some items I felt would enhance shareowner value, including paying larger dividends. Since when I began my correspondence with IIJ's board in early 2010, the board went on to hike IIJ's dividend four times for a total increase of 50% over the next year.

Going back to Buffett, he stated during his Japan visit his main focus is on companies that have some kind of sustainable competitive advantage. A look at Berkshire Hathaway's portfolio and its (as well as Buffett's) track record prove the merit of investing in high-quality companies at *good* or better prices. Of course it would be foolish to think that he ignores management, as he entrusts substantial responsibility in the executive officers of Berkshire's subsidiaries. Japanese management mirrors the situation at Berkshire. While more can always be done to enhance shareholder value, by and large Japanese management consists of longtime company employees with long-term investment horizons. There are comparatively very few cases of discontent or disgust where investors or the public have felt they've been exploited. We'll take a look at executive compensation next. Finally, to reiterate Buffett's focus on competitive advantage, reflect on his oft-quoted statement: "When a management with a reputation for brilliance tackles a business with a reputation for bad economics, it is usually the reputation of the business that remains intact."

## Executive compensation

Since 2010 Japan's Financial Services Agency (FSA) has required disclosure of executives receiving annual compensation in excess of Y100 million (US$1 million at Y100/$ parity). Although belated, not limiting such disclosure to only the top-5 executives is a plus over the disclosure requirement in the U.S. The Y100 million (or $1M for simplicity's sake) is a serious milestone representing significant executive compensation in Japan, whereas in the U.S., it would be half of the year 2010 average CEO pay at small-cap firms (corresponding to constituents of the S&P 600) and less than one-tenth of the $11M-plus average CEO pay at large-cap (S&P 500) companies.[132] What investors can be certain of is that there will be little to no dilution of shareowners due to equity-based compensation, thus share repurchases are highly-effective in reducing share count. What's more is that Japanese companies have been known to retire treasury stock, reducing risk to investors that shares repurchased may be reissued at a later date. One could argue that equity-based compensation is grossly underused to the potential detriment of corporate value. The challenge is how to compensate talent and outsized achievement without upsetting the largely egalitarian, still seniority-grounded system.

---

[132] S&P 600 pay amount per compensation research company, Equilar; S&P 500 pay amount per the AFL-CIO's "Executive Paywatch" analysis, http://www.paywatch.org.

Let's review the compensation practices at Nintendo and of company president Satoru Iwata. After a multi-year string of phenomenal revenue and profit growth on the back of the popular Wii and DS gaming systems, Nintendo has since faced a sharp decline in its stock price, taking it to pre-Wii and DS launch levels. (See chart below.) Following its annual meeting in late-June 2011 and the implementation of a painful but necessary price cut to its then slow-selling 3DS handheld gaming device, Mr. Iwata and company directors volunteered to take pay cuts of 20% to 50%. Some may be thinking, yeah, big deal. But it is a big deal. For all the negative hits Japan takes for its corporate governance, it's a shame there is not more publicity of some of the many positives, which includes compensation practices. In addition, "pay for performance" is a controversial topic in the U.S. Shareowners may not mind the lavish executive pay packages if companies were delivering performance-wise. The problem is that even when companies do not deliver, executives, and especially CEOs, are still paid very, very well, and their bonuses are likely still paid to some extent, as well as other forms of compensation including pension accruals, and perhaps most importantly, equity (option) grants. At Nintendo – which a couple years ago was among the largest of Japanese publicly traded companies and today is still the 29th largest ($20B at mid-February 2012) – the company has achieved a very transparent, truly pay-for-performance system of compensation.

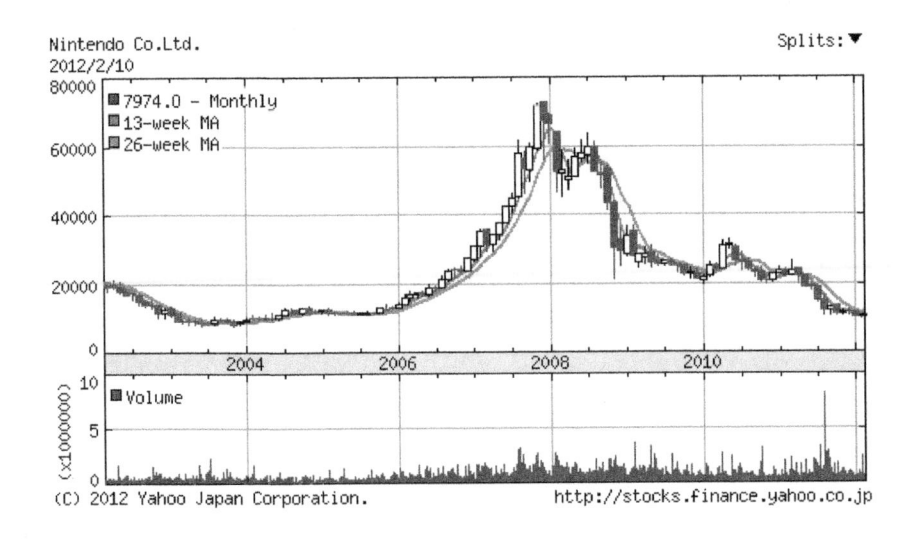

Nintendo has fixed president Satoru Iwata's salary at Y68 million (for simplicity let's use a Y100/US$1 rate, meaning it equates to $680,000). Pay-for-performance entails executive officers and directors sharing 0.2% of operating profits, but the grand total payout is capped at Y600 million ($6M). Nintendo does not issue stock options or any non-cash compensation. Therefore, in good years, the president of one of Japan's largest and most storied companies can earn several million dollars; in a year of declining financials but a still profitable one for the company, he may earn between $1M - $2M, and in a year of losses, his pay will not exceed $680K. It goes without saying that in most, if not all, cases he will be the highest paid employee.

For a quick comparison, not quite apples to apples, but one that clearly makes a point, I reviewed compensation at Electronic Arts (EA) for 2010. EA has also been struggling in recent years (though its decline is most pronounced looking back four to five years, in which its stock is down nearly two-thirds) and as of mid-February 2012 it had a market capitalization approaching $6B (two-thirds smaller than Nintendo's). Amongst EA's top-five executives, cash salaries ranged from $591K - $800K, but when factoring in bonuses and stock awards, total compensation ranged from $2.9M to $5.9M. Compensation was similar or higher in previous years despite the sharp stock price decline in 2008 and a mostly sub-$20 stock price since then. (See chart below.) So how about pay cuts at EA? Nope. Pay has increased since fiscal 2009 for all, and increased for three of the top-five since fiscal 2010.

**Electronic Arts Inc.**
■ EA

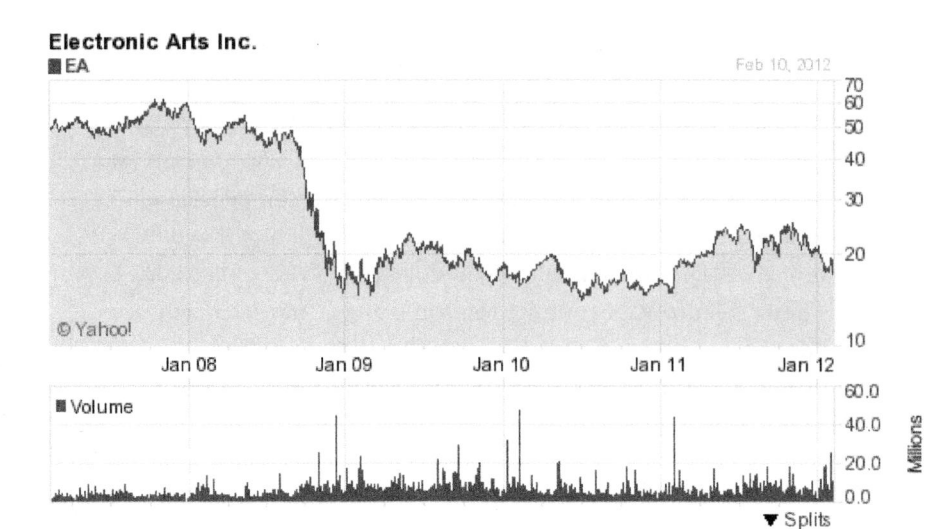

Feb 10, 2012

Pay cuts also happen at the prime minister-level. On October 31, 2011, some seven months after the March 11th disaster, Prime Minster Yoshihiko Noda issued the following statement (excerpted) on his blog as PM:[133]

> "Insofar as I am asking the people of Japan to shoulder a certain portion of the burden associated with reconstruction, first of all I myself will return close to 12 million yen in salary without waiting for the passage of the related bills, in order to demonstrate my keen preparedness impacting myself. In the future as well, there await a large number of issues that will be hard to maneuver around, but I am determined that I will never run from these issues, from my sense of duty derived from that resolve."

One last example of compensation, pay cuts, and the difference in attitudes of leadership, involves Japan Airlines and American Airlines. In 2006, due to ongoing struggles at Japan's largest airliner, newly appointed president and CEO Haruka Nishimatsu (a career JAL employee) would soon voluntarily cut his annual base salary by 60% to Y9 million ($90K) with no supplementation via bonuses or equity grants, and none of the common executive perks. News reports said he ate at the company cafeteria, rode the

---

[133] See: http://nodasblog.kantei.go.jp/2011/10/20111031.html.

city bus to work, and never wore designer suits. A flight attendant commented that she felt close to the president and "encouraged." Japan Airlines was nevertheless forced into bankruptcy a year later, but as of early 2012, it is planning to relist its shares as it has returned to profitability. Mr. Nishimatsu was replaced as CEO ahead of JAL's widely expected filing for bankruptcy protection. Prior to its filing, American Airlines proposed making a billion dollar-plus investment in JAL as part of its turnaround; they were both members of the same air alliance.[134]

Compare Japan Airlines to the situation at American Airlines, where the airliner's stock had traded as high as $45 in 2007 before it dropped to single-digits in 2008, where it effectively stayed until falling into bankruptcy in 2011. Although salaries were frozen for four of the top-five executives disclosed in American's 2011 proxy statement, salaries ranged from $424K - $670K and had been rising incrementally in years prior. On top of these payments came $912K - $3.28M in stock awards and $330K - $1.185M in option awards, and increases in pension values of between $316K and $721K. While the equity is now effectively worthless, consider the pay levels and practices in light of claims of needing to pay other employees less and make cuts to their pensions. Research by the *Star-Telegram* shows the (real) big payouts for executives are in fact likely forthcoming as the airliner will be more able to cut costs under bankruptcy protection, while the executives will continue to be paid well and most importantly could receive outsized equity grants if/when American relists.[135]

Research by the AFL-CIO found that 2010 CEO pay at large companies (i.e. S&P 500 constituents) was a staggering 343:1 of the average worker,

---

[134] "Sink or swim: Haruka Nishimatsu, chief executive, Japan Airlines," Mar. 19, 2007. http://www.flightglobal.com/news/articles/sink-or-swim-haruka-nishimatsu-chief-executive-japan-212611/; "Japan Airline Boss Sets Exec Example," Feb. 27, 2009. http://www.cbsnews.com/stories/2009/01/28/eveningnews/main4761136.shtml; and "Japan Airlines gets new CEO as bankruptcy looms," Jan. 13, 2010, http://www.reuters.com/article/2010/01/13/us-jal-idUSTRE60B04H20100113.

[135] "If American Airlines unions objected to executive pay before, just wait," Dec. 14, 2011. http://www.star-telegram.com/2011/12/14/3595805/if-american-airlines-unions-objected.html

representing CEO pay in excess of $11 million.[136] At the opposite end of the spectrum, CEO pay at small companies (i.e. S&P 600) was $2.2 million, still 44-times that of a worker earning $50,000 – the latter figure is a generous amount, higher than any study on national worker compensation. The ratio at mid-sized companies (S&P 400) is nearly double that of small companies.[137] I have found the difference in CEO pay in the U.S. versus Japan is roughly 30-times; even at the Y100M or $1M level we're still talking about a difference of around 10-times. Often cited figures in Japan include a government study of CEO pay at "large companies," where the average CEO pay totaled Y31 million ($310K). A study by the Chingin Kanri Research Center reportedly eliminated smaller companies in the government's study and arrived at a range of Y35 million to Y40 million ($350K - $400K).

In 2010, amongst 1,337 TOPIX 1st Section companies there were 213 executives that earned compensation greater than Y100 million ($1M), and 84.5% of them fell within the Y100 million – Y199 million range ($1M - $1.99M).[138] The number of companies that paid an executive Y100 million-plus totaled only 113. Total executive compensation averaged Y286 million ($2.86M) amongst TOPIX 1 companies, which is in the neighborhood of what CEOs earn at small-cap companies in the U.S. Base salaries accounted for over 66% of Japanese executive compensation, followed by bonuses at 14%, and both stock options and pension benefits at 7% each.[139]

---

[136] AFL-CIO comment letter to the SEC dated Aug. 11, 2011.

[137] The S&P 400/600 pay data is per compensation data research company, Equilar, and is referenced in the nongovernmental organization, the United States Proxy Exchange's, August 3, 2011, report: "Shareowner Guidelines for Say-on-Pay Voting." See: http://proxyexchange.org/wp-content/uploads/2011/08/standards_2.pdf. The author is a co-author of the Guidelines.

[138] "2010年3月期決算　東証1部上場企業　役員報酬開示企業調査　役員報酬1億円以上は113社・213人," Jul. 1, 2010. http://www.tsr-net.co.jp/news/analysis/2010/1203232_1612.html

[139] "社長の報酬は高すぎる？　安すぎる？," Jun. 27, 2010. http://webronza.asahi.com/synodos/2010062600001.html; "社長の平均年収3200万円," Mar. 2006, http://www.money-box.org/2006/03/18141021.html

The highest-paid executive in Japan is Nissan's (7201) Carlos Ghosn at Y891 million ($8.9M). He often leads publicly-traded Japanese companies in compensation and has seen his pay continue to increase annually despite Nissan's woes during and after the financial crisis. It also turns out that the ratio of his pay to the average employee at Nissan, 143:1, is the highest in Japan. Only three other companies had ratios exceeding 100:1. Among the top-10, the only other company with a non-Japanese head was Sony (6758), with Howard Stringer, where his company's ostensibly well-paid employees made his Y800 million-plus compensation look a bit less excessive at 93:1. That may not assuage employees and it certainly won't make investors feel better given Sony's floundering share price. Number ten is Yamada Denki (9831), a leading consumer electronics retailer, where the ratio is 65:1.

These ratios, even at the high-end are much narrower than ones in the U.S. So much so that in Mr. Ghosn's case, when questioned/criticized at Nissan's 2010 Annual Shareholder Meeting for his and other officers' large compensation while the company skipped its annual dividend payment, he answered that *his pay may be high in Japan but it's not based on a world standard*. Mr. Ghosn said he relied on a consulting company to review compensation of CEO's in the US and EU and argued his pay was not high at all compared to the average Y1.09 billion (Y90/$1 approximate average yen rate in June 2010, equates to $12M) paid to large auto company CEOs and Y1.18 billion ($13M) paid to non-auto large company CEOs.[140]

In 2010, the Tokyo Stock Exchange also implemented a new rule requiring all listed companies appoint at least one independent director. Under Japan's Company Law, such a director is subject to more stringent criteria for independence than an outside director or auditor. Corporate boards have long been targets of Western investor criticism. While I share some of the frustration, I also think it's unfair to criticize Japan so heavily given the chimera or illusion of independent directors in the U.S.; actual

---

[140] "赤字経営者と年収格差100倍以上でも文句なし日本のサラリーマン、「豊か」の基準は?," Aug. 4, 2011, http://moneyzine.jp/article/detail/198123; Carlos Ghosn comments at Nissan 2010 Annual Meeting per http://www2.ttcn.ne.jp/honkawa/5455.html which sites *Tokyo Shimbun* article dated June 24, 2010.

independence is far from reality. A review of board directors in the U.S. will show there are valid concerns over independence, which include board members that are corporate officers, former officers, have long tenures on the board, have too much cash compensation coming from their directorship, and also cases where directors have too many other director and/or executive obligations. Thus, my message to readers is to not be so quick to judge or fall for the status-quo criticism of Japan's corporate governance, and instead know that nowhere is there a perfect system; there are pros/cons to the established ways in Japan, the U.S., and elsewhere.

## Shareowner rights

For readers' information and reference, the following is a selection of shareowner rights that in most or all cases would exceed the rights available to minority shareowners in U.S. equities. One major shortcoming involves Article 303 below, which unlike the U.S., where the hurdle to submit shareowner proposals is essentially owning $2,000 worth of stock for the past year and a commitment to hold it for the coming year, in Japan the ownership value hurdle is much higher, effectively squeezing out most individual investors. Another fault of the Japanese system is that investors have a very limited time to review proxies, sometimes only two or three days, due to the high concentration of meetings as mentioned earlier and correspondingly tight deadlines. This is apparently changing however thanks to software and technology, and hopefully what will turn out to be a mutually beneficial arrangement between demand from institutional investors and supply by proxy services companies. Know also that shareholders only have rights to attend an annual meeting and/or vote if they hold at least one minimum unit. For example, if a company's minimum unit is 1,000 shares and a shareowner owns 500, the shareowner will not be able to attend a shareowner meeting or vote on proposals or director elections. Therefore, references to shareowners below are deemed to be ones that are entitled to vote by way of owning a requisite minimum trading unit.

- **Article 40 – Method of Election of Officers at Incorporation** – includes among a number of provisions that elections are determined by majority votes (as opposed to plurality vote as is found commonly in the U.S., per state law, where a director wins an election with the highest number of votes irrespective of the number of votes withheld). *Article 43* holds that dismissal of directors is also determined by majority vote. *Articles 89 & 342* establish that any shareholder can request a company allow cumulative voting. *Article 309* states that unless provided for otherwise in the articles of incorporation, resolutions at a shareholder meeting are determined by majority vote – note that certain situations unrelated to more routine matters of resolution may be subject to two-thirds majority vote. See *Article 854* mentioned below regarding seeking dismissal of an officer.

- **Article 125 – Keeping and Making Available for Inspection of Shareholder Registry** – any shareholder with a valid reason (i.e. not having an illegitimate one) can receive access a company's shareholder list.

- **Articles 210 and 247 – Demand Cessation of Share and Warrant Issuances** – Any shareowner can request such, arguing an issuance would be disadvantageous, so as long as the shareowner has owned shares for at least six consecutive months.

- **Article 297 – Demand for Calling of Meeting by Shareholders** – unless a company's articles of incorporation allow for a lesser requirement, company shareholders of greater than 6 consecutive months that own 3% or more of shares outstanding are able to call a shareholder meeting by making such a request to the Board. *Article 367* also allows for the calling of a meeting but has as the underlying reason for doing so concerning a director's violation of laws (or the articles of incorporation) or having a conflict of interest with the company.

- **Article 303 – Shareholders' Right to Propose** – unless a company's articles of incorporation allow for a lesser requirement, company shareholders of greater than 6 consecutive months that own 1% or more of shares outstanding (or 300 votes) may submit a shareowner proposal. *Article 304* stipulates that proposals must be of matters ordinarily voted on at annual meetings; they cannot be in violation of any law or the articles of incorporation. It also establishes that the same proposal has not been submitted within the past 3 years unless said proposal previously garnered 10% or more support.

- **Articles 371 and 442 – Inspection of Board Meeting Minutes and Financials** – Any shareholder can submit a request to a company to review its board meeting minutes for the purpose of exercising shareholder rights, however, court permission is required. The same applies for inspection of financial statements (*Article 442*).

- **Article 833 – Seeking Dissolution of a Company** – Shareowners controlling at least 10% of a company's voting rights may file for dissolution in cases where a company faces extreme difficulty as a going concern and is likely to suffer irreparable harm, or in cases where management itself or a disposition of assets is extremely unreasonable and jeopardizes a company.

- **Article 854 – Seek Dismissal of an Officer** – The ownership threshold to request such is 3% or greater, held for six consecutive months (or less in either case if so provided in the articles of incorporation). The procedures to do so are beyond the scope of this book.

# Parting words of wisdom from Graham & Dodd

"Sound investment in common stocks requires sound attitudes and actions by stockholders. The intelligent choice of securities is, of course, the major factor in successful investment. But if the stockholder is to regard himself as a continuing part-owner of the business in which he has placed his money, he must be ready at times to act like a true owner and to make the decisions associated with ownership. If he wants his interests fully protected he must be willing to do something of his own to protect them. This requires a moderate amount of initiative and judgment." --- Excerpt from Graham & Dodd's 1962 edition of *Security Analysis*

# INDEX

## 3
33 industry sectors, 32

## 5
5% rule, 156, 157

## A
Active in Asia, 31, 32, 147, 149
Aderans, 40
ADRs, v, 6, 12, 26, 46, 47, 48, 49, 68, 85, 87, 93, 97, 105, 130, 136, 148
advance-decline ratio, 72
Advantest, 46, 89
Aeon, 98, 115, 116, 121
Aica Kogyo, 168
Aiphone, 168
Alliance Bernstein, 157
Aloka Corp., 163
American Airlines, 184, 185
analyst coverage, 86, 87, 106
annual meetings, 91, 100, 190
Anritsu, 57, 58
Aozora Bank, 171
Arrows, 32
Asahi Glass, 148, 149, 150
Asahi Tec, 171
Asia, 15, 19, 31, 32, 55, 90, 129, 147
Asian financial crisis, 79
Astellas Pharma, 49
Asuka Asset Management, 157
AT&T, 28, 95, 96, 117, 120
Autobacs, 168

## B
Bain & Co., 122
balance sheet recession, 2, 78
Bank of Japan, 8, 9, 53, 65, 69, 70, 77, 79, 139, 142
Bank of Yokohama, 40
Belle Investment Research, 86, 87
BlackRock Japan, 157
BOJ, 8, 53, 69, 70, 77, 79, 81, 139
Brandes, 26, 39, 40, 157
Brillance Capital, 157
buybacks, 94, 99, 105, 114, 146

## C
candlestick chart, 71, 73, 111, 128
Canon, 37, 38, 39, 40, 42, 46, 66, 68, 88, 97, 109, 117, 149, 150
Capgemini report, 139
Capital Research, 157
CEO pay, 181, 185
China, 8, 14, 15, 17, 18, 19, 20, 23, 55, 68, 78, 90, 123, 127, 133, 134, 139, 147, 170, 174, 176
China Investment Corp., 176
Chiyoda, 168
Chiyoda Integre, 168
Chubu Electric Power, 114
Chugai Pharma, 171
Chuo Mitsui, 158
Coca-Cola West, 99
Company Law, 92, 155, 187
corporate governance, viii, 120, 179, 180, 182, 188, 200
cost of capital, 1, 2, 3, 128, 129
Credit Saison, 175
Credit Suisse, 158
cross-shareholdings, 95, 106, 108, 110, 112, 143
CurrencyShares Japanese Yen, 50

## D
Dai Nippon Printing, 49
Dai-ichi Life, 68

Daiichi Sankyo, 49
Daikin, 148
Daiwa SBI Small Cap value, 59
Daiwa Securities, 42, 49
Dalton Investments, 158
Deere, 117, 120
demographic disaster, 17
DeNA, 89
Denso, 67
depreciation, 144, 145
Deutsche Bank, 158
Dividend Focus 100, 32, 99, 149
dividend yield, 32, 42, 53, 60, 98, 99, 112, 113, 119, 120, 130, 131, 141, 142, 150, 153, 154, 165, 166, 172
dividends, 26, 51, 91, 92, 93, 97, 98, 101, 103, 111, 113, 146, 180
Dodge & Cox, 39, 40
DOE, 98

## E

earnings yield, 141
East JP Railway, 67
EDINET, 155, 156, 157
Effissimo Capital, 107, 158, 161
Electronic Arts, 183
executive compensation, 181, 186
Ezaki Glico, 110

## F

false starts, 52, 74
Fanuc, 49, 66, 149, 150, 151
Fidelity Japan fund, 37
Fidelity Japan Smaller Companies, 38
Fidelity Trust, 158
First Eagle, 26, 39, 42
FISCO, 171
FMR, 158
Ford, 13, 48, 117, 118, 119
foreign ownership, 170

Fujifilm, 40
Fujitsu, 40, 104
Fukuoka Stock Exchange, 102

## G

GDP, 5, 14, 17, 20, 21, 22, 23, 80, 135, 147, 152
General Motors, 48, 117
Genky, 59, 60, 61
Gilead, 117, 120
GMO Payment Gateway, 38
Goldman Sachs, 54, 158
Goodman Japan, 171, 172
Graham & Dodd, 4, 11, 191
Gree, 58, 125

## H

HappiNet, 168
Harris Associates, 158
HERCULES, 30
Hiday Hidaka, 98
Hirose Electric, 42, 43
Hitachi, 46, 58, 67, 68, 89, 107, 117, 148, 150, 151, 163, 164, 175
Hogy Medical, 98
holidays, 81, 137
Honda, 12, 35, 38, 39, 40, 46, 48, 66, 67, 68, 92, 93, 97, 100, 101, 118, 119, 149, 150, 151
Hoya, 97

## I

IBM, 28, 117, 123
Ichigo Asset Management, 158, 165, 167, 168, 177
Ichigo Group, 167, 168, 171
IHI, 162
independent director, 187
Infomart, 166

Inpex, 89, 148, 152
Internet Initiative Japan, 46, 47, 68, 93, 94, 180
Invesco Asset Management, 158
investor trends, 172
IPO, 41, 62, 63, 103, 121, 122, 130
iShares MSCI Japan Index fund, 37
ISM, 69, 71
Itochu, 38

## J

Japan Airlines, 121, 184, 185
Japan Asia Group, 171
Japan Equity Fund, 50
Japan ETFs
  DXJ, 45
  EWJ, 8, 15, 16, 37, 38, 39, 40, 43, 44, 50, 125
  ITF, 37
  JSC, 50
  NKY, 43
Japan Pension Fund Association, 131
Japan Post, 36, 80
Japan Real Time, 79
Japan Smaller Cap Fund, 50
Japan Trustee Svcs, 67
Japan-focused mutual fund, 27, 35, 36, 37, 39, 50
Japan-focused mutual funds, 27, 35, 36, 39, 50
JASDAQ, 29, 30, 32, 45, 59, 64, 84, 87, 103, 135, 139, 143, 168
JF The Japan fund, 57
JGBs, 80, 125, 139, 141, 142, 174
JPMorgan, 49, 65, 68, 159
Jupiter Telecom, 30

## K

Kagome, 111, 112, 113, 114
Kajima, 114, 175

Kao, 49, 129, 130
KDDI, 49, 66, 95
Kikkoman, 105
Kirin, 12, 89
KLab, 57
Kokusai, 56
Komatsu, 37, 49, 67, 89, 114, 115, 120, 148, 150
Konami, 46
Konica Minolta, 89
Kroger, 117, 121
Kubota, 12, 46
Kyocera, 12, 40, 46

## L

large shareholding report, 155
Lawson, 89
Lazard Asset Management, 159
LeoPalace21, 58
Levi Strauss Japan, 171
limit-up, 83
Lion, 97
listed subsidiaries, 106, 107, 146
LITE-ON Japan, 171
Livedoor, 36
long margin balance, 83
Longleaf, 39, 40, 41
lost decade, 14, 20, 52, 79, 140
low ROE, 143, 145, 147

## M

Makita, 46
margin of safety, 3, 11, 27, 146
Marubeni, 88
Master Trust Bank JP, 67
Matthews Japan fund, 37, 38
MBO, 161, 163, 164
mega banks, 35, 65
Meiji Yasuda Life, 67
Mikuni Coca-Cola Bottling, 99

millionaires, 139
mini share lots, 101
minimum trading increments, 84
minimum trading units, 51, 92, 100, 101, 102, 103
Ministry of Finance, 67, 173
Mitsubishi, 12, 34, 37, 38, 39, 40, 46, 47, 64, 65, 66, 67, 88, 113, 114, 159, 175
Mitsubishi UFJ, 37, 38, 39, 46, 47, 64, 65, 66, 67, 88, 113, 159, 175
Mitsui, 38, 66, 89, 159, 167, 175
Mizuho, 37, 46, 47, 54, 64, 65, 66, 68, 104, 115, 118, 121, 137, 141, 159, 175
MK Capital Mgmt, 171
monetary policy meeting, 81
MonotaRo, 171
Morgan Stanley, 44, 126, 159, 167
Morningstar, 29, 39, 45, 50, 53, 54, 55, 56, 57, 58, 74
Morningstar Japan, 29, 53, 54, 55, 56, 57, 58, 74
most-watched stocks, 113, 114
Mothers, 29, 30, 57, 58, 87, 103, 156, 166, 172, 173
moving averages, 71, 72, 73
Moxley & Co., 68
Mr. Market, 4, 72
Mrs. Watanabe, 53
Murata, 149, 152

## N

Nagawa, 165
Nagoya Stock Exchange, 102
Nanao, 168
NEC, 89, 117, 175
NEO, 30
net buyer, 140, 173
Net One Systems, 58
net seller, 140, 173

New Tachikawa Aircraft, 161
NGK Spark Plug, 40
Nidec, 47, 88, 105, 149, 150, 151
Nikkei 225, 5, 13, 20, 27, 28, 35, 36, 43, 50, 52, 55, 56, 58, 73, 74, 75, 76, 79, 132, 133, 135, 142, 161
*Nikkei Financial*, 87, 128, 129
Nikkei Weekly, 51, 52, 83, 92, 101, 102, 112, 113
Nikki, 168
Nikko, 55, 56, 88
Nintendo, 29, 37, 38, 40, 48, 115, 117, 136, 137, 138, 182, 183
Nippon Life, 67, 159
Nippon Steel, 148, 167
NishiMatsuya Chain, 168
Nissan, 34, 38, 48, 66, 68, 89, 97, 118, 119, 171, 172, 187
Nitori, 41, 42
Nitto Denko, 149, 150, 151, 175
Nomura, 2, 37, 46, 47, 55, 56, 64, 78, 88, 92, 97, 104, 110, 111, 113, 114, 117, 159, 175
NTT, 38, 40, 47, 66, 67, 68, 95, 105, 109, 110, 115, 120, 175
NTT DoCoMo, 47, 66, 68, 105, 109, 115, 120, 175

## O

Oakmark, 39, 42, 43
Ohashi Technica, 168
Oji Paper, 175
Olympus, 40, 42, 127, 178, 179
Omron, 149
Oracle, 2, 116, 117, 171, 172
Orbis Investment Management, 159
ordinary shares, 12, 48
ORIX, 38, 46, 175, 176
Osaka Securities Exchange, 29, 103
Osaka Steel, 167, 177
over-capacity, 144

## P

Panasonic, 12, 46, 47, 97, 115, 117, 149
Park24, 45
patents, 144
pay-for-performance, 182
PGM Holdings, 171
PIMCO, 39
Pink Sheets, 48, 49, 85
Plaza Accord, 80
population, 18, 19, 21, 23, 24, 120, 145
Prestige International, 62
price-to-book, 64, 117, 120, 133, 146, 147, 148, 152, 172
price-to-earnings, 60, 118, 119, 147, 148
price-to-sales, 134
Prospect Asset Management, 159
psychologically important, 71, 74, 75, 76

## R

Rakuten, 30, 84
real estate, 20, 59, 62, 130, 140, 143, 152, 168, 172
Relo Holdings, 62
Renaissance Technologies, 160
Renault, 68, 172
Renesas Electronics, 89
repurchases, 99, 104, 105, 108, 181
resource conversion, 27, 103, 146
returns on equity, 128, 129, 143, 150, 164
Riso Kyoiku, 98
Rohm, 43, 149, 150, 152

## S

Sanjo Machine Works, 163, 164
Sanrio, 58
Sapporo Securities Exchange, 102
Schroders, 160, 162
Scudder/Nomura Japan fund, 37, 38
Seeking Alpha, vii, 6, 16, 118
Sega Sammy, 49
Sekisui House, 49
Senshu Electric, 60, 63
Seria, 59, 60, 61
service sector, 20, 21
Seven & I, 40
SFP Value Realization, 160, 163
Shaklee Global, 171
shareowner rights, 188, 200
Shinsei Bank, 171
Shiseido, 49, 89
shorting stock, 83
Showa Shell Petro, 171
Silchester International Investors, 160
Simplex Asset Management, 160
Skymark Airlines, 58
SMC, 148, 152
Softbank, 66, 109, 114, 116, 120, 175
*sokaiya*, 100
Sony, 6, 10, 35, 37, 38, 46, 47, 48, 68, 97, 113, 115, 117, 129, 130, 138, 175, 176, 187
Sony Financial, 129, 130
Southeastern Asset Management, 160
spinoffs, 107, 108, 146
Square Enix, 43
SSBT OD05, 174
SSTOD05 Omnibus, 68
Star Mica, 60, 63
State Street, 67, 174
Steel Partners, 40, 110, 180
Step, 60, 63
Sugi Holdings, 43, 98
Sumida, 98
Sumitomo Metal, 37, 148, 150
Sumitomo Mitsui, 37, 38, 39, 46, 47, 65
**Superinvestors, 1, 4, 10**
Suzuki, 35, 84, 94, 123, 149

## T

Tachihi Enterprise, 161
Taisei Corporation, 175
Taiyo Fund, 160
Taiyo Pearl, 160
Takeda Pharma, 49, 66, 89, 114, 117, 175
Takuma, 58
*tankan*, 69, 70, 71
taxation, 22
TDK, 149
technical analysis, 71, 72, 111
Teijin, 175
Templeton, 160
*The Manual of Ideas*, 168, 170, 177
The Pack Corp., 99
Third Avenue, 26, 39, 119, 120, 160
ticker system, 34
Toba, 168
TOKAI, 59, 60
Tokio Marine, 49, 68
Tokyo Electric Power, 114
Tokyo Electron, 149, 150, 151, 152
Tokyo Kohtetsu, 165, 167, 168, 169, 177
Tokyo Stock Exchange, 28, 31, 32, 44, 84, 85, 86, 99, 100, 101, 103, 116, 121, 122, 144, 147, 149, 155, 156, 172, 173, 176, 187
Tokyo Theatres, 153
Tokyotokeiba, 154
TOPIX
    Core 30, 31
    Large 70, 31
    TOPIX 1, 28, 30, 31, 32, 39, 50, 64, 74, 87, 88, 102, 103, 114, 139, 162, 173, 186
    TOPIX 1st Section, 28, 64, 74, 88, 102, 103, 114, 139, 162, 173, 186

TOPIX 2, 28, 30, 59, 64, 87, 143, 162, 164, 173
TOPIX 2nd Section, 28, 59, 162, 164, 173
Toray, 148, 150
Toshiba, 89, 148, 150, 151, 176
Tower Investment Advisors, 160
Toyota, 6, 12, 13, 14, 34, 35, 37, 38, 39, 40, 42, 46, 47, 48, 66, 67, 68, 87, 97, 110, 113, 114, 117, 118, 119, 120
Toyota Group, 110, 119
Toyota Industries, 43, 68, 119
Trade Myths, 15
treasury stock, 181
Trend Micro, 171
*TSE Magazine*, 122, 156
Tsukui, 59, 60, 62
Tweedy Browne, 26

## U

UBIC, 57
Uchida Yoko, 168
Undervalued Japan Stocks fund, 64
unemployment, 22, 24, 141, 144, 145
Unicharm, 89

## V

valuation, 1, 42, 64, 97, 107, 111, 127, 129
Vanguard Pacific Stock, 50
Verite, 171

## W

Wacoal, 47
Watts, 59, 60, 63
widow-maker trade, 125
WisdomTree, 44, 50

## Y

Yamada Denki, 187
Yamaha, 149
yen carry trade, 53, 130
Yomiuri Land, 153

*yutaiken*, 98, 101, 111, 112, 113, 114, 141

## Z

ZIRP, 2, 52, 77
Zuiko, 165

# ABOUT THE AUTHOR

Steven is a value investor and shareowner rights proponent. He splits his time between balance sheets and proxy statements. Active in both Japan and the U.S., Steven enjoys researching value investment ideas as much as he does reviewing corporate governance matters. He is a member of the United States Proxy Exchange, a non-profit organization dedicated to facilitating shareowner rights.

Visit his website at http://steventowns.com

Printed in Great Britain
by Amazon